C00 165 314X

CANCELLED

KU-750-640

BOARDS AT WORK

Boards at Work

How Directors View their Roles and Responsibilities

PHILIP STILES
and
BERNARD TAYLOR

OXFORD
UNIVERSITY PRESS

OXFORD
UNIVERSITY PRESS

Great Clarendon Street, Oxford OX2 6DP

Oxford University Press is a department of the University of Oxford.
It furthers the University's objective of excellence in research, scholarship,
and education by publishing worldwide in

Oxford New York

Athens Auckland Bangkok Bogotá Buenos Aires Cape Town
Chennai Dar es Salaam Delhi Florence Hong Kong Istanbul Karachi
Kolkata Kuala Lumpur Madrid Melbourne Mexico City Mumbai Nairobi
Paris São Paulo Shanghai Singapore Taipei Tokyo Toronto Warsaw

with associated companies in Berlin Ibadan

Oxford is a registered trade mark of Oxford University Press
in the UK and in certain other countries

Published in the United States
by Oxford University Press Inc., New York

© Philip Stiles and Bernard Taylor, 2001

The moral rights of the authors have been asserted
Database right Oxford University Press (maker)

First published 2001

All rights reserved. No part of this publication may be reproduced,
stored in a retrieval system, or transmitted, in any form or by any means,
without the prior permission in writing of Oxford University Press,
or as expressly permitted by law, or under terms agreed with the appropriate
reprographics rights organisation. Enquiries concerning reproduction
outside the scope of the above should be sent to the Rights Department,
Oxford University Press, at the address above

You must not circulate this book in any other binding or cover
and you must impose the same condition on any acquirer

British Library Cataloguing in Publication Data
Data available

Library of Congress Cataloging in Publication Data
Stiles, Philip.
Boards at work : how directors view their roles and responsibilities /
Philip Stiles and Bernard Taylor.
p. cm.
Includes bibliographical references and index.
1. Directors of corporations–Great Britain. 2. Corporate governance–Great Britain.
3. Boards of directors–Great Britain I. Taylor, Bernard, 1931– II. Title.
HD2745 .S755 2001   658.4'22'0941–dc21   00-068839

ISBN 0–19–828876–X

1 3 5 7 9 10 8 6 4 2

Typeset by J&L Composition Ltd, Filey, North Yorkshire
Printed in Great Britain
on acid-free paper by
Biddles Ltd., Guildford & King's Lynn

DUNDEE CITY
COUNCIL

LOCATION

CT

ACCESSION NUMBER

C00 165 3140

SUPPLIER

DAWSON

PRICE

£30.00

CLASS No.

658.422

DATE

4.7.01

Preface

On 1 December 1992, when Sir Adrian Cadbury and his committee published their final report on 'The Financial Aspects of Corporate Governance', they started a train of events that changed the face of British boards and led to a worldwide movement for the reform of corporate governance.

In Britain the Cadbury Report was followed by the Greenbury and Hampel reports, and by a Combined Code of Practice that had the backing of the London Stock Exchange. Later, in 1998, the government initiated a comprehensive review of Company Law—the first in over 100 years. Many of the OECD countries produced their own Corporate Governance Guidelines. (The OECD report on *Corporate Governance* (1998: 105–7) lists twenty-four Corporate Governance Guidelines and Codes of Best Practice from fourteen countries.) Following the collapse of the Russian economy and other emerging markets in 1998, the World Bank, the International Monetary Fund, and leading investment banks have made corporate governance reform a condition of lending to the countries of Eastern Europe and the developing economies. The European authorities are also insisting that the countries of central Europe should establish appropriate controls and auditing systems to protect the interests of shareholders and other stakeholders before they will be allowed to join the European Union.

The last decade of the twentieth century also saw the emergence of corporate governance as a growing field of study and research in universities and business schools around the world. We met as part of the Henley research team that later produced *Standards of Good Practice for Boards of Directors* (IOD 1995), an investigation into the roles and responsibilities of boards of directors commissioned by the Department of Employment and sponsored by the Institute of Directors. Each of us has continued to explore the nature of board activity, both through in-depth research of boards and shareholder and stakeholder groups, and through the creation of forums and resources for executive development. This work has convinced us of the complexity of the issues in corporate governance and the multifaceted nature of the board's roles and responsibilities. A major aim of this book is to present a detailed picture of how British boards operate. The dominant theory suggests that boards are the agents of the shareholders, and the public debate about corporate governance emphasizes the need for the non-executive directors (NEDs) to protect the interests of the shareholders, the employees, the customers, and society as a whole by controlling potentially greedy and irresponsible chief executives. But what do the directors themselves think? Is this how they see their role or do they believe they have other functions—and, if so, what are they?

A central problem facing researchers and writers on corporate governance is to discover how boards work and in particular what happens when the board is in session. Board discussions are confidential and board agendas deal with matters that are vital to the future of the business. With some issues such as acquisitions and divestments, or closures and restructuring, it would be illegal or unethical for directors to tell researchers or journalists what they have been discussing. Also the board is a political forum. Boards are concerned with the exercise of power. They invest in some divisions and disinvest in others. They can make or break careers, create or destroy jobs, contribute to the development of a region, or damage its quality of life.

So most books about boards are based either on the author's personal experience working as a director on a small number of boards, or on surveys of the data published in company reports about the composition and structure of boards, directors' remuneration, and so on. There are also a number of blow-by-blow accounts of companies in crisis that draw on the reports of public inquiries and lawsuits such as the Maxwell case and the Guinness affair. These are concerned with 'the pathology of corporate governance', the investigation of fraud and criminal behaviour.

In *Boards at Work* we set out to discover how the main boards of large British companies operate using the reports of directors at first hand. In doing so, the study responds for repeated calls for greater insight into board process (Pettigrew 1992) and highlights the importance of building relationships within and around the board in developing cohesive corporate governance.

Following the Cadbury Code, most large quoted companies changed their board structures (see PIRC 1998), reducing the size of boards, separating the roles of chairman and chief executive, appointing a new group of 'independent' non-executive directors, and establishing board committees. The compliance of organizations with these structural reforms has been an enduring theme of writing on corporate governance, but the actual working of boards has remained a 'black box'. It was our intention to shed some light on this curiously underresearched area. A fundamental issue that was the focus of heated public debate in Britain during the 1990s centred on the accountability of boards of directors. The need for transparency in financial reporting, risk management, executive pay, and social responsibility placed strong expectations on boards of directors. Ensuring transparency and openness of communication and information is no simple task, and much of the process revolves around the development of positive relationships between the board of directors and investors and stakeholders. Outside the few set-piece mechanisms for communication—the annual general meeting, the provision of the annual and half-yearly report and accounts—it is the strength of informal ties between the board and external constituencies that can be all-important. Frequent meetings, timely and accurate information, can develop a sense of personification between the various groups and enhance the legitimacy of the board, creating mutual trust. Exploring the nature of internal and external forms of accountability is also a central purpose of this book.

Though our focus is on the board of directors as a whole, we were in particular concerned to discover the nature of the role of non-executive directors. They are the linchpin of Britain's corporate governance system. They have been introduced as a new resource for the board. A central question is: 'How do they add value?' There are limits to what non-executive directors can contribute to the company, because they work part-time for, say, twenty days a year, and the information that they have about the company can be limited. There is clearly a danger that their grasp of company affairs will be superficial, and they may become too dependent on the executive team. In some companies the Executive Committee will become the Management Board and the Main Board, while the non-executive directors will simply act as a 'rubber stamp', as the Supervisory Board often acts in the German system.

This would be unfortunate, because a strong chief executive should be able to use his or her other board as a 'sounding board' of senior advisers. The non-executives should be able to contribute common sense, good judgement, and creative ideas, based on experience in business or government, and specific expertise and contacts in international affairs, finance, and technology. We were anxious to see how non-executives managed their structural limitations and actively contributed to the running of organizations. Through this research study we aimed to discover what are the key elements that enable chairmen and chief executives, non-executives and executives, of major companies to manage their interrelationships, to handle inevitable conflicts, and to ensure that the board operates efficiently and effectively.

Boards sit at the apex of organizations and have to deal with complex business problems in a short time-span and often with incomplete information. Their roles are multiple and often conflicting. In major organizations, boards control huge resources and employ large numbers of people. The processes by which boards operate are therefore of major significance, not just to the individual companies but to the wider society. The purpose of this book is to show the nature of these processes and how they are enacted.

In writing this book, we have been helped by many colleagues and friends. We would like to extend our thanks in particular to Jay Lorsch, John Stopford, Lynda Gratton, and Nigel Nicholson for providing detailed advice on drafts of the book. We would like to thank Keith Macmillan, Peter Herbert, Vic Dulewicz, John Roberts, Patrick McGovern, and Patrick Flood for their interest and encouragement. We would also like to express our gratitude to David Musson, Sarah Dobson, and Hilary Walford of the OUP for their expertise and patience. Our greatest debt, however, is to the directors who kindly gave their time to this project.

Contents

List of Tables

Abbreviations

ALI	American Law Institute
CEO	chief executive officer
EDC	Executive Directors' Committee
ICAEW	Institute of Chartered Accountants of England and Wales
ICSA	Institute of Chartered Secretaries and Administrators
IOD	Institute of Directors
ISC	Institutional Shareholders' Committee
NADC	National Association of Corporate Directors
PIRC	Pensions Investment Research Consultants
ROE	return on equity
RSA	Royal Society of Arts
TCE	transaction-cost economics

1

The Changing Expectations of Boards of Directors

Expectations of boards of directors are changing. The popular media as well as corporate governance experts have characterized boards largely as rubber stamps for management. However, a number of high-profile cases have shown non-executive directors flexing their muscles, while, at the same time, those 'slumbering giants'—the institutional investors—have also received a 'wake-up call' following celebrated instances of corporate malfeasance or incompetence. A reconcentration of ownership in the hands of a relatively small number of financial intermediary institutions such as insurance firms, banks, and pension funds—in the UK, 60 per cent of the ordinary shares of listed UK companies are held by institutions (Charkham and Simpson 1998)—has given such groups considerable potential leverage to influence the direction and accountability of their portfolio companies (Parkinson 1993; Charkham 1994a; Short and Keasey 1997). The introduction of numerous codes of conduct and best practice, too, has brought reforms in board structure and composition. The widespread introduction of a non-executive cadre, the splitting of the roles of chairman and chief executive, and the setting-up of a board committee structure to handle audit and remuneration issues have increased the potential influence of the board.

But these developments have failed to allay the popular perception of boards as ineffectual. For example, non-executive directors have been described variously as poodles, pet rocks, or parsley on the fish, and the proliferation of the 'corporate governance industry' is seen in some quarters as counterproductive.

The major theme of this book is that, contrary to much of the work on boards of directors that stresses the notion of boards either as rubber stamps or as simply a monitoring device, the role of the board has indeed far more potential for active involvement in the running of the organization, and this involvement depends on the degree of cooperation and trust that exists between board members and in the relationships the board has with management and shareholders/stakeholders.

The dominant view of boards, a view that has underpinned the majority of reform activity, is that the board acts as a control mechanism to reduce the potential divergence of interests between corporate management and shareholders. Non-executive directors, because of their supposed independence and objectivity, provide an important check and balance to the power of the chief executive and his or her executive team. The notion of 'contestability' in the boardroom has become central, and the model for boards is unmistakably adversarial (*The Economist* 1994). Against this view, this book argues that close working between the executive and non-executive cadres promotes enhanced strategic discussion, greater information flow between members, and a lack of dominance of any one individual or subgroup over the board as a whole.

One major problem with the adversarial view is that it downplays the role boards can play in the strategy process and in shaping the identity of the organization. For such a role, the adversarial model is clearly unsuitable, with its generation of an 'us and them' mentality between executives and non-executives. Board involvement in the strategy process entails a much higher degree of collaboration between executives and non-executives and in a real sense a relaxing of the constraints of independence in order for trust to be generated and social cohesion to be established. We do not argue that boards should be characterized by close ties between all members such that disagreement is absent or that the requirement for monitoring withers away. The dangers of groupthink (Janis 1983) have been well documented and there are clearly occasions when boards in general, or individual board members in particular, demonstrate all too obviously that the assumptions of agency theory—opportunism, self-seeking behaviour—are warranted under certain circumstances. What we advocate here is that trust and control need each other (Roberts 1998). The central role of trust as a foundation for effective collaboration (where trust is defined as an expression of confidence between parties in an exchange—(Jones and George 1998)) has been shown in studies on high-performance teams (Leavitt and Lipman-Blumen 1985), cooperative problem-solving activity in groups (Friedlander 1970), conflict management (Deutsch 1973), negotiation activity (Sheppard 1995), reputation management (Tsui 1994), and knowledge and information exchange (Jones and George 1998). In the case of boards, there is a dynamic tension between trust and distrust (distrust equated with questioning and differences in perspective (Lewicki *et al.* 1998)). There is a tension between the forces driving heterogeneity—predominately institutional pressure to appoint non-executive directors for their expertise and knowledge of conditions 'outside' the organization in order to increase effectiveness of decision-making—and the forces of homogeneity—promoting harmony in the board 'team' and reducing the potential for internal conflict and factionalism. Such a tension, we will see, is handled in different ways, but both trust and distrust co-exist and are inseparable and are a necessary condition for effective boards.

The adversarial model of boards is rooted in rather narrow assumptions of human nature, primarily that individuals are utility maximizers, are self-seeking and opportunistic. On this view, executives are not to be trusted, not because these individual characteristics are always played out, but because the difficulty and cost involved in identifying trustworthy agents are so large that organizations should rationally seek to structure themselves as if all employees cannot be trusted (Hosmer 1985; Williamson 1985). This agency view depends on an atomistic view of individuals, depicting persons as entirely separate and independent from one another, their identity somehow complete, with a fixed patterns of motives and beliefs (Roberts 1998). But this is to ignore the centrality of relationships in the formation of identity. Identity is not fixed, but is moulded by the daily interaction with others; indeed, it can be argued that the individual 'is constituted only in and through relationships with others'

(Roberts 1998: 7). If relationships, rather than the individual, are the basic unit of analysis, then there are a number of implications for the study of boards. One implication is that, the institution of the board can be seen as a social construction, exemplifying what Giddens calls the duality of structure. The board structure is both a condition and a consequence of action and interaction. The board sets the conditions within which members operate, but its structure is also affected by the interaction of its members, and the negotiation of power and influence over time. But, if relationships are central, and the self is constantly shaped by interaction with others, this in turn implies two things. The first is that balance and consistency between parties over time are unlikely; the complexity of relationships means that different pressures and contexts will serve to produce changes within relationships that will bring tension, inconsistency, and dissonance and, with the exercise of skill, resolution. In terms of boards, we can say that relationships within the board, and those between the board and management and between the board and shareholders/stakeholders, are constantly shifting and fluid, indeed the wealth of new information and changing circumstances that the board experiences makes prolonged balance and consistency unlikely; the real status quo may be characterized by imbalance and uncertainty. Secondly, relationships are generally characterized as involving experiencing others in multiple ways. The richness of relationships means that we can hold complex, highly detailed information about others, enabling us to hold simultaneously different views of each other (Lewicki *et al.* 1998). This richness enables board members to hold different views of one another at the same time. Importantly, this provides the potential for directors to combine trusted relationships between board members with operating control systems to ensure accountability. Trust and control are not polar opposites but are separable and distinct concepts and can coexist. The interdependence of trust and control is crucial in board endeavour, since boards undertake a number of (potentially conflicting) roles, and the multifaceted nature of relationships within the board provides different grounds for trust and control to develop. Carrying out the strategic role requires a strong degree of trust, with members needing to feel valued and respected when making contributions. Ensuring accountability to shareholders and stakeholders requires vigilance and monitoring within the board. Both require to be balanced and both can be mutually strengthening (Luhmann 1979).

The focus of this study looks closely at how directors perceive their roles and responsibilities and the enabling and constraining forces that impact on their fulfilment of these tasks. A good deal of work on boards has examined the role of demographic characteristics of board members or the structure and composition of boards to make judgements about performance (indirectly) of the board and (directly) of the firm. But the beliefs and behaviours of board members cannot be reliably inferred from demographic variables alone (Forbes and Milliken 1999), and the use of composition variables also fails to illuminate what exactly goes on within the board. Specifying outputs of the board is extremely difficult. Because boards are not responsible for implementing strategic decisions or for day-to-day administration (Fama and Jensen 1983), their output is entirely cognitive in nature (Forbes and

Milliken 1999). By studying board process, we can gain insight into how boards operate and what factors contribute to effective working of the board in terms of the carrying-out of duties and also in terms of how board members work as a group.

The board's domain

The description of what a board of directors is for varies depending on which particular theoretical approach scholars take (see Chapter 3), but in formal terms the board is the link between the shareholders of the firm and the managers entrusted with undertaking the day-to-day operations of the organization (Monks and Minow 1995; Forbes and Milliken 1999). Boards, by general agreement, have three key roles: strategy—responsibility for monitoring and influencing strategy; control—maintaining control over the management of the company; and service—providing advice and counsel to executives, and providing an institutional face for the organization (Mintzberg 1983; Zahra and Pearce 1989; Goodstein *et al.* 1994; Johnson *et al.* 1996). In this book, we will be looking at UK boards of directors in large organizations. A distinctive feature of these boards is that they are unitary —there is no supervisory tier, as in Germany or France. A non-executive cadre, who serve on a part-time basis and have limited exposure to the host firm's activity, sits with full-time executives of the organization as a single board, which meets on average ten times a year at formal board meetings, while board committees (such as remuneration, nomination, and audit) provide other opportunities for board members to interact. In most cases, the role of the chairman of the firm is distinct from that of the chief executive (a separation recommended by the Cadbury Report 1992 and subsequently in a plethora of other prescriptive studies) and the chairman's status is usually non-executive. The chief executive, as the title implies, heads the executive group, while the chairman is typically the lead non-executive director. The board, then, is internally differentiated and we can already see some of the dimensions of interaction that must be managed if the board is to perform effectively. Not only must the non-executive and executive groups cohere in a real sense, but chairman and chief executive must also develop a working relationship both between themselves and also with the respective executive and non-executive cadres.

A major problem with generating board cohesiveness and an ability to work together is that boards meet only infrequently. Also, since the board is partly composed of part-time members whose main allegiance is outside the host organization, problems of lack of in-depth knowledge, incomplete access to information, and sheer time pressures on non-executives become crucial. The relationship of non-executives to the board as a whole can be characterized, therefore, as one of 'partial inclusion' (Weick 1979; Forbes and Milliken 1999). The extent to which this both enables and constrains board process will be a key theme of this book.

The board is arguably the central instrument of governance (Demb and Neubauer 1992). Though the board is certainly not the only governance mechanism—the role of the shareholder and other stakeholders, the market for corporate control, systems of corporate finance, and national and international regulation all interact in complex ways to affect the governance of large firms (Monks and Minow 1995; Tricker 1995; Deakin and Hughes 1997a)—the board is certainly the most promising source for monitoring management, with greater flexibility than external controls to adjust managerial behaviour. It collects and processes information more quickly than external mechanisms, which enables it to identify problems before they become serious, and, through its (supposed) control on the selection of directors, it can improve the overall quality of management without the drastic consequences of a takeover (Parkinson 1993). For these reasons, boards have become the focus of efforts to reform corporate governance, and this policy interest provides a further reason for the emphasis of this book.

The rise of corporate governance

The corporate governance touchpaper was lit in the 1980s' takeover boom, when managers sought to entrench themselves in office by adopting a variety of anti-takeover devices, such as poison pills, greenmail, and golden parachutes, which certainly did not serve the interests of shareholders. The wave of takeovers also promoted renewed debate on the nature of corporate governance systems and how, in the face of a highly active market for corporate control, pressure on management to produce short-term results was increasing, discouraging long-term planning and investment (Marsh 1990; Lipton and Panner 1993; Paul 1993; Kay 1994).

These concerns were compounded at the turn of the decade by a series of corporate frauds—Maxwell, Polly Peck, the Bank of Credit and Commerce International, Barlow Clowes—and failures—Ferranti, Coloroll, British and Commonwealth—that showed dramatically the huge financial consequences of unfettered power, and the failure of the board to provide adequate checks to safeguard the interests of investors, employees, and customers. The spate of scandals and failures also called into question the role of the auditor in ensuring accountability of organizations. The collapse of a number of well-known companies that, according to their duly audited accounts, were healthy focused attention on the considerable scope for the distorted presentation of financial information (Whittington 1993; Smith 1996).

The executive pay bonanza has also shown up the wilder excesses of management, with executive directors awarding themselves huge pay increases, often unrelated to the performance of their organizations, showing for many a lack of restraint that was difficult to justify. The 'fat-cat' phenomenon emerged with a series of celebrated examples, notably Cedric Brown at the recently privatized British Gas, whose 75 per cent pay rise in 1994 (to £480,000) caused widespread condemnation—though this was dwarfed by the 203 per cent rise in pay for Sam Chisholm of BSkyB (to £2.03 million) and the 170 per cent rise (to £1.72 million) for Carlton's Michael Green a year later (Buckingham and Whitebloom 1996). The supposed link between executive pay and performance has become a central theme in corporate governance research (e.g. Cosh 1975; Cosh and Hughes 1987; Szymanski 1992; Forbes and Watson 1993; Gregg *et al.* 1993; Main 1993; Conyon *et al.* 1995; Bruce and Buck 1997; Conyon 1997; Ezzamel and Watson 1997).

The result has been increasing scrutiny from regulators, investor groups, and the business media on how corporations in general, and boards of directors in particular, operate. Policy initiatives have mushroomed. The Cadbury Report in 1992, which sought to improve standards of corporate (and board) behaviour following widespread concern over financial reporting and auditing, attempted to prescribe best practice in board structures and composition. Cadbury has been augmented by the Greenbury Report (1995) into executive pay, which attempted to link directors' earnings more closely to corporate performance, and the Hampel Report (1998), a successor to Cadbury that stressed the board's role in improving the prosperity of its companies. A London Stock Exchange Combined Code was introduced in July 1998 (Combined Code 1998), and has been followed by the Turnbull Report (1999) into internal control, recommending that directors are made responsible for the effective risk management of their organizations. This intense policy activity has been reflected throughout the world, with at least fourteen countries with published codes of corporate governance (Cadbury 1997).

Though corporate governance as a subject has attracted widespread recent interest, the nature of the debate on corporate governance—the system by which companies are directed and controlled (Cadbury 1992)—is shaped by Berle and Means's 1932 analysis of the American firm, which documented the split of ownership and control, and with it the dispersion of shareholdings in large corporations. As organizations grew, the number of shareholders increased, diminishing the voice of the individual investor, whose stake would be so small compared to the collective number of shares issued as to be almost negligible (though the financial value of a small stake could be considerable). The result was that corporate wealth was held by shareholders as a 'passive' instrument, while managers controlled the organization (Roe 1996: 6) The fragmentation of ownership and the shift of power towards managers and in particular the chief executive had many advantages—including the growth of professional managers and the efficiency of risk-sharing, but also brought with it problems in terms of management accountability. In formal terms, the shareholders elect the board (and the board elects the CEO) to ensure that their interests are safeguarded, but it is a commonplace now to suggest that boards are controlled by management. For example, Roe (1996: 6) argues:

everyone knew that in the public firm the flow of power was the reverse. The CEO recommended nominees to the board. Board members were often insider-employees or other CEOs, who have little reason to invest time and energy in second-guessing the incumbent CEO . . . the CEO dominated the election and the firm. Even today, many directors 'feel they are serving at the pleasure of the CEO-Chairman'.

The belief that managers control boards rather than boards controlling management has been a dominant theme in both academic and practitioner writings. The lack of accountability of senior managers has been manifest in a number of areas, which have coalesced to bring the corporate governance debate into prominence.

This book began just after the Maxwell affair and has witnessed not only the introduction of Cadbury and other policy initiatives, but also the rise of investor activism both in the UK and the USA (Coffee 1991; Drucker 1991; Bhide 1994; Blair 1995; Hawley and Williams 1997) and the increase in societal pressures. As Demb and Neubauer (1992: 21) state: 'the regulatory framework would remain an empty shell without the public's willingness to bring direct pressure for corporate conformity. And the pressure would amount to little more than whistling in the wind if the there were no consequences for the company.' The level of social activism has risen considerably in recent years. Organizations such as Business in the Community, the Per Cent Club, and the Action Resource Centre have emerged (Parkinson 1993), which have augmented pressure groups such as the Pension Investment Research Consultants (PIRC), a corporate governance watchdog, and environmental groups such as Greenpeace and Friends of the Earth. The currency of the 'stakeholder' concept, too, has steadily grown, aided by its adoption in the political arena (Donaldson and Preston 1995; Plender 1997).

Despite these developments, managers are still seen as insufficiently constrained by owners and the board of directors. Though there is evidence that the proportion of holdings by institutional investors has increased, and that investors sometimes do act in some cases of blatant mismanagement, there is little to suggest that direct investor influence on companies is widespread. The costs of monitoring a portfolio of companies and the dangers inherent in receiving price sensitive information from the companies monitored, which may infringe against insider dealing regulations, are such that shareholder activism on a systematic scale is unlikely to occur at the level of individual companies (for involvement at a macro-level, with institutions forming a clearing house of suitable non-executive directors to improve the corporate governance system (see Gilson and Kraakman 1991; Parkinson 1993)).

The problem in trying to assess the contribution of boards to the running of organizations, and hence the expectations we realistically have of them, lies in the fact that basic grounded research is 'still in its infancy' (Pettigrew 1992). There is a dearth of strong descriptive data on how boards of directors perceive their role and in what respects they can influence the performance of the firm. Shedding light on accountability is not the only aim here: how boards can enhance the performance of companies is also a pressing need, a need emphasized in policy terms through the Hampel Report (1998). The conformance aspect of boards' roles has been to the fore in much literature—unsurprising given the pathology of factors cited above. Yet the board's position at the apex of the firm, nominally at least overseeing the strategy, control, and institutional functions of the firm (Zahra and Pearce 1989), provides it with considerable potential for shaping the organization's performance.

In the empirical work of this study, we look at the experience of boards of directors in large UK companies. In view of the widespread activity in the UK on corporate governance matters, together with the complexity of many of the key issues, it was felt a UK sample would represent a distinctive contribution at both an academic and a practical level. The growing debate over whether the UK (and US) model of corporate governance has greater advantages over the Rheinian model, operated in parts of Europe and also Japan (Franks and Meyer 1991; Porter 1991; Working Group on Corporate Governance 1991; Kester 1992; Albert 1993; Prevezer and Ricketts 1994; Meyer 1997), has added considerably to the literature, but this is not a comparative study. Given the dearth of fine-grained research of UK board practice, a bounded UK study remains the most pressing need (Pettigrew 1992). However, filling in the picture here may provide the basis for informed comparative research at a later stage.

This study draws on several disciplines—economics, finance, accountancy, sociology, law, as well as corporate strategy and organizational behaviour. However, though the literature on corporate governance is burgeoning, there are few studies that are based on the actual reports and behaviour of directors themselves. This study is driven chiefly by interviewing the primary sources—directors—and developing a model that emerged from the data. This model is then related back to other research studies to compare the findings and to place its contribution within the context of existing theories. The primary aim is to build theory on boards of directors and secondly to contribute to the policy debate on improving practical corporate governance.

The structure of the book

The book focuses on the actual operation of the board of directors. Issues such as the involvement of the board in the strategy-making process, how monitoring and the accountability of the organization are ensured, how boards settle issues of selection and succession, and to what extent boards act as the institutional face of the organization, are discussed. Chapter 2 outlines the major theoretical issues pertaining to boards of directors' research. We argue that much of the empirical work supporting the theories sheds little light on the actual operations of the board. Based largely on secondary data or anecdotal evidence, these studies eschew detailed analysis of what directors do and how they conceive of their influence. This chapter also argues that the theories themselves may not be mutually exclusive and that there is strong potential for synthesis. Chapter 3 outlines the methodological approach of this study, specifically involving interviews with individual directors over a broad sample of companies, investors, and stakeholder groups, and case studies of Allied Domecq, BAA, Burmah Castrol, and Securicor. Chapters 4–6 describe the findings of the research. Chapter 4 focuses on the strategic role of the board, and argues that, though the board is not involved in strategy formulation, it determines the strategic context within which the firm operates. Chapter 5 examines the board's involvement in control, and shows how, in addition to monitoring past and present performance, directors also actively diagnose opportunities for the firm through data from control systems, thereby facilitating organizational change. The board's role in assessing managerial performance also represents a strong element in its control role. Chapter 6 describes the institutional role of the board, which details how the board builds links with key investors and stakeholders. At the end of each of these chapters, we present some of the detailed case study findings for further illustration of the key issues. In Chapter 7, the nature of board process in terms of the key relationships among members is explored. Chapter 8 seeks to assess the implications of the study and presents thoughts on future directions for boards of directors.

2
Perspectives on the Contribution of Boards of Directors

How boards of directors influence the performance of organizations has been a central topic of the corporate governance literature. As a result of the highly publicized cases of corporate fraud and failure, there has been a strong focus on policy issues (Cadbury 1992; Greenbury 1995a; Hampel Report 1998; Combined Code 1998; Turnbull Report 1999). This work has generated substantive recommendations about how boards of directors may best serve their corporations. The presciptive emphasis has been echoed by a growing number of commentators (usually practising directors) who have described ways in which boards can better be configured to add value to the organization (G. Mills 1981; Loose and Yelland 1987; Lipton and Lorsch 1992; Charkham 1999a; Monks and Minow 1995; Garratt 1996). This work has been characterized, however, as action-oriented, and concerned primarily with offering practical insights than with developing theory (Pettigrew 1992: 3). Theoretical, conceptual, and empirical work has attracted scholars from a broad range of disciplines, including economics, finance, management, and sociology (Zahra and Pearce 1989). Whilst this variety of research has produced a vibrant academic field, different methodological approaches and research agendas have resulted in findings that are largely inconsistent and non-additive (Pettigrew 1992). Further, this fragmentation in research paradigms has led to a lack of consensus on what boards of directors are actually supposed to do. The nature of a board's contribution (and therefore the expectation placed upon it) depends crucially on which theoretical perspective is adopted. In this chapter, six major theoretical traditions are identified from the literature and discussed. These are agency theory and transaction-cost economics (which, as they share key assumptions and approaches to conceptualizing boards, we shall examine together); stewardship theory, resource-dependence theory, class-hegemony theory; and managerial-hegemony theory (see Table 2.1).

The main argument of this chapter is that the first five theories described are limited in scale and scope and lack grounding in descriptive empirical research—they give little clue as to how boards actually work in practice and how directors perceive their role within organizations. We shall then move on to examine work in the board process area, focusing primarily on the dominant theoretical strand, the managerial-hegemony theory. We shall argue that this theory, with its claims of managerial dominance over boards and its construction of a general picture of board passivity, is unduly pessimistic and ignores a good deal of the board's potential for active influence in the running of the organization.

TABLE 2.1. *Perspectives on boards of directors*

Dimension	Theoretical perspective				
	Agency TCE	Stewardship	Resource dependence	Class hegemony	Managerial hegemony
Board role	Ensure match with managers and owners	Ensure the stewardship of firm assets	Reduce environmental uncertainty, boundary-spanning	Perpetuate ruling elite and class power	Board a 'legal fiction'
Theoretical origin	Economics and finance	Organization theory	Sociology	Sociology	Organization theory
Detail on board activity	Low	Low	Low	Low	Moderate
Empirical support	Equivocal	Limited	Moderate	Moderate	Moderate
Limitations of theory	Assumptions too narrow; ignores the complexity of organizations:	Largely untested	Focus on resource attainment, not resource use, interlocks not shown to influence behaviour	Partial view of board motivation	Problems over definitions of 'control', owner networks underestimated

Source: Adapted from Zahra and Pearce 1989.

Before we begin discussion of the theories of boards of directors, it will be helpful to examine what boards are required to do by law. Intuitively, this ought to frame the boundaries of board responsibilities; however, the legal requirements of boards give no clear indication as to the extent of board endeavour.

Theories of boards

The legal view

In the UK, as in many countries, boards are a legal requirement for public limited companies. Directors' legal responsibilities derive from (1) the legal status of the body on behalf of which they perform them, and (2) the functions they perform (IOD 1996). The legal status of public limited corporations is governed by The Companies Act 1985, which states that directors' duties are owed to 'the company' 'and may have to take account of the interests in the company of people who may reasonably be expected to become shareholders as well as those of present shareholders' (IOD 1996: 11). The board is thus legally required to act in the interests of *shareholders*, a view reinforced by the Cadbury (1992) recommendations. The Companies

Act requires public companies to have at least two directors, but the Act does not define the functions of directors (Parkinson 1993: 56). These are described by the Articles, where

the almost universal practice is to vest in the board all the powers necessary for the management of the business bar those required by the Act to be exercised by the shareholders in the general meeting. From the board, powers are frequently delegated to committees of directors or to individual board members, and thence down the managerial hierarchy. As to the functions retained by the board itself, *there is no consistent practice.* (Parkinson 1993: 57; emphasis added).

   The board's functions, therefore, are described in the most general terms by the Articles, and, in practice, there is wide variation between companies on how the board's role is to be interpreted and how many powers are to be delegated to the executive. In terms of individual directors, UK law describes two main duties: a duty of skill and care (taken to mean the care expected from a reasonably diligent person possessing the skills appropriate to a director entrusted with the function entrusted to the director in question (IOD 1995)), and a fiduciary duty, to act bona fide in the interests of the company, which includes the duty to act within one's powers and not allow personal interests to conflict with the company's (Coopers & Lybrand 1986).
   Again, the legal emphasis is on safeguarding the interests of shareholders, and this reinforces a narrow view of corporate purpose. Parkinson (1993) states that the fiduciary duty of directors is to act in the interests of shareholders, which is usually taken to mean maximizing profits. Apart from the fact that directors have a duty to acknowledge the interests of employees in their deliberations, there is no specific guidance given as to the rights of other interested parties affected by corporate decisions (Tricker 1984: 98).
   Consideration of the legal duties of directors takes us only a small way towards understanding the work of directors and boards, for at least two main reasons. First, though boards may have de jure control of the organization, the de facto control may rest with management. A large literature has grown up around the managerialist thesis that boards are ineffective monitors of management (Mace 1971; Lorsch and MacIver 1989). The looseness of the specifications of directors' duties encourages this view. The duty of care says that directors must act in accordance with the standard of the 'ordinary prudent man', which provides a low standard and one that has been accused of being devoid of content (Parkinson 1993). The fiduciary duty is framed in terms of subjective intentions, and 'any plausible assertion that a course of action is designed to increase the company's financial well-being will be enough to protect it from attack' (Parkinson 1993: 96). The notion that boards are ineffective has fuelled the efforts of reformers, efforts that are redoubled following every major corporate scandal. Secondly, the legal notion of boards has also been attacked because it pays insufficient attention to the interests of *stakeholders* other than shareholders. Representation of workers, ethnic minorities, and females have all been urged in calls for reform of board practice. Greater democracy at the apex of

the company is a popular refrain for those with an interest in the social role of corporations.

The question surrounding the effectiveness of the board of directors as a mechanism for reconciling the interests of shareholders and management is the starting point for the theories under discussion here. There is recognition, particularly from the economic theories of the board, that the board is but one instrument in the effecting corporate control, but one that has the greatest potential for ensuring good corporate governance.

Organizational economics: Agency and transaction-cost theories

The application of economic theories to the study of organizations in general, and boards of directors in particular, has grown in popularity in recent years and organizational economics is now regarded as the major framework in organizational studies (Donaldson 1995). This rise to prominence has stemmed largely from the contributions of two major theories: agency theory (Ross 1973; Jensen and Meckling 1976) and transaction-cost economics (TCE) (Williamson 1975, 1984, 1985). Together, these have been called the organizational economics approach (Barney and Ouchi 1986; Donaldson 1995).

The key idea of agency theory is that of the agency relationship, where one party (the principal) delegates work to another party (the agent), who performs that work (Eisenhardt 1989a).[1] In research on boards of directors, agency theory has traditionally focused on the relationship between shareholders and managers of large public companies (Berle and Means 1932). The theory defines the relationship between principal (shareholders) and agents (managers) as a contract in which the behaviour of the agent is conditioned by incentive structures (Kosnik 1987). The separation of ownership and control underlines the concept that organizations are both work-sharing and risk-sharing entities (Eisenhardt 1985; Baysinger and Hoskisson 1990). The shareholders contribute capital and bear the risk of the organization, while the managers are usually wholly responsible for decision management (Jensen and Meckling 1976; Fama and Jensen 1983). This separation, though deemed economically efficient by agency theory, can give rise to conflicts of interest between executives and shareholders, in particular through the opportunism of agents. For example, Jensen and Meckling (1976) mention the excessive use of managerial perks and

---

[1] Agency theory addresses two concerns that can arise in this relationship: that there may be partial goal conflict between principal and agent, and that there may be a problem of risk-sharing, which can occur when the principal and agent have different risk preferences (Eisenhardt 1989a). Because of the pervasiveness of the agency relationship, agency theory has been used in many disciplines that are concerned with co-operative behaviour. Two streams have developed: the principal agent and corporate control. The principal-agent literature is concerned with constructing a formal theory, largely technical in form, that can be applied to a number of agency relationships, including employer–employee, lawyer–client, and buyer–supplier (Eisenhardt 1989a). The second stream, corporate control, by contrast, focuses almost wholly on the contract between shareholders and their agents in large companies (Eisenhardt 1989a; Rumelt *et al.* 1991). It is the corporate-control branch of agency theory, then, that has been influential in the debate on corporate governance.

Kosnik (1987) cites managers pursuing diversification strategies in order to increase the firm's size and, with it, their associated prestige. Other costs may arise because, as managers, unlike shareholders, cannot readily diversify their employment risks across a range of investments, they tend to be more risk averse than may be in the interests of shareholders (Fama 1980; Knoeber 1986; Baysinger and Hoskisson 1990; Prentice 1993). Further, one of the assumptions of agency theory is that agents operate with bounded rationality—that is, managers will satisfice rather than profit maximize (Eisenhardt 1989*a*; Prentice 1993).

Agency theorists argue that it is corporate governance mechanisms in general, and the board of directors in particular, that can harmonize these agency conflicts and safeguard invested capital (Fama and Jensen 1983; Williamson 1984). The board ensures that managers are not the sole evaluators of their own performance (Baysinger and Hoskisson 1990) and the board's legal responsibilities to hire, fire, and reward executives are seen as key elements in controlling conflicts of interest. The mechanisms for harmonization of the interests of the two parties can be classed as both internal and external. The internal devices include setting the premises of managerial decision-making (Mizruchi 1983; Eisenhardt 1989*a*), introducing performance-related executive remuneration packages, increasing the firm ownership of the managers (Lambert and Larcker 1985; Jensen and Meckling 1976), and increasing the information the board has about managerial behaviour (Fama and Jensen 1983; Eisenhardt 1989*a*). Examples of external measures are the impact of competitive forces in the product market and the labour market (Fama 1980; Williamson 1984) and the threat of takeover (Kosnik 1987).

Agency theory, therefore, highlights the role of the board as a monitor of management activities in order to minimize agency costs and thereby protect shareholder interests. What effect does this have on what the board is expected to do: in other words, what are the operational consequences of agency theory for the board of directors? It is clear that reducing agency costs and maximizing shareholder wealth are key roles of the board according to the theory. So too is evaluating the performance of the chief executive and the performance of the company as a whole (Fama and Jensen 1983). This will typically extend to involvement in selection, renumeration, and, on occasion, dismissal, of the chief executive (Zahra and Pearce 1989). What is also important in agency theory is the strategic role of the board (Mizruchi 1983; Zahra and Pearce 1989).

In transaction-cost economics (TCE), the key issue is: when do firms produce to their own needs and when do they purchase in the market (the 'make-or-buy' question) (Coase 1937; Williamson 1975, 1985)? The different costs between the hierarchy of the organization and the market (the transaction costs) determine whether the market is used for some transactions and the internal hierarchy of the organization for others (Williamson 1985).

While agency theory regards the firm as a nexus of contracts, TCE considers the firm to be a governance structure. Agency theory and TCE differ chiefly in the choice of the basic unit of analysis. TCE regards the transaction as the basic unit of analysis, while in agency theory the basic unit of analysis is the individual agent. The two theories also differ in the contractual focus: agency theory holds that there is an irreducible agency cost in the move away from ownership to managerial discretion and the realignment of incentives to reduce these costs are *ex ante* costs. TCE, by contrast, 'emphasizes ex post costs' (Williamson 1984: 21). TCE attempts to reduce the costs of misaligned transactions 'through judicious choice of governance structure (market, hierarchy or hybrid), rather than merely realigning incentives and pricing them out . . . ' (Williamson 1984: 21).

Though there are these differences (for others, see Williamson 1984, and Eisenhardt 1989*a*), transaction-cost economics is 'increasingly intertwined' with agency theory (Doz and Prahalad 1991) and there are strong similarities between the two, particularly in regard to their assumptions. Both theories are concerned with managerial discretion, and both assume that managers are given to opportunism (self-interest seeking) and moral hazard, and that managers operate under bounded rationality (Simon 1976). Another common point of contact between the two theories is their view of the role of the board of directors. Both agency theory and TCE regard the board of directors as an instrument of control: 'the board is principally an instrument by which managers control other managers' (Williamson 1984: 22).

Stewardship theory

Stewardship theory takes off directly from considerations about assumptions inherent in both agency theory and TCE, specifically, arguing against the assumptions of opportunism and, drawing on organizational psychology and organizational sociology, putting the case for a different form of motivation for managers (Donaldson 1990; Fox and Hamilton 1994; Davis *et al.* 1997). The theory is developed by Donaldson (1990: 372), who states:

The 'model man' underlying agency and organisational economics is that of the self-interested actor rational maximising his own personal economic gain. The model is individualistic and is predicated upon the notion of an in-built conflict of interest between owner and manager. Moreover, the model is one of an individual calculating likely costs and benefits, and thus seeking to attain rewards and avoid punishment, especially financial ones. This is a model of the type called Theory X by organisational psychologists.

Donaldson's thesis is that these assumptions are extreme and there are alternative theories concerning what motivates human behaviour. He accepts that bounded rationality, one of the key assumptions of agency theory and TCE, is not problematic, but argues that, according to a number of theoretical considerations, there may be no inherent problem of managerial motivation. Citing McClelland (1961) and Herzberg *et al.* (1967), Donaldson claims that managers are motivated by non-financial motivators: they feel 'a need to achieve, to gain intrinsic satisfaction through successfully performing inherently challenging work, to exercise responsibility and authority, and thereby gain recognition from peers and bosses' (1990: 375).

Stewardship theory argues, therefore, that, rather than managers being seen as opportunistic, self-interested actors, they should be regarded as wanting to do a good job, 'to be good stewards of corporate assets' (Donaldson 1990: 376). The facilitation of effective performance by an executive is, on this view, determined by the contingencies of the organizational structure and how these help or hinder the implementation of plans and reinforce responsibility and authority.

A key consequence of the debate between organizational economics and stewardship theory concerns the issue of chief-executive duality. According to agency theory, the combining of the two roles in one person will lead to a concentration of power and consequently, owing to the agency costs involved in this, lower returns to shareholders. Stewardship theory, on the other hand, believes that unifying command at the head of the company—that is, combining the chief-executive and chairman roles—can have a beneficial effect on shareholder returns, by providing greater unity of direction and strong command and control.

Resource-dependence theory

The resource dependence theory stems from streams in economics and sociological research concerned with distribution of power in the firm (Zahra and Pearce 1989). These streams explored the phenomenon of board interlocks and their effect on the rivalry of industries, and the pattern of new director selection. In both streams, the general conclusion was that new directors were invited to sit on boards in order to enhance a firm's ability to raise funds, to add to the reputation of the company through recognition of their name in the community, and to deal with threats in the external environment (Zald 1969; Pennings 1980; Pearce and Zahra 1992).

Pfeffer (1972, 1973) used these streams of research to develop a strategic contingency theory of board composition. This theory claims that boards serve as a 'co-optative' mechanism for a company to link itself with the external environment to secure resources and, on occasion, protect itself against environmental adversity. For example, firms may strengthen their boards by inviting acknowledged leaders in different sectors of the firm's environment to serve on the board. As Pfeffer (1972: 222) writes: 'Business organisations (and other organisations) use their boards of directors as vehicles through which they coopt, or partially absorb, important external organisations with which they are interdependent. The strategy of co-optation involves exchanging some degree of control and privacy of information for some commitment for continued support from the external organisation.' Board structure is therefore seen as an institutional function, and theorists have argued that, by increasing the size and diversity of the board, the links between the organization and its environment and the securing of critical resources (including prestige and legitimacy) will be strengthened (Pfeffer 1972, 1973, 1987; Burt 1980; Pearce and Zahra 1992; Goodstein *et al.* 1994).

The resource-dependence theory is seen as having important links to Lawrence and Lorsch's (1967) thesis that successful organizations have internal structures that match environmental demands (Pfeffer 1972). Board size and composition are viewed as 'rational organisational responses to the conditions of the external environment' (Pfeffer 1972: 223). The theory is also intended to acknowledge the open systems nature of organizations, transacting with environments, and constrained by networks of interdependencies with other organizations, rather than understanding the behaviour of organizations simply in terms of rational, intentional managerial action (Pfeffer 1987).

The commonest forms of reducing environmental uncertainty resulting from dependence on external constituencies include mergers, joint ventures, contracts, and interlocking directorates, with interlocking directorates the most widely used environmental strategy (Bazerman and Schoorman 1983). There is a large literature on board interlock (see Pennings 1980), which, as Pfeffer (1987: 27) states, 'has probably been the most empirically studied form of intercorporate relation'. This theme is clearly complementary to the resource-dependence tradition. But there is one major difference, highlighted by Zahra and Pearce (1989), which is that, in board interlock theory, the interlock is usually between competing firms, whereas, with resource-dependence theory, directors help to link to both competitors and other environmental constituents.

The role of the board, on this view, is to provide information to reduce environmental uncertainty and to extract resources for company operations. However, as Mintzberg (1983) and Donaldson (1995) argue, the process of co-optation is wholly inferred. Donaldson (1995: 153) claims: 'Whether or not outsiders on the board are in fact drawn from powerful environment bodies or are in a position to influence those bodies, and whether they do so and are successful at making the competitive environment easier and more munificent for the focal organization—all of this remains unmeasured and unverified.'

Class-hegemony theory

The class-hegemony model developed from sociological research, mainly in the USA, which was generally Marxist in origin (C. W. Mills 1956; Nicols 1969). This research identified a cohesive upper class within the USA characterized by self-consciousness and consensus on social issues (Bazerman and Schoorman 1983). According to this model, power is shared by an elite at the head of large companies, an elite that holds similar views of reality. Boards of directors, on this view, seek to perpetuate this ruling elite and encourage the strengthening of it through interlocking directorates. As Stanworth and Giddens (1974) argue: 'Britain made gentlemen of businessmen and businessmen of gentlemen', with the result that a 'consolidated and unitary upper class in industrial Britain' was formed (cited in Useem 1984: 183).

This approach, like resource-dependence theory, focuses on intercorporate relations and there are close similarities in the predictions that both theories make (Mizruchi and Schwartz 1988; Pfeffer 1992). Both theories, too, have strong links to the theory of interlocking directorates, which class-based theorists view as a strategy to construct elite class networks (Zeitlin 1974) and which can be viewed as indicators of 'intraclass integration, co-ordination and control' (Soref and Zeitlin 1988: 77). Useem, using a comparison of US and UK companies, argues that the individuals who form the interlocks are an 'inner circle, [who] constitute a distinct, semi-autonomous network, one that transcends company, regional, sectoral and other politically divisive fault lines within the corporate community' (1984: 4).

The key difference between the two theories is that resource-dependence theory is characterized by an 'emphasis on actions serving the interests of and being organised by organisations rather than families, individuals or a social class' (Pfeffer 1992: 27). Class theory, therefore, adopts the view that organizations are the agents of individuals, families, or a social class rather than being agents of organizations (Pfeffer 1987).

According to this theory, the role of the board will emphasize selecting the 'right' directors (in terms of social status and influence). Useem (1984: 5) says: 'In considering an executive for promotion . . . it is not only reputation that has come to count. The executive's standing within the broader corporate community—as cultivated through successful service on the boards of several other large companies, leadership in major business associations, and the assumption of civic and public responsibilities—is increasingly a factor.'

A successful director, on this account, must also represent the capitalist elite (C. W. Mills 1956; Zahra and Pearce 1989) and, through the network, promote legislation favourable to all big business (Useem 1984). Strong competition will be discouraged (Bazermann and Schoorman 1983) and there will be unwritten rules on corporate conduct (Koenig *et al.* 1979).

Managerial-hegemony theory

The managerial-hegemony theory describes the board as a de jure, but not the de facto governing body of the organization. The real responsibility of running and controlling the company is assumed by corporate management. According to this theory, the board of directors is, in effect, a legal fiction and is dominated by management, making it ineffective in reducing the potential for agency problems between management and shareholders (Mace 1971; Vance 1983; Kosnik 1987).

This debate finds early expression in the work of Berle and Means (1932), whose thesis of the separation of ownership and control argued that, as companies grew and increased their share capital, the proportion of shares held by the largest institutions would decrease (Berle and Means 1932; Tricker 1984). As a result, the power of large shareholders to control corporations was diluted. The ensuing weakness of shareholder control means that the discretion afforded to management over the control of the company would increase, and, since managers are likely to be self-serving, they may pursue objectives of their own choosing (Parkinson 1993). The outline of the managerialist thesis shows that much depends on the definition of the term 'control'. There have been a number of conceptual difficulties around this issue (Herman 1981; Mizruchi 1983), but there is now a strong body of work in this area (Pettigrew 1992). Managers are expected to exercise day-to-day operating control, which gives them an intimate knowledge of the business, putting the board at a disadvantage. In addition to this specialized knowledge, managers in profitable companies are able to finance investments from retained earnings, thus allowing them to weaken the dependence on shareholders for capital (Mizruchi 1983). This allows them to pursue aims other than profit maximization. A further cause of managerial dominance stems from the procedure for selecting directors. As Pfeffer (1972: 220) writes: 'The selection procedure by which board members are chosen guarantees that, in most cases, board members are handpicked by management. In many practical respects, management is, therefore, in control of the board.'

This has led Mace (1971: 3) to state that 'boards are the creatures of the CEO'. There is a strong argument which states that, because insiders work for the chief executive, report to him or her regularly, and are generally dependent upon him or her for career advancement and rewards, it is unreasonable to expect a subordinate director to challenge a chief executive at a board meeting. Though outside directors do not suffer from this handicap to such an extent, the problem remains. The ineffectiveness of the board to monitor the performance of management stems, it is claimed, from the lack of independence of its outside directors. The selection of outside directors is controlled by management and, given the prestige and financial rewards of a seat on the board, typically means that the outside directors are unlikely to criticize management. Outside directors are unlikely to know a great deal about the business and management will frequently restrict information to them (Mace 1971). This will lead to the board adopting merely a 'rubber-stamping' function (Herman 1981). The size of board is another consideration. Large boards are 'weak' boards (Herman 1981), since large boards make in-depth discussion unlikely and increase the prospect for diversity and fragmentation.

The role of the board, therefore, on the managerial-hegemony approach is limited by the domination of management, and, as a result, the board is passive and has no input into organizational decision-making. Nor does it exercise control over the performance of the chief executive or the company as a whole, which, in the eyes of shareholders, makes the board ineffective. However, Zeitlin's (1974) attack on managerialism remains powerful, arguing that an increased concentration of ownership and interlocking directorships has created the conditions that considerably reduce the managerial problem. The increase in ownership concentration in recent years has strengthened this argument and Scott's (1985, 1997) thesis of the constellation of ownership interests constraining the scope for managerialism provides further support for this line of reasoning.

Scope and limitations of the theories

There are degrees of overlap between the six theories. Agency theory shares a number of assumptions with TCE, in particular bounded rationality, opportunism, and self-seeking behaviour. These theories, like managerial-hegemony theory, assume the problem of corporate control and the divergence of interest between shareholders and managers. Resource-dependence theory and class-hegemony tradition share with organizational economics the assumptions of self-interest at the individual level and goal conflict at the organizational level (Eisenhardt 1989*a*). The conflicts, of course, are settled differently, with the sociological models emphasizing the power of co-optation and coalitions while agency theory uses the alignment of incentives (Eisenhardt 1989*a*). Resource-dependence and class-hegemony theories also both focus on intercorporate relations and the use of the interlocking directorates research tradition. Given these overlaps, a number of authors have urged a methodological pluralism in relation to research on boards of directors. For example, Kosnik, whose 1987 study merged agency theory with managerial hegemony, concluded: 'The fact that both frameworks were found to offer relevant insights into the contingencies that might affect board performance in corporate governance illustrates how the integration of different research traditions can provide new insights into the functioning and performance of corporate boards of directors' (1987: 182). Eisenhardt recommends that agency theory be used with complementary theories because agency theory 'presents a partial view of the world that, although it is valid, also ignores a good bit of the complexity of organisations. Additional perspectives can help to capture the greater complexity' (1989*a*: 71). Barney (1990) urges a methodological linkage between TCE and traditional management theory, including stewardship theory, while Donaldson and Davies argue that, regarding stewardship theory and agency theory, the key issue might not be which one is more valid, for 'each may be valid for some phenomena but not for others. Then the question is what are the switching rules between agency and stewardship theory?' (1991: 11).

The view that one theory by itself does not illuminate the whole spectrum of board endeavour receives strong support from examination of the shortcomings of the various positions described. Agency theory's key assumption about the opportunism of management and their non-alignment with shareholders' interests has been criticized as too narrow and failing to take account of alternative views on the nature of human motivation. Perrow argues that the theory's view of individuals as opportunistic and self-seeking is dehumanizing, and too simplistic to have any practical import (Perrow 1986; Hendry 1997). TCE has been criticized on similar grounds (Ghoshal and Moran 1996). Difficulties over board composition measures and firm performance measures have meant that empirical findings have been inconsistent and associations have at best been modest (Johnson *et al.* 1996). A further shortcoming concerns the fact that the nature of the strategic role of the board, highlighted as crucial by agency theory, has had little empirical support (Henke 1986; Zahra and Pearce 1989).

TCE also gives little detail as to how the board should be composed or organized beyond providing a strong control role. Stewardship theory suffers from lack of empirical support and, like agency theory and TCE, does not document how boards make decisions. Resource-dependence theory, though it tells us much about the external fit between boards of organizations and the environment, largely ignores the details about the inner workings of boards—for example, their involvement in strategy-making, or how directors are chosen to sit on the board (Zahra and Pearce 1989). Further, as Provan (1980) points out, resource-dependence theory focuses almost entirely on resource attainment as the criterion of board effectiveness, rather than (or in addition to) resource use. Managerial-hegemony theory has some empirical support, but its theoretical basis, that boards of directors are ineffective governing mechanisms, has run into problems over the definition of the word 'control' (Mizruchi 1983). Further, Mizruchi argues that, even though the board may have little knowledge of the workings of the company or its day-to-day running, nevertheless it 'is able to set the limits within which management will act' (1983: 433). The board has what Mizruchi calls 'bottom-line' control, primarily the ability to hire and fire the chief executive, though he accepts that there is little evidence on whether boards do in fact carry out such a role. The work by Zeitlin (1974) and Scott (1997) has also cast doubt on the claims of managerialism by invoking the constraining powers of investors and the structure of finance capitalism. Class-hegemony theory has moderate empirical evidence to support it, but, like resource-dependence theory, suffers from a general lack of detail on what it is that boards actually do and the characteristics of actual corporate governance practices. A major problem for both class theory and resource-dependence theory lies in their reliance on the phenomenon of interlocking directorates. Interlocking directorate research has been criticized as focusing largely on the method of network analysis without providing an adequate explanation of what the consequences are of the ties that are identified: in other words, empirical evidence on the effects of interlocks on what firms actually do is virtually nil (Zajac 1992; Pettigrew 1992).

Board process studies

The central problem with research on boards of directors has been that the majority of studies have been conducted at one remove from board activity (Pettigrew 1992). That is, much energy has been expended in testing theoretical models, using secondary data chiefly on company performance, while few descriptive studies have actually been carried out with directors themselves. As Tricker states in an editorial to the journal *Corporate Governance: An International Review*: 'the gap between the contributions of theory and what practitioners are interested in seems to be widening. Rigour and relevance should not be mutually exclusive' (1994: 55).

Pettigrew lends his weight to a move away from the study of boards 'several paces from the actors, process and issue' (1992: 177) to one that opens up the black box of board behaviour. As he argues:

the study of boards and their directors has not been helped by over-ambitious attempts to link independent variables such as board composition to outcome variables such as board and firm performance. The research agenda here need not be guided just by studies testing the relative explanatory power of agency theory or theories of managerial hegemony. The task is perhaps a simpler one, to redress the overwhelmingly prescriptive bias in this literature and begin to provide some basic descriptive findings about boards and their directors. (1992: 178)

Though some research has centred on issues of board power and control over management, this work has tended to focus on structural aspects of power. However, these aspects—formal authority position, legislative right, control over rewards and sanctions—must also been seen in conjunction with relational sources of power and influence—abilities, personal prestige or status, quality of contacts—if a rounded picture of board activity is to be developed (Finkelstein 1992; Pettigrew and McNulty 1995).

As Finkelstein (1992) argues, power is a relative concept, capable of being understood only in particular contexts. Pettigrew and McNulty's work supports this claim, stating that 'power displayed on one occasion may not be transferable to other settings. Because power is inherently situational, it is dynamic and potentially unstable' (1995: 852). Because strategic decisions are by their nature uncertain and laden with ambiguities, they leave space for the exercise of power, with different board members pursuing their own preferred choices (Finkelstein 1992). These structural and relational forms of power have been viewed, particularly in the light of Giddens's theory of structuration, as simultaneous and complementary (Giddens 1977; Brass and Burkhardt 1993; Pettigrew and McNulty 1995). A study of board process will therefore examine not just the structural arrangements of the board, but crucially the behaviours and relationship-building processes that are involved in carrying out board tasks.

There have been a number of studies that have undertaken descriptive analysis of boards of directors (Mace 1971; Pahl and Winkler 1974; Fidler 1981; Lorsch and MacIver 1989; Demb and Neubauer 1992; S. Hill 1995; O'Neal and Thomas 1995; Pettigrew and McNulty 1995), studies that have tended to support the thesis of the managerial domination of the board, while stressing that there are certain contingencies that may alter the balance of power between executives and non-executives and so may provide for a more influential role for the board. Mace (1971) found that, in a sample of US boards (where non-executives are usually in the majority), the board's involvement in such roles as strategic decision-making, monitoring the company, and evaluating the president was minimal, unless the organization was undergoing a crisis. Lorsch and MacIver's (1989) study confirmed the picture of board passivity in normal conditions. Pahl and Winkler's (1974) UK research reported similar findings, with boards presented as legitimating institutions rather than decision-making ones. The work of Fidler (1981), Demb and Neubauer (1992), Ferlie, Ashburner and Fitzgerald (1994), and Pettigrew and McNulty (1995) also supports the managerial-hegemony view of the organization, but identifies further contingencies that can influence the degree to which the board becomes involved. External contingencies—concentration of ownership, the external environment, industry type—and internal contingencies—phase of life cycle, chief-executive style, company size, and corporate resource situation are cited, together with the composition of the board, its structure, the nature of board process and the characteristics of the directors—will all have an important influence on how involved the board will be in the management of the organization. Hill's (1995) findings also emphasize the influence of the executive, in particular the chief executive, and how an established boardroom culture can limit the influence of non-executive directors. But Hill concludes that evidence for the divergence between the interests of owners and those of managers was scant, with managers wanting to be seen to be good professionals running the company, lending support to the stewardship theory of boards.

A series of studies by Westphal and Zajac has highlighted how the interpersonal influence processes in the board/chief-executive relationship can help trust and cooperation develop within the board and help problem-solving and decision-making activity (Westphal and Zajac 1995a, 1997; Zajac and Westphal 1996).

These studies provide some insight into the nature of boards in operation and the norms of conduct present in the boardroom. However, some deal with only part of board activity (for example, strategic involvement), and some deal only with US experience, where non-executive directors are in the majority, unlike the situation in the UK, where the reverse is generally the case. This has resulted in a concentration on the role of the non-executive at the expense of the executive director, who, from the writings of some researchers, is seen to have an important role in monitoring the CEO (Baysinger and Hoskisson 1990; Johnson *et al.* 1996). A number of studies are based on questionnaire data alone, which removes the researcher a little further from the boardroom; and some were written before the major changes in corporate governance of the early 1990s, which considerably altered the profile of the issue and potentially the approach of many boards of directors.

This book examines board activity as a whole and seeks to understand directors' views of their own role and the contexts and processes that influence the degree to which they can carry out their functions. The research is grounded in the experience of directors and aims to examine the nature of relationships within the board as well as, to some extent, the board's relationships with shareholders and stakeholders. In the next chapter, the methodology that framed this research will be described.

3

Researching Boards of Directors

There is only a small body of primary research on boards of directors from which to draw any methodological insights. In this chapter, we discuss the methodological approach used in this book. The field of boards-of-directors' research gives rise to a number of problems in terms of methodology. First, there is the problem of access—achieving contact with directors and securing their participation can be difficult. The issue of research instrument also has a strong bearing here; directors tend to refuse to complete questionnaires, and are reluctant on the whole to cooperate with participant observation studies (Fidler 1981; Moyser and Wagstaff 1987a). Secondly, there are defensive responses—many directors, particularly of large firms, are used to being under the media spotlight, and have as a consequence developed a wariness in discussing their company and their activities with external parties. There is always a danger of the researcher receiving very little information, or information that constitutes merely a public-relations exercise, designed to show the director and firm in as good a light as possible, which may not reflect the underlying reality. Thirdly, there is the problem of holding directors to the script (Hill 1995)—directors may deem other issues more interesting and pertinent than those on the interview schedule, and so may impose their own agenda, something that they are well used to in their corporate lives.

These issues have been encountered by most researchers working on elites. In the following sections, we discuss the research approach we have used to study boards of directors

Methods

The shortcomings of the individual research methods can be overcome to some extent by adopting a multi-method approach to research design (Jick 1979). This approach has been used to good effect in boards-of-directors' research chiefly using the triangulation model, where the multiple methods converge on a single 'answer' (Snow and Thomas 1994). For example, Lorsch and MacIver, in their 1989 study of US boards, interviewed eighty directors and supplemented this with four case studies and a questionnaire ($n=1,100$). Demb and Neubauer (1992) also took a multi-method approach, interviewing seventy-one directors from eleven multinational companies and using the results from a questionnaire, whose sample ($n=137$) was taken from a number of board-level courses the authors ran at IMD in Lausanne. Interviews lasted two to three hours. Judge and Zeithaml (1992) used a combination of qualitative and quantitative data in their work on board involvement with strategic decisions, interviewing in the main the chief executive, an insider, and an outsider using a semi-structured format in forty-two organizations for a total of 114 interviews, but, instead of employing a questionnaire, they used directors' responses to two seven-point scales introduced in the interview to gain measures of board involvement. Peck (1995) provides a rare example of a study that uses observation, minutes, and questionnaires to study the performance of an NHS Trust board. Fifteen board meetings were observed and board papers and minutes gathered, and, at the end of this process, a questionnaire was sent to the members of the Trust board with items measuring 'members' perceptions of the roles that the board had been most successful at undertaking during its initial months' (Peck 1995: 146). Multi-method approaches are also common in related fields such as strategy (Pettigrew 1973; Eisenhardt and Bourgeois 1988) and human resource management (Truss *et al.* 1997). The reward for use of such multi-method use is 'likely to be increased validity' (Snow and Thomas 1994: 474) and robustness in the findings. For this reason, this study used between-method triangulation to try to ensure the rigour of the research. The methods chosen were open-ended interviews with main board directors, interviews with shareholder groups and stakeholder representatives, and case studies with four UK public companies involving interviews with on average five main board directors; and the gathering of extensive secondary and archival data.

Construction of sampling frame

Because of concern that access to main board directors would be a problem, it was decided that the sampling frame should be as large as possible within three constraints: (1) the directors had to sit on the main board (functional directors who were not on the main board, directors of subsidiary firms, and retired directors were therefore excluded); (2) the companies had to be UK owned; and (3) the companies had to be public companies. The reasons for these constraints are straightforward. With regard to the first constraint, the primary focus of the research was to examine the perceptions of directors concerning their own roles. This was felt to be best achieved by studying directors who took large resource allocation decisions, who had, in some sense, real power within the firm (Fidler 1981). The second constraint enabled the study to circumvent issues concerning differing corporate governance systems and structures. There is a real need for cross-cultural research in this area, but this book had a more modest intent and did not set out to address those issues. The third constraint ensured that the issue of ownership and control would surface—a central plank of the corporate governance debate—and that the degree of specialization and diversity within the firm owing to size and presence in various markets would be reflected in the make-up of the board. In particular, studying the public company would bring forth the debate over the role of the non-executive director, again, a key focus in both academic and prescriptive literatures.

The sampling frame was initially constructed, like Fidler's (1981), from *The Times'* list of the 1,000 largest companies, with foreign firms excluded. The strategy to gain access was composed of a number of strands, which together produced a workable sample. Pettigrew and McNulty (1995) have shown that gaining access to the top echelon of companies may be difficult, but, with perseverance, one can achieve good results. The principal methods used in this study have followed a similar pattern to Martin's approach (1985): (1) direct approach using third-party contact; (2) direct approach by letter; (3) direct approach through personal contact; (4) indirect approach through referral, though the order was changed.

The first approach was to begin, not by direct approach by letter, but to try to push on an open door through the use of a third-party contact. If successful, this would constitute a 'warm' contact and the interviewee could then recommend a subsequent interview with another director. This method was used sparingly but it certainly had reasonable success. For this approach, a personal contact who knew or was working with a director of a public company would offer to talk to that director and tell him or her about the project. This was followed by a letter outlining the research and citing the mutual contact, and requesting a meeting. Most useful in this regard was the help of senior academic colleagues who helped by giving leads into a number of organizations.

The direct approach by letter brought surprising results. This was sent to the first 500 on *The Times'* 1,000 list (excluding foreign firms), with a subsequent mailing put on stand-by. Several leading companies responded very positively to a tailored letter, enough to postpone the next mailing, and were willing to arrange an interview with a main board director. These letters were usually addressed to the chairman of the companies concerned, and this is where the bulk of interviews with chairmen originated. This type of approach certainly reinforced the original conviction that the subject of boards of directors was one that was stimulating great interest among practitioners, and it also served, indirectly, to instil confidence in the research programme as a worthwhile study.

The third approach relied on personal contacts; though this was the easiest method, it required a large degree of caution. Gaining contacts in this area is a difficult process, and, once they are achieved, one is wary of jeopardizing them. Therefore, approaching contacts for interview must be done on the basis that the project is clearly explained, that the interviewees feel they will not be wasting their time, and that their trust is not abused by asking for highly sensitive information.

The fourth method is a very effective one and perhaps lends some weight to the theory of director networks. This is to ask an interviewee if he or she can propose anyone else who might be able to help with the research. Invariably they can, and this leads to a further approach using method 1.

The sample, therefore, in common with most qualitative research on business elites, was chosen with a degree of opportunism. As Hill (1995: 248) argues, 'successful sampling does not appear to be feasible in research on directors'. The only stipulation was that sufficient numbers of different types of director—chief executive, chairman, executive, and non-executive—were represented.

Design of the interview schedule

The schedule was drawn from an analysis of existing literature. There was broad agreement from the prescriptive literature that the board has three main roles: strategic, control, and institutional (Zahra and Pearce 1989). The strategic role is said to be the defining role of the board, giving the term 'director' its true meaning, and playing an important part in determining the organization's effectiveness. The control role refers to the key responsibility of the board to safeguard the company's assets and resources, to ensure survival, and to avoid corporate trauma or consistent poor performance. The institutional role is concerned with the board as the perceived apex of the company, the figurehead in terms of public perception and accountability. The institutional role also includes the board's ability to span boundaries and form networks with other companies and influential bodies (for example, the government), thus enhancing credibility and legitimacy and potentially securing scarce resources more efficiently.

These three broad roles formed the outline of the interview schedule. On the basis of previous research in the area (Mace 1971; Henke 1986; Lorsch and MacIver 1989; Demb and Neubauer 1992), a number of questions and prompts were included under each heading. The interview schedule was piloted with five directors (three executives and two non-executives who were participants of a Henley Management College Directors' course). One of the executive directors invited us to sit in on a board meeting, which allowed the schedule to be refined further. Following the revision of some questions to avoid ambiguity or framing, a schedule of twenty questions was settled upon. Questions focused on the extent of board involvement in strategy, the nature of strategy discussions (for example, formal and informal, frequency, and so on); how the board adds value, how the board monitors the health of the company, the control measures it has at its disposal, and how the board links with the external environment.

Directors were invited to talk around the questions and develop any points they believed were important, either to them as individuals or companies, or about the wider concerns of boards of directors as a whole. The principal point guiding the data collection was that there should be enough flexibility to encourage new ideas to emerge, to look for unexpected contingencies, and to gain new insights.

In addition, interviews were also carried out with a number of stakeholder groups. One of the themes of the book concerns the expectations of boards of directors and it was felt important to gain the views of a number of 'stakeholders' on the perceptions of the role of the board. A number of key informants were chosen from a variety of institutions, including the Institutional Shareholders' Committee, the Consumers' Association, the Stock Exchange, the Bank of England, analysts, environmental groups, and journalists. There were twenty of these interviews in total, lasting usually one and half hours, and the data collected helped considerably in terms of understanding the contextual frame surrounding the board of directors.

Interviews were conducted with fifty-one directors of public companies in the UK. The directors came from a wide variety of sectors, so that a general picture of board endeavour could be built up that was not industry specific. The sample also ranged across types of director (see Table 3.1). These interviews lasted between one and two hours each. After fifty-one interviews, it was judged that 'theoretical saturation' had occurred (Glaser and Strauss 1967) and that additional interviews were not providing new or divergent information.

TABLE 3.1. *Interviews: Breakdown by type*

Director type	Number
Chief executives	11
Chairmen	16
Executives	13
Non-executives	11
TOTAL	51

Case studies

The second strand of the research was to conduct case studies into four large UK businesses—Allied Domecq, BAA, Burmah Castrol, and Securicor—in order to deepen the understanding of board process. Though cases are often portrayed as somehow inferior to other social-science methods, with sufficient rigour, case studies can yield rich data that are capable of standing on an equal footing with any other research method (Eisenhardt 1989*b*; Parkhe 1993). Indeed, as Parkhe (1993: 258), citing Eisenhardt, argues: 'one of the strengths of building theory from cases is that the constant juxtaposition of conflicting realities forces individuals to reframe perceptions into a new gestalt and tends to "unfreeze" thinking and so the process has the potential to generate theory with less researcher bias than theory built from incremental studies.' Traditional concerns over the case study as not yielding generalizable findings rest on a confusion between replication logic and sampling logic. The use of multiple cases allows for replication, with multiple cases analogous to multiple experiments, so that, if similar results occur in the cases, replication can be said to occur, making the findings more robust and increasing validity (Yin 1984; Eisenhardt 1989*b*). An individual case is, therefore, similar to a single experiment and 'the analysis must follow cross-experiment rather than within-experiment design and logic' (Yin 1984: 48). The replication logic stands in contrast to sampling logic, where a number of respondents are assumed to represent a larger population, 'so that data from a smaller number of persons are assumed to represent the data that might have been collected from the entire pool' (Yin 1984: 50). Sampling logic is inappropriate for case studies, because cases are not intended to assess the incidence of phenomena and because a sampling logic would entail the production of a huge number of cases, as the researcher attempts to cover both the phenomena and their context (Yin 1984: 52).

The cases were chosen primarily because they are large and complex companies that have strong reputations but have also experienced periods of turbulence and change. As Pettigrew (1990: 270) states, in site selection: 'a judicious mixture of forethought and intention, chance and opportunism, and environmental preparedness play their part'. The forethought and intention of this research were to choose companies from different sectors that were highly visible and that could provide critical incidents and social dramas (Pettigrew 1990). What was wanted was for the company to allow access to a number of board members, ideally five, so that a rounded picture of board activity could be gained. A number of leading companies were approached to ask if they would take part in the research. Twelve agreed to take part initially but two dropped out because of business pressures, and five said they would take part, but with only the chairman or the chief executive willing to speak on behalf of the whole board. This left four companies, and, for the purposes of the study, this was felt to be a sufficient number of cases. In theoretical terms, studying structurally complex, diversified companies is appropriate if the research is to be able to examine the nature of the board *vis-à-vis* management, the use of board committees, the relationship between the board and shareholders, and the issues of control associated with large companies.

In addition to interviews with several board members, company documentation and secondary data were gathered. Company annual reports, mission statements, policy documents, reserved powers statements, public-relations material, as well as analysts' reports, press cuttings, and other archival information provided a rich source of data with which to assess company activity and the role of the board.

Data analysis

Interviews

The data analysis procedure followed the grounded theory approach expounded by Glaser and Strauss (1967), which requires that data and theory be constantly compared throughout the data collection and analysis period. The process of evolving theory in this research began before the actual data collection, primarily through the review of literature. Ideas gathered from this source served to orient the fieldwork, but these ideas were held 'lightly' and were constantly compared and contrasted with the notes from the interviews and other pieces of information collected during the data collection. The result was a set of initial categories used to organize the data, examples being: the mandate of the board, the strategy process, control issues, the role of the non-executive director, the role of the chairman, dialogues with external constituencies. These categories were modified as the data collection continued in order to account for new evidence. Certain themes or key phrases that emerged as common across interviews (for example, gatekeeping and diagnosis) made for strong additional categories.

Following an interview, a transcription would be produced. This would be supplemented by making a contact summary sheet, which would highlight the main concepts, themes, and issues from the interview (Miles and Huberman 1994). The contact summary sheet was usually no more than a page in length, but the regular production of these sheets helped the researcher not to get bogged down in a mass of material. Elementary codes were applied to the salient points on the sheet. This speedy method of data reduction was very helpful in sorting out initial thoughts and impressions. Interview transcripts were analysed sentence by sentence and coded against the provisional category list. The initial categories were adhered to for the first five or six interviews, and then some were revised in the light of fit and descriptive power (Miles and Huberman 1994). Some overlapping themes were merged and second-order theoretical labels were assigned to the emergent themes to capture the categories at a higher level of abstraction (Van Maanen 1979).

Case studies

The process of analysing the interviews from the case-study phase followed that of the initial round of interviews. Patterns were matched to the model, with checks made for new information of potentially new categories. This buttressing of the original findings through exploration in four different research sites affords a further element of triangulation into the study, with the new data from the cases testing the validity and generality of the initial findings. This corroborative work is advanced by Yin (1984) and Eisenhardt (1989b) as an important source of validity and reliability. A further source of confidence in the findings rests on the fact than a draft of the findings was sent to the case companies, who were invited to give any comments. The comments were incorporated into the final draft and served as a valuable reality check to the initial interpretations of the data.

Conclusion

The methodological approach chosen in this study has attempted to reflect and understand the complexity of the functioning of organizational elites. This study has incorporated interviews with multiple constituencies and four case studies, as well as extensive analysis of secondary data, to provide a rounded picture of board involvement in large UK companies. In the next chapter, we shall turn to the empirical data, focusing first on the role of the board in the strategic process.

4
The Strategic Role of the Board

Greater pressure for corporate accountability in the light of increased shareholder activism and public scrutiny has prompted an examination of the board's role in strategic decision-making (Judge and Zeithaml 1992). Policy initiatives have urged boards to become more involved, and major institutional shareholder groups have also issued guidelines that have encouraged boards to challenge the strategic leadership provided by management (ISC 1991). Further, the board's involvement in the strategic decision-making process has been called the best defence against hostile takeover bids (Weidenbaum 1985). Though there is some evidence that boards are becoming more involved (*The Economist* 1994), the overwhelming impression, certainly from the business press, is one of board passivity and reluctance to introduce contestability into the boardroom.

The view that boards fail to realize their potential in the strategic decision-making process receives theoretical backing from the managerialist tradition. The work of Mace (1971) and Lorsch and MacIver (1989) found that boards were often willing to become involved in the strategic process, but were either constrained from doing so, or else were availed of the opportunity only in times of crisis. However, in much of the literature, the nature of involvement remains undifferentiated. The two basic questions, 'what does strategy-making mean', and 'what constitutes involvement in strategy' usually remain unaddressed: it is assumed that 'strategy' and 'involvement' are perspicuous concepts, but this is far from being the case. The purpose of this chapter is to examine the nature of boards' perception of strategy, and involvement therein, and to discuss the enablers and constraints to the board playing a more active role in organizational decision-making. In brief, the main arguments are as follows.

The board's role in large organizations is not to formulate strategy, but rather to set the context of strategy. It does this in a number of ways: through setting and actively reviewing the corporate definition—the 'what business are we in' question; through the gatekeeping function—actively assessing and reviewing strategic proposals, and often *changing* proposals through comment and advice; through confidence-building—encouraging managers with good track records in their strategic aims; and through the selection of directors—the outcomes of which send strong signals to the rest of the organization concerning the type of person who succeeds and the standards others have to attain.

These roles are important in shaping the domain of discretion for managers, and are crucial strategic mechanisms for the company, for at least three reasons. First, the board is the ultimate arbiter of what constitutes the focus of the company. Secondly, through selective screening and confidence-building, the capacity for innovation and entrepreneurship can be regulated and motivated. Thirdly, through constant examination of the business definition and corporate strategy, the commitment to certain strategies or business sectors may be questioned and so boards may be instrumental in breaking organizational habits and forcing change.

The evidence of this research, therefore, is that, contra the managerialist theory, the board does play a valuable role in the strategic process within an organization. Supporting evidence from the control role of the board and from its institutional role (see Chapters 5 and 6) will show the board's potential for strategic activity through the use of feedforward systems of control—diagnosing situations that can bring about change—and through boundary-spanning activity, which can bring new information and bring changes in strategic direction.

This chapter is structured as follows. First, a brief overview of relevant theory will be examined and then various models of strategy will be discussed. This will be followed by the major findings of the research: the board's role in setting the strategic context and its involvement in the strategic content. The chapter is concluded by a discussion and implications for theory.

Theoretical debates

The strategic role of the board is often used as the defining characteristic of board endeavour, the role that separates the work of the board from that of management (Tricker 1984; Lorsch and MacIver 1989; Hilmer 1994; Hilmer and Tricker 1994). Though the Companies Act does not set out specific roles for directors, the board's fiduciary duty is usually taken to include responsibility for the monitoring and assessment of strategic proposals. Tricker (1984) states that direction involves the formulation of strategy, the acquisition and allocation of resources, and the setting of policies. The Institute of Directors' *Guidelines for Directors* (IOD 1995) also states that the board takes responsibility for determining the company's strategic objectives and strategic policies.

The role of the board in strategy is usually taken to include identifying what business the company is in, developing a vision and mission, assessing threats and opportunities, strengths and weaknesses, and selecting and implementing a choice of strategies (Tricker 1984; Pearce and Zahra 1991; Hilmer 1993a). The strategic role of the board has been clearly identified as a major factor in strengthening a company's competitive position and in ensuring the alignment of company purpose with shareholders' interests (Mintzberg 1983; Parkinson 1993). Andrews (1980) has argued that boards should actively determine the future direction of the company, labelling this a key part of the leadership role of the board. He says: 'Effective board participation in strategic processes could make an important long-term difference in a company's performance' (1980: 31). The board's strategic role is also said to encompass acquiring resources (Pfeffer 1972, 1973) and taking decisions on strategic change that enable the organization to achieve fit with environmental change (Mintzberg 1978; Pearce and Zahra 1991; Goodstein *et al.* 1994). Goodstein *et al.* (1994) argue that heightened periods of environmental turbulence or declines in company performance provide boards of directors with the potential for full mobilization and the initiation of strategic change.

Agency theory (see Eisenhardt 1989a for a full review), resource-dependence theory (Pfeffer 1972, 1973; Pfeffer and Salancik 1978; Provan 1980) and stewardship theory (Donaldson 1995) agree on the usefulness of boards contributing to the strategic discussions within a company (see Chapter 2 for details). Agency theory, as Zahra and Pearce (1989: 302) state: 'places a premium on a board's strategic contribution, specifically the board's involvement in and contribution to the articulation of the firm's mission, the development of the firm's strategy and the setting of guidelines for implementation and effective control of the chosen strategy'.

Stewardship theory views the strategic role of the board as contributing to the board's stewardship of the company, while resource-dependence theory argues that, by increasing the size and diversity of the board, the links between the organization and its environment and the securing of critical resources (including prestige and legitimacy) will be strengthened (Pfeffer and Salancik 1978; Pearce and Zahra 1991; Goodstein *et al.* 1994) and this boundary-spanning activity can bring new strategic information.

Empirical support for the strategic role of the board comes from Demb and Neubauer's (1992) study of seventy-one directors, which revealed that over three-quarters of those interviewed saw the board's main task as setting strategy and overall direction. However, the nature and type of involvement were not examined in this study (O'Neal and Thomas 1995). Tricker's series of studies in UK companies (1984) supported the view that boards are involved in the strategic process, though again the exact nature of the board's role is not specified. The Conference Board of America (1993, 1996) found boards giving a significant proportion of meeting time to strategic issues, though these studies based on surveys failed to differentiate the nature of 'involvement'. Judge and Zeithaml (1992), following interviews with 114 board members from four US industry sectors, found that board size, levels of diversification, and insider representation were negatively related to board involvement, and organizational age was positively related to it. Board involvement positively related to financial performance, after controlling for industry and size effects. For Tashakori and Boulton (1985), board involvement in strategy is positively correlated with information availability, board performance evaluation, and a majority of outside directors.

Hill's (1995) study of forty-two UK directors in eleven companies confirmed that strategic direction is what directors see as their main purpose, with non-executive directors seeing a wide role for themselves, including bringing breadth of vision, scanning the environment, and acting as a sounding board for the chief executive. The issue of the forcefulness and ability of non-executives to make a significant contribution was a key theme of Pettigrew and McNulty's (1995) study of twenty UK non-executives. They characterize some board cultures as minimalist, others as maximalist, depending on the part-time members' will and skill, and also the presence of contextual factors, such as crisis conditions or changing board dynamics. A similar story was depicted in Ferlie, Ashburner, and Fitzgerald's (1994) research into eleven NHS boards, where three levels of board involvement were identified—rubber stamping, probing and questioning of strategic options, and active involvement in deciding between options, including shaping the vision. Factors influencing progression through levels include the experience, expertise, and confidence of the non-executive director, and whether the executives want non-executives to make the transition.

There are numerous dissenting voices in the debate over the board's strategic contribution, notably Mace (1971), who found that boards were not involved in strategic planning and that the basic objectives, corporate strategies, and broad policies of the company are not in fact established by the board in most large and medium-sized companies: 'For example, a management proposal for approval of an annual capital budget, involving $10m to $50m or more, will take roughly thirty minutes of a board meeting of one and a half hours. And it would be a rare board member who would do anything except go along with management' (1971: 31). Mace did discover, however, that, in crisis situations, boards became heavily involved in the decision-making process within the organization. Lorsch and MacIver's study (1989) of eighty directors and four case companies also supported the managerialist view. Norburn and Grinyer's research into twenty-one British boards found large-scale disagreement in the establishment of corporate direction: 'The entire picture of objective setting is one of confusion and is in marked contrast to the recommendations of the academic and consultancy world' (1974: 38).

Pahl and Winkler (1974), who conducted research in nineteen companies using a variety of qualitative techniques, found that boards collectively do not decide or discuss anything, with most proposals 'going through on the nod,' and concluded that the board is a legitimating institution rather than a decision-making one. Rosenstein (1987) examined four US corporations and stated that the board is 'not a proper locus for making or originating strategy', though he did say that a major role is to monitor and dismiss the chief executive. Henke's survey of 234 US manufacturing firms showed that almost every board influenced the decisions of numerous strategy-related issues, though surprisingly 'the majority of boards do not recognize that they are involved in the strategy decision-making' (1986: 93).

This last point illustrates some of the difficulties in researching this area. Debates over what constitutes 'strategy' are a staple of the strategic management literature, and, while single definitions have proved elusive, a number of theoretical schools have developed that have become influential. In the next section, we shall examine some of the most important.

Models of strategy

A powerful underlying conception of strategy has been that strategy is the result of formal planning—an analytic process that establishes long-term objectives, a process usually initiated by top management and undertaken by staff strategists (Chandler 1962; Ansoff 1965). Though this view of strategy has had enormous influence among businesses, particularly in the 1970s and 1980s (Hendry *et al.* 1993), descriptive analysis of the complexity of the strategy process within organizations led to this view being challenged (Mintzberg and Waters 1985; Noda and Bower 1996). A number of conceptual and empirical problems were raised. Planning for optimal solutions is highly problematic, given environmental uncertainty (Cyert and March 1963) and the bounded rationality of managers (Simon 1976). Ethnographic studies demonstrated that clear objectives are often not set (Pettigrew 1985) and that political activity often constrains the choice of organizational goals (Hickson *et al.* 1971). Organizations usually have multiple constituencies, each with varying degrees of power, whose objectives can often conflict with the goals of the organization (Tsui 1990). The role of managers at lower levels in the strategy process, providing a bottom-up contribution to organizational goals, is also important (Bower 1970; Burgelman 1983, 1991; Mintzberg 1983). Finally, the strategic planning model gave no account of how strategies might be effectively implemented (Hendry *et al.* 1993).

The recognition of these concerns has brought a clear focus in strategy research on the process of strategy, and a move away from prescription towards a descriptive understanding of the complexity of strategy formation and implementation. Mintzberg's series of studies (Mintzberg 1973, 1978; Mintzberg and Waters 1985) has researched the process of strategy formulation based on the definition of strategy as 'a pattern in a stream of decisions'. Strategy, in this view, is emergent rather than planned, and involves multiple levels within the organization (Burgelman 1983, 1991; Noda and Bower 1996). Though scholars in this tradition are critical of the strategic planning model and regard it as seriously limited, nevertheless there is recognition that no strategies will be perfectly emergent, and some planning element will remain: 'It is difficult to imagine action in the *total* absence of intention—in some pocket of the organisation if not from the leadership itself' (Mintzberg and Waters 1985: 2). Deliberate and emergent strategies, then, 'form the poles of a continuum along which we would expect real-world strategies to fall' (Mintzberg and Waters 1985: 3).

Though some companies may lack an articulated corporate level strategy, it would be rare for any organization to have no rough strategic direction. The determination of this corporate-level variable is usually thought to be undertaken by top corporate executives (Mintzberg and Waters 1985; Noda and Bower 1996). In addition, top-level executives are also responsible for the structural context of the firm, which includes determining the organizational architecture, performance management, and information systems (Burgelman 1983, 1991; Noda and Bower 1996). These top-down processes, however, are not completely detached from the influences of managerial activities at lower levels of the corporate hierarchy. From the field data, the picture that emerged was one of multiple and interlocking activities throughout the organization. Managers within the hierarchy interpret and amend broad top-down strategic and structural direction and, through feedback and the development of strategic initiatives at the front line of organizational activity, provide a bottom-up strategic process to combine with the broad overlay.

In research on boards of directors, discussions of the strategic role of the board have largely ignored the emergent nature of strategy and its implications for board involvement. Demb and Neubauer (1992) briefly mentioned the issue and asserted that, the more an organization is characterized by an emergent strategy-development process, the less likely it is that the board will be involved; the more fluid and fragmented the decision-making process, the less chance there is for non-executive directors to intervene or to submit their opinions (1992: 73–82). However, given the importance of the emergent strategy view, further examination of the board's role when faced with such conditions would be valuable.

Levels of strategy involvement

The concept of involvement in strategy has proved difficult to define. A common distinction is based on the largely accepted view of specific strategy decisions as being composed of a formation phase and an evaluation phase (Judge and Zeithaml 1992). In both formulation and evaluation, there are levels of involvement, which can be represented as continua (Zahra and Pearce 1989; Pettigrew and McNulty 1995). In formulation, the board's involvement ranges from working with management to develop strategic direction to merely ratifying management's proposals. In evaluation, boards can be classified as to whether they probe management's evaluations of resource allocations or whether they simply accept the evaluation top management provides (Judge and Zeithaml 1992). Unpacking this concept is rare in the literature, but it serves to heighten our awareness of the potential for boards and to base expectations of board endeavour on a more realistic footing. In general, the literature has drawn a broad distinction between 'passive' and 'active' boards (see Table 4.1)

In an entirely passive board, the only contribution made by directors is to satisfy the requirements of company law. The simplest (and limiting) case is where the board is entirely composed of executives and the board is simply a legal fiction. In such cases, the board is identical with the top management team, but it nevertheless initiates formal board meetings in order to comply with its statutory duties. We shall ignore these cases for the reason that Parker (1990) gives—namely, that a board without non-

TABLE 4.1. *Studies on strategic involvement of the board*

Strength of involvement	Description	Studies
Passive	Statutory boards	Pro-forma (Pahl and Winkler 1974)
		Minimalist (Pettigrew and McNulty 1995)
		Statutory (Aram and Cowan 1986)
		Managerial control (Molz 1985)
		Ratifying (Wood 1983)
		Legalistic (Zahra and Pearce 1989)
		First-level board (Ferlie *et al.* 1994)
	Review boards	Review and approve (Molz 1985)
		Review and analysis (Zahra 1990)
		Second stage board (Ferlie *et al.* 1994)
		Third party (Herman 1981)
Active	Partnership	Collegial (Vance 1983)
		Shared leadership (Herman 1981)
		Participative (Wood 1983)
		Normative/strategic (Molz 1985)
		Maximalist (Pettigrew and McNulty 1995)
		Partnership (Zahra 1990)

executives is not really a board. Where non-executive directors are present, in this type of board they serve only as rubber-stampers or as ornaments to the organization. To all intents and purposes, this kind of board is an irrelevance to the functioning of the company (Pahl and Winkler 1974). Directors do not take part in any significant decision-making and recommendations from managers go through on the nod.

An active board is one that does play some role in the functioning of the organization. This involvement is a matter of degree. At one extreme, the board may act to review and ratify management proposals. At the other, the board may be a full partner in developing the content of specific strategies and decisions. The degree of activity of a board (its place along the continuum) is the result of a number of factors that we shall describe in Chapter 7. The finding that some boards are ambivalent about adopting a role in the strategic process is set against the dominant normative strand in the literature, which states that boards should be so involved.

Setting the strategic context

For this study, prior exposure to the literature and to experiences of other large corporations had brought some expectation that the strategy process would involve both a top-down and a bottom-up approach to the development of strategy, with broad strategic frameworks being issued by top management, and business-unit and divisional management teams making strategies for their own businesses, congruent with the overarching framework.

Table 4.2 shows the frequency scores to the issue, 'what is the role of the board in

TABLE 4.2. *The role of the board*

Interview responses	Frequency
Involvement in strategy	32
Responsibility for monitoring the health of the firm	20
Hire, appraise, and fire executives	7
Converse with shareholders/stakeholders	6
Ensure corporate renewal	5
Development of the corporate vision	5
Responsibility for ethical framework	4
Ensure corporate survival	3
Determine risk position	3
Lead strategic change	2
Review social responsibilities	2
Act as ambassadors for the firm	2
Understand current and forthcoming legislation	1
TOTAL	92

Note: Multiple responses allowed.
Source: Interviews (n=51).

your company?'. Clearly, strategy involvement is an important element of board endeavour. The obvious concern with these data is that they leave the nature of board involvement indeterminate. For this reason, a finer-grained analysis of the interview responses to the issue of strategy involvement was undertaken. Sentences that contained reference to the board's involvement in strategy were analysed and key verbs or qualifiers were highlighted to ascertain the mode of involvement. This analysis is given in Table 4.3.

The closest a respondent came to stating that the board formulated strategy was with the phrase 'help formulate'. The picture that emerges, therefore, is that boards in large companies do not appear to be *directly* involved in strategy *formulation*. But this does not entail the board being an entirely passive mechanism in the mould of the managerialist theory. From the discussion of the strategy process, and the role of the board within it, there emerged a clear picture of board activity. In broad terms, the board's role has less to do with strategy formulation than with setting the strategic context and acting as gatekeeper for strategic proposals. This view stands between managerialist views of the board—which state that boards have little involvement in determining the strategic content of the corporation—and the more optimistic views of board activity presented by the largely prescriptive literature on boards.

Business definition

The strategy process does not operate in a vacuum; every firm has a set of factors that impinges upon it and constrains the strategic choices open to it. These factors include the administrative heritage of the business, the industry sector, the size of the firm, the capabilities of its workforce, the strength of competition, the level of technology, and so forth. A firm is also constrained by its commitment to former and existing strategies (Ghemawhat 1991). Within these constraints, firms must focus to gain competitive advantage: the decision as to 'what business are we in' is fundamental,

TABLE 4.3. *Mode of strategic involvement*

Involvement in strategy	Frequency
Review	10
Discuss	9
Approve	3
Ratify	3
Decision-taking	2
Monitor	2
Define strategic framework	1
Guide	1
Help formulate	1
TOTAL	32

Source: Interviews (n=32).

and it is a question that is asked continually of firms, particularly in circumstances of change. From the interview data (see frequency scores, Table 4.2), the setting of the overarching direction of the organization appeared to be a defining characteristic of the board's role. For example:

The board sets the corporate direction, the corporate strategy. The business strategies are the responsibility of the operating units. Directors are responsible for the overall direction of the company—who else should do it? (executive director)

The first order strategy, deciding what areas of business to be in, what is the core business, what should be divested or bought, how resources are to be allocated around the organization, is in the domain of the board. Specific strategies to do with subsidiaries or business units have to be delegated. (chairman)

The board is the tiller of the organization: it is setting the broad direction, steering the right course. But many things are going on at the same time in the boat, which are the responsibility of the crew. (non-executive director)

The responsibility for determining corporate strategy at this very broad level is linked to the board's role in setting the vision and mission of the organization. As Johnson and Scholes (1988: 8) state, a mission 'is a "visionary" view of the overall strategic posture of an organisation and is likely to be a persistent and resistant influence on strategic decisions'. One executive director said: 'The mission is why we are in business. The vision is where we want to be. These are fundamentally the responsibility of the board.'

Boards also set the ethical tone with regard to their monitoring and accountability roles. What is expected of management, both by way of performance and behaviour, is ultimately the responsibility of directors (Pettigrew 1992). The board is thus recognized as crucial in the process of developing an ethical framework, implicit or explicit, for the formulation of strategy and policy, monitoring management and ensuring accountability (Andrews 1980; Parker 1990; Pettigrew 1992). A common manifestation of this role is the production of corporate codes of ethics, which are intended to capture succinctly the guiding principles of the organization. The efficacy of such codes, and the problem of how their values are communicated and enforced, are important issues.

The board's role in determining the mission and values of the company was a recurrent theme in discussions with directors. The role of mission statements in terms of identifying priorities and aligning the workforce to a common set of goals has been well attested (Campbell and Yeung 1990; Demb and Neubauer 1992). Boards were also viewed as responsible for enshrining the corporate values by the interviewees—for example, 'The values of the company must come from the top. The board must set the tone, and they must live the values; only if they do this will the values come alive' (executive director).

The mission and values were frequently driven by the chairman. There was a view that a mission or a set of values could not be written by committee; there had to be a succinct coherent simple view. Of course, once the chairman had drawn up this list, it would be circulated and agreement on the content would be secured and, if necessary, changes made.

The establishment of a clear framework of corporate direction and values exercises a critical influence on the activities of managers by defining the parameters of strategic decisions. This is akin to Burgelman's notion of the *concept* of strategy, a concept that 'provides a more or less shared frame of reference for the strategic actors in the organization, and provides the basis for corporate objective setting in terms of its business portfolio and resource allocation' (1983: 1350). The findings of this part of the research suggest that it is the board's responsibility largely to determine this concept of strategy. In a formal way, this is undertaken largely at the annual review, where progress on strategic plans and budget will be analysed by the board, and new strategic directions—for example, acquisitions and divestments, alliances activity—will be explored. For example, 'An opportunity arose to buy a chain of stores which we felt had potential, but had a poor brand image. We discussed it at the December board meeting, but the board rejected the idea because it was felt the acquisition would dilute our image of being a high-quality provider' (chief executive).

One of the reasons why all major acquisitions have to go to the board is that, apart from the considerable costs involved that have to be signed off, an acquisition has the potential to change the focus of the business and in some sense alter the organizational identity and strategy. Discussions about business definition occur *informally*, too. It was common for managers who were entrepreneurial to sound out executives on particular ideas. If these look promising, an informal discussion will go up the line, with the executives sounding out non-executives about the feasibility of the proposed plan. One executive director said: 'We like to give our non-executives a clear idea of what is in the pipeline. We want no surprises when things come to the board meeting. Sometimes, at an early stage, a non-executive will say "I don't think that's really us", or "that's the sort of thing (a competitor) would do".'

Maintaining the strategic framework

The board plays a number of roles to ensure that the company's focus is maintained and that management does not stray too far from the strategy framework (the degree to which activity outside the strategic framework is tolerated is discussed later). We shall describe three roles: gatekeeping, confidence-building, and selecting the chief executive and other directors in general.

Gatekeeping

To determine the parameters of strategic activity within the organization, it is important that there be a mechanism by which proposals for strategic or operational goals are screened and those that lie outside the current concept of strategy are eliminated. At the highest level, it is the role of the board to act as this screening mechanism. This mechanism acts, therefore, to ensure that the concept of strategy outlined by the board is matched by strategic behaviour at operational levels (Burgelman 1983).

An important issue that affects the potential for non-executive director involvement in strategy is the information asymmetry between executives and non-executives. The non-executives clearly have less involvement in the company than do the executives, rendering them at a disadvantage regarding information about the company, particularly where information is used as grounds for strategic decision-making. This may make non-executives less effective or, in the worst case, redundant in the strategy-making process. Even though many non-executives are executives of other companies (and usually chief executives at that), and are well used to participating in strategic discussions, they are unlikely to be as familiar with the business of the company in which they are non-executives than the incumbent executive management. The executives, then, are in control of the information that a board receives, and this is an important element of their power. Pahl and Winkler (1974: 108) state that, in all companies that have an active board, management adopts a manipulative strategy *vis à vis* the board. The intention, on the part of management, is to seek generalized approval of proposals and operate without constraints from the board. This does not entail the managerialist thesis, but tends to imply a rather routinized view of board endeavour and the lack of substantial disagreement at board meetings.

There is a certain pragmatic logic to this process. Because time at board meetings is relatively brief, and because the board cannot be expected to listen to every strategic option that has been generated on a single or several issues (the decision-making process would be dramatically slowed), there is usually some screening of strategic options before they are presented to the board. The forum where this is most likely to happen is the executive committee (or chief executive's committee, or management committee). The great majority of directors interviewed stated that their organization had this type of committee, and it typically comprises the chief executive and the executive directors, together with, perhaps, the head of corporate planning and, depending on the strategic issues coming before the committee, the relevant head of an operating unit or functional head.

The executive committee is usually a formal committee, with delegated powers assigned to it, giving it the power to decide certain issues without the necessity of taking them to the board for approval (for example, an executive committee may be allowed to decide on capital expenditure up to, say, £1 million in a large company, but a figure higher than this must go to full board for approval). Should a proposed strategic initiative be considered initially promising, the proposer of the idea (for example, the head of an operating unit) will undertake to write a proposal for presentation to the executive committee. This will happen, of course, in the normal planning cycle, but the case of a proposed acquisition makes the procedure a little clearer. Should the head of an operating unit consider the purchase of another firm a good idea, he or she will have to present his case in the best possible light. This would entail costings, forecasts, potential synergies, tangible and intangible benefits, and so on. He or she may be helped in this by the corporate planning department. Once such detail has been collected, he or she will make his presentation to the executive committee. At this forum, there will be the normal choices of outright rejection, revision, or immediate acceptance and referral to the board. Acceptance by the executive committee will mean that the chief executive and the other executive directors are satisfied with the strategy and are content to approve it at the full board meeting.

In this way, then, only the strongest strategic proposals survive, and, when they reach the board, the executives can display a united front for their adoption. This raised a number of questions from the interview data. The first concerns a point that was discussed briefly earlier—that many strategic proposals come from the chief executive him or herself. There were doubts expressed as to the level of criticism to which these ideas are subjected:

A powerful chief executive is used to getting his way and other executives may be fearful of citing objections to his plans. This is the real benefit of the non-executive directors, who, if they are tough enough, will ask the difficult questions. But it is hard to expect the executives to get tough with the chief executive, because he appoints them, rewards them and potentially fires them. (chairman)

Apart from the reasons cited in the quotation above, there is also the belief of some directors that the chief executive has a great deal of influence on the performance of the business, and, if the company is successful, they may see the chief executive's touch as sure on all ideas, with a consequent lowering of the critical faculty by his or her team. The second criticism of the use of the executive committee as a strategic options filter is that the non-executives do not see the process of strategic discussion and decision that contributed to the choice of the final option(s). When the chosen option appears at the board meeting, the non-executives are presented with virtually a *fait accompli*, a proposal that has the unanimous backing of the executives and that is in a highly polished state. One non-executive director said: 'For most large decisions, the non-executives really only rubber stamp the decisions made earlier by the executives. We can ask about timing or cost, but it is difficult to second guess what alternatives were available and the merits of them.'

This criticism, however, was voiced by only three directors. Most said that the strategies that appeared at the board meeting for discussion and the genesis of those strategies were familiar to all directors. 'There is a rule which our board adheres to: there should be no surprises at the board meeting. The directors should be familiar with what comes before them and they should not be asked to decide upon a large issue without having knowledge of it well beforehand' (chairman).

This prior knowledge comes in a variety of forms. One is formal. A device used by a number of boards is to invite proposers of strategies to make a presentation at the full board meeting, and not just at the executive committee. If the non-executives are considered to be powerful, this may be a good precautionary move to allow advice and comment at an early stage and reduce potential embarrassment should the non-executives reject an executive committee-recommended project out of court. A second method is the informal approach mentioned earlier, keeping non-executive directors informed of ideas currently in the pipeline and sounding them out as to their suitability. One non-executive director said:

The idea to divest one of our main businesses was developed jointly by the chairman and the chief executive, I think. They both saw the logic behind it, but it was a huge step, because it would mean selling off some major brands. But the shape of our business, and a recent major acquisition, made it the right move. But they asked us all, individually, what we thought of the basic idea. They spelled out their reasons and took on board some of our comments, I believe. They had already done their homework and they were confident of their forecasts. When the final proposal came to the board, we were of course all familiar with the contents and we agreed it.

The third form stems from the provision of timely information to the non-executives, usually through the minutes of the executive committee meeting. Given that non-executive directors have limited access to information (and the cost of gaining full access and processing all information would be very costly), and have limited time to discuss all proposals and debate all decisions, the board acts essentially in a gatekeeper role. This role is governed by normative rules, and each board has certain criteria, usually based on quality, feasibility, and strategic fit, with which non-executive directors can ground their judgements on specific proposals. To the extent that non-executive directors perform this task well, it focuses the activities of managers on producing high-quality proposals that are based on sound reasoning and presented in a rational and clear manner. As Parkinson (1993: 197) claims, the obligation to report to a higher authority can lead to efficiency gains. Mace (1971: 80), too, concurs:

Presidents and other members of management, in describing the discipline value of boards, indicated that the requirement of appearing formally before the board of directors consisting of respected, able people of stature, no matter how friendly, causes the company organisation to do a better job of thinking through their problem and of being better prepared with solutions, explanations or rationales.

Mace concludes that boards have an important role to play acting as the organization's conscience. The gatekeeping role figured prominently in the field data. For example:

As part of the business planning cycle, the units put in their strategies and we review them. This is a very important process, since it is both part of the strategic planning process and also part of our process of monitoring the performance of management. We can look for synergies across the various plans and advise on other possible avenues for the units concerned and also check to see whether, in the targets they have set themselves, they are looking for an easy time. If we feel the targets they have set are not very demanding, we just hike them up. They must be demanding.   (executive director)

This review is particularly important where the head of the operating unit is not a member of the main board. Where he or she is represented on the main board, regular presentations will be made to the board on the unit's progress and performance against targets, both financial and strategic.

But there are a number of problems with the gatekeeper role. First, it tends to encourage conformity. New or radical ideas are likely to be discouraged. Secondly, the gatekeeping role is replicated throughout the organizational hierarchy. A proposal from a business unit will have to meet criteria set by the management teams at each level. If it reaches executive committee stage, the proposal may have been through several iterations. Once the proposal has the blessing of the chief executive and his or her team, it is very difficult for the board to turn it down. Only two directors (of fifty-one) in the first sample could remember the board turning down a proposal approved by the management team (rather than asking for amendments). Such an action violates a key unwritten rule in the boardroom: confrontation should never be made public, but should be resolved in private. The two examples both involved a dominant chief executive who was urging approval, in one case, for an acquisition, and in the other, for a disposal. In both cases, the directors reported that the chief executive had put a 'three-line whip' on the executive team and attempted to 'strong arm' the board into acceptance.

Nevertheless, the board's *potential* for refusing to sanction management's proposals affords it strong latent power (see Herman 1981), and management's reluctance to face tough questioning or appear foolish under fire in the boardroom ensures that strategic proposals are of a high standard in companies where the non-executive directors are active and carry weight and respect. This discipline function is explored further in Chapter 5.

Confidence-building

Though proposals rarely get turned down, it is usually the case that the non-executive directors will question details of the plans and in some cases ask for further information to be provided or recommend changes. Though this is hardly the proactive role envisaged by many prescriptive writers on boards, nevertheless it is very important both as a discipline to strategic decision-making and also as a signal concerning the standard of proposal that will be tolerated. Because boards that operate in this way are not merely rubber-stampers, their approval of strategic plans is not automatic. In making judgements on proposals or resource allocations, the board will be influenced not only by the strength and logic of the particular case, but also by (1) the credibility of the proponent of the plan and (2) the track record of proposals of similar type. At interview, a number of non-executives said that the personality of the person who raised the proposal was an important variable in determining the worthiness of the plan: 'If X or Y suggests a course of action, I know that it will be thoroughly thought out and very soundly reasoned. They are the type of people who have a very good grasp of detail and do not overlook anything. They have also been with the business for years and they know what works' (non-executive director). As for the track record of previous similar proposals, this naturally figured prominently in the non-executive directors' evaluative schemes, since this kind of information is readily available, at least in large firms, which are closely monitored by external agencies, such as the press. One non-executive told of the case of a diversification strategy that came before the board of an organization which, five years earlier, had moved away from its core business, with almost disastrous effects. 'It took us [the non-executive directors] a lot of convincing that we should go down this road again. We were sure the market wouldn't like us doing this. I remember the chief executive had to go away and refine the proposal and sell it to us again, taking into account all our doubts.'

The degree to which the board feels confident in the proposals that come before it will influence the degree to which it is likely to take risks (Noda and Bower 1996). The onus, therefore, on lower-level managers who are attempting to initiative bottom-up strategy is to convince the board of their performance. Again, this may increase efficiency and serve as a useful discipline for managerial activity (though, of course, some managers may choose to distort their own performance or hide the possible adverse effects of an intended strategy).

There was also evidence concerning the internal selection process of competing strategic proposals (Burgelman 1983, 1991) that the particular corporate context of each organization would determine to a considerable extent the choice of plan or decision. In one company, which could be described as a financial-control firm (Goold and Campbell 1987), there was a strong desire to 'stick to the knitting', and proposals that adhered to the narrow strategic direction of the business, particularly if they could show short-term benefits, would tend to be successful. Alternatively, in a fast-moving consumer goods business, innovation was being actively sought and the constraints on strategic ideas were relaxed, allowing for the possibility of generating growth from new (and unexpected) sources.

Through the setting of the strategic parameters, therefore, the board is able to determine the degree of renewal an organization may undertake. Tolerance of activity outside the existing context of strategy may produce new resource combinations that may generate competitive advantage for the firm. Insistence on narrow conformity to the strategic parameters, conversely, will tend to dampen entrepreneurial activity and reduce the potential for new (as opposed to incremental) combinations of productive resources (Burgelman 1983).

Selecting directors

The strategic parameters of an organization, its shared frame of reference, are to a large extent influenced by the character and style of the chief executive. The board's role in selecting the chief executive gives it power of a very high order, and again reinforces its potential for setting the strategic context of the organization. As Mintzberg (1983: 70) states:

This is the one decision the board can never fully delegate (except, of course, to one of its members, who might in fact be the outgoing chief executive). And the power to appoint of course constitutes the power to dismiss as well. Were the board to possess no power other than this one—and truly to possess this one—then it would be a potent force indeed in the organisational power system.

Mace (1971) and Herman (1981) believed the board did not fulfil this role, but there is growing evidence that, as far as *dismissing* the chief executive is concerned, boards are exercising this role with increasing regularity (the process of disciplining directors is explored in Chapter 6).

The *selection* of a chief executive is a relatively rare occurrence. The data that did emerge expressed the view that, if the turnover of the chief executive was in the normal run of things (usually retirement), then it was typically the person recommended by the outgoing chief executive who would succeed to the position. This candidate was usually known to other board members as the heir apparent. However, this is not always the case. In one example, a chief executive, in conjunction with the chairman, believed that either of two men could take the role after the chief executive's retirement. In the period up to the retirement (six months), the two candidates were encouraged to stake their respective claims—one was the marketing director, the other the finance director. In the end, the marketing director secured the position: 'We were going for expansion overseas. What we needed was a big push on our marketing strategy and our marketing focus. X was in a real sense the right man at the right time' (chairman).

The process of selecting a new chief executive, though often a foregone conclusion, still follows certain 'rules'. The chief executive will consult with his or her chairman (or, in the case of chief-executive duality, the most senior member of the 'inner cabinet', usually the finance director). They will speak about the appropriateness of a number of internal candidates. Even if one candidate is to be chosen with certainty, nevertheless a list will be prepared by the two senior board members. This list may include an outsider, a person from another company who is deemed to have exceptional ability and whose profile appears to match the requirements of the company's aims and could fit in with other board members.

Interviews will be held with the shortlist of candidates, normally conducted by the chief executive and the chairman. The candidate's vision for the future, leadership qualities, track record, and the potential impression he or she would make to major investors will be scrutinized. So, too, will the signal the appointment would make to the rest of the company. In broad terms, would the appointment signal continuity or a change in management style? Informal soundings will also be made, not only internally but, on occasion, with important investors. It is largely through these informal conversations that the board members have the opportunity to give their opinion. The vote in the board meeting as to the appointment is usually a *fait accompli*, with the unwritten rule being to express no dissent.

For managers to be selected to executive director positions, the chief executive again tends to dominate the process. Though most large firms have succession systems in place for the top cadre of managers, it is the chief executive who decides who makes it to the board. For non-executive directors, too, the process is not radically different. However, it is often the *chairman* who will decide that the appointment of a non-executive is necessary: 'It is my job to make sure we have balanced team. If I feel we are under strength in an area, or could use some expertise in a particular discipline, I may decide that we need someone to join us. It could be a consultant, or it could be a non-executive' (chairman). The chairman, or chief executive, will seek approval from the board that a non-executive is required. Once this approval is secured, the chairman and chief executive will draw up a job specification for the role and this will be usually be given to headhunters, who will conduct a search and report back with a list of names. The chairman will sift through the names and arrive at a shortlist. Interviews will be undertaken, again with the chairman and chief executive, and the candidates will normally meet all the executive and other non-executive directors informally over dinner. After informal soundings with other directors, the chairman and chief executive will make the decision. Another favoured route to the selection of non-executives is for the chief executive simply to nominate contacts or personal acquaintances: 'I picked this board. They were my appointments, We had particular needs to fill and I knew people who could do the job. They have all been excellent' (chief executive).

This is rare, however (this was the only mentioned occurrence of a chief executive hand-picking all the non-executives). Directors are now conscious of the need to appear objective in their selection process: 'Because of our brand and reputation, we have to appear whiter than white. We can't afford to be seen loading the bases. We have to be transparent; we can't get away with an old school tie method of getting directors on board' (chief executive). The danger is that, from the external point of view, the chief executive is seen as selecting a cosy club, or a team of 'yes' people for the board. But the majority of directors spoke of their desire to have a diversity of opinion within the board and wanting genuine debate. A chief executive said:

I don't expect to be agreed with all the time. I want my executives to challenge me, to come up with their own ideas. I can't do everything on my own, the business is too complex for that. I need good people around me, and that includes the non-executive. They have to earn their money here and that means speaking up at board meetings and telling us things we didn't already know.

But were a chief executive to hand-pick all the board members, this is no guarantee that, because these directors owe their position to the patronage of the chief executive, they will always support him or her. One executive director said: 'As long as we are sailing in the right direction, everyone is happy with the captain. But if we look like we are going to run aground, we will ask serious questions of the captain's fitness to continue. His every decision will be scrutinized.'

Strategic content

The process of strategy in large firms is characteristically determined by a top-down and bottom-up approach, with the board providing much of the strategic context within which strategic behaviour may be monitored. The data from this study support the view that strategic activity occurs at multiple levels within the firm, a view that provides for a broader view of strategy than the traditional rational planning model assumes. Given that the board has some input in establishing the strategic boundaries of the organization, what input can the board have in determining strategic *content*? Our discussion thus far shows that it is through the manipulation of the strategic context of the organization that the board makes its major contribution to strategy, rather than through a substantive contribution to the decision-making process. Let us explore this in a little more detail.

The genesis of strategic proposals

The formal strategy formulation process—the determination of corporate objective setting in terms of business portfolio and resource allocation (Bower 1970; Burgelman 1983, 1991)—derives its content chiefly from the deliberations of the executive committee. Strategies proposed by the business units or divisions will usually pass before the executive committee; it is at this stage that deficiencies in content and presentation of the proposed strategy will be highlighted and conformance or divergence from the overall strategic aim of the company will be assessed. Emerging from this process will be strategic proposals that have the endorsement of the executive committee. At the board meeting, therefore, it is highly unlikely that the non-executives will overturn the choices made by members with the greatest firm and industry-specific knowledge, who have access to the fullest information, and who have the opportunity to consider the choices in the greatest detail. Such a view comes, for example, from Pahl and Winkler (1974), who state that much pre-board activity constitutes a screening mechanism, often defended on the grounds that, without such a strategy, there would be too much information given to non-executive directors (though managerial theorists would posit that the information asymmetry involved leads to managerial manipulation of the company, a theme discussed below). Serious discussion of strategic options and related decision-making are therefore not the norm. Sometimes, the executive committee will call a formal planning committee to assess strategic options. A number of companies have a specialist corporate planning department, which examines strategic trends and undertakes competitor analysis, the results of which are normally presented to the board at regular intervals, but more normally are fed straight through to the chief executive. Much of this work is routine. The illuminating fact to emerge from the interviews is that initiatives to investigate the feasibility of new strategies usually come from either the chief executive or the chairman. In other words, the planning department was not seen as a form of brainstorming department or skunkworks, where new ideas would be aired or tested as a matter of course. The reality is, it seems, more mundane. Their involvement in innovation springs directly from the ideas (typically) of the chief executive or the chairman. On occasion, of course, discussions at board meetings will throw up interesting thoughts or problems that will need to be investigated further in order to ascertain their potential effects. But the majority of interviewees whose companies did have planning departments said that they were largely reactive to the insights of the chief executive or the chairman. One chief executive said:

I, or one of my team, but usually me, will ask the corporate planners to assess the merits and demerits of a particular proposal. Often it will be just an idea, something I've thought of, which sounds interesting and which might be worth checking out. They come back with a brief report and if it looks promising, we'll develop a full proposal and put it to the management team for their comments.

These and other comments are interesting in that they show the emergent nature of strategy within organizations. A number of directors stated that some of the key business strategies, and perhaps even the corporate strategy, were results of flashes of individual insights rather than outcomes of formal planning processes and methods. The chief executive director of an engineering firm said:

We were looking at ways to meet the targets we had set. We had grown organically throughout our history but, just at that time, I had noticed a nice business, not directly in our core business, but which would represent a useful piece of vertical integration. I wrote the strategy basically on the back of an envelope and gave it to the planning director and his team to investigate. They reacted very positively and we bought the company.

Inner cabinet

With regard to the political aspect of decision-making, this study found that boards tend to be dominated by an inner circle of directors. This inner circle, or cabal, typically comprised the chief executive, the chairman, and the finance director. This accords with Pahl and Winkler's (1974) study, which described the notion of positional elites—that is, directors who form a circle of members responsible for decision-making (1974: 106). One chairman said: 'Much of strategy-making and vision comes from the key triumvirate of the chairman, chief executive and the finance director. Don't make too much of democracy in the boardroom.'

Of course, this triumvirate did not always comprise the dominant elite. Sometimes, directors spoke of a particular function (for example, marketing or operations), whose executive would be part of an inner cabinet, or else the head of the main division or business unit might also be afforded this status. The evidence of this research is that, though these inner cabinets certainly exist, this does not entail that other directors are irrelevant to the decision-making of the organization. The reality is that these members, who are normally the most experienced in the firm, talk to each other a great deal outside the board meeting on strategic issues. Often these discussions will be the early test bed for future proposals, and agreement among the inner cabinet will ensure that a plan will be investigated further. In this sense, the inner cabinet is less a circumventing device against board procedure, or a subversive of the power of the board, than a key part of the informal strategic control process, where key directors will discuss progress and assess opportunities without the formality of convening either the executive committee or the board:

I will talk to the chairman every week about all kinds of things, much of which would not be appropriate to bring to the exec committee. Some of it will be gossip, some blue sky theorizing, we might talk about how so and so is doing in the division. There's no set agenda but I find this meeting invaluable, particularly on a personal level.   (chief executive)

Certainly, in terms of who the *shareholders* want to meet to discuss the progress of the firm, it is normally the chief executive, the chairman, and one other, usually the finance director. Some directors are marginalized, of course, in terms of power, and the views of some directors were listened to more intently than others: 'Martin is an expert when it comes to law, and I would always consult him in the event of a legal problem. But as for strategy, he needs to take a broader view. I find he doesn't think deeply enough about it' (chief executive). The extent of a director's marginalization depended on the knowledge and behaviour of the individual director and the degree of confidence he or she enjoyed with colleagues. It did not always break down along functional or divisional lines, nor in the director's position in the resource allocation process.

Crisis conditions

Though we found little evidence to suggest that the board is involved to a great extent in formulating the content of strategy, in times of crisis the board does become much more proactive in its activities. In two companies, the threat of takeover saw an increase in board activity. The number of *formal* board meetings did not increase, but there was a great deal more informal activity, with many telephone conversations, *ad hoc* meetings between executives and non-executives, and a strong concerted action to build the best defence: 'The board has to act as a board and not as a management committee. This is particularly so in crisis situations. For example, in bid circumstances, the board should present a united front and each member, including the non-executives, should have a specific task to perform' (chief executive). This approach has affinities with the type of control labelled 'control by exception' (Molz 1985). This view holds that 'the board would make most decisions on a review and approve basis, but under cataclysmic conditions, the board would take independent action. The most frequent occurrence of such an action is when the board decides to terminate the chief executive officer involuntarily' (Molz 1985: 90).

The decision to remove a chief executive is dealt with in Chapter 5. In terms of an increase in board activity, the event certainly does increase the number of conversations between directors, again usually outside the regular board meeting, particularly prior to the decision to fire the chief executive. These meetings will be coordinated by the chairman (or, in the case of chief-executive duality, the leading non-executive director), as executive directors themselves will find it difficult to stand overtly against the incumbent chief executive, since they may not wish to appear disloyal or commit 'regicide' or indeed want to be perceived to be staking a claim for the job themselves. The enforced turnover of a chief executive is normally due to serious underperformance of the company, or malfeasance, or a catastrophic failure of a project. One executive said:

For five years we had done exceptionally well under X. We could do no wrong. Then he wanted to expand, to build on our good fortune. We bought a large US firm, paid way over the top, though we didn't know that at the time. It just never performed for us, but the CEO couldn't see it. He was wedded to his plan. On top of it all, one of the US execs was arrested for fraud. The firm became a serious drain on our resources. Most of us wanted to cut and run, but X wouldn't hear of it. A group of us met the chairman and canvassed the other non-execs and said, 'Look, X can't turn things around'. We were helped by some conversations I had had with a few big investors. We put the case to X and he took it very calmly. It was like he was relieved. It was a great shame, because he had a terrific mind.

Boundary spanning

Another area that could be construed as involving non-executives as partners in the strategic arena is boundary-spanning activity, primarily concerning non-executive directors using their access to information external to the company to feed into strategic discussion and, as a result, reduce environmental uncertainty. One director said: 'One of our non-executives was for many years a senior civil servant. His knowledge about the workings of Whitehall has been of considerable benefit to us, particularly as we operate in a very sensitive market and we need to be able to influence the right people.' This element of board behaviour will be examined in Chapter 6.

Discussion and conclusions

The board's involvement in strategy is often taken as the defining characteristic of its role. The prescriptive literature urges a clear link between the degree of the board's involvement in strategy and organizational effectiveness (see e.g. the Cadbury Report (Cadbury 1992)). The managerial theory, however, has stressed the passive nature of board activity. In terms of the other major theories, the board's strategic input is regarded as an important and potentially effective mechanism in ensuring good corporate governance. In this research, we have tried to explore the realities underlying these normative strictures. In terms of strategy formulation, it is at the corporate level that the board is expected to make a contribution, helping the executive team to craft corporate objectives. But, as was made clear from the interview data, the strategy-making process in large companies does not proceed in a purely top-down fashion, with the corporate centre taking the lead. This study supports the findings of Bower (1970), Burgelman (1983, 1991), and Mintzberg (1983), which demonstrate that strategy is typically developed both at executive committee and business-unit level. The board is largely responsible for setting the strategic parameters within which strategic activity can take place.

Given that there is a predominately bottom-up movement in most strategy-making, the role for the board appears to be limited to activities of coordination and checking for consistency and coherence among proposed strategies. In some cases it appears that the role of the board is no more than the sign-off on the strategies of business units or divisions, but, from our interview findings, this minimal activity appears to be rare. The review and analysis of strategic proposals are very important factors both in maintaining the quality of corporate objective setting (the gatekeeping function) and in instilling confidence among those executives who demonstrate the required quality of thinking and presentation (the confidence-building function).

The board's role in determining and maintaining the definition of the business, in conjunction with its gatekeeping role and confidence-building activity, is important in shaping the domain of discretion for managers. Though these roles may be interpreted as constraints on management activity (and so constituting an important element in the board's control role), they are also crucial strategic mechanisms for the company, for at least three reasons. First, the board is the ultimate arbiter of what constitutes the focus of the company ('what business are we in?', 'what areas should we go into?'). Secondly, through selective screening and confidence building, the capacity for innovation and entrepreneurship can be regulated. Thirdly, through constant examination of the business definition and corporate strategy, the commitment to certain strategies or business sectors may be questioned and so boards may be instrumental in breaking organizational habits and forcing change, a finding that supports a key conclusion of Judge and Zeithaml (1992).

These activities of the board are certainly more limited than some commentators would prescribe, and we saw little evidence of the 'partnership' model of board activity, except in times of crisis, a view that accords with the findings of other writers (e.g. Lorsch and MacIver 1989; Demb and Neubauer 1992; Pettigrew and McNulty 1995).

There are a number of implications for theory from this analysis. First, what of managerialist theory? The story we encountered was one of managers developing strategic proposals but within a framework of corporate objectives approved by the board. Mizruchi's (1983) thesis that boards remain controllers of the strategic agenda finds support from this data. The managerialist view also does not seem to square with the finding that the directors interviewed said that they ran their companies in the interests of shareholders. This accords with the findings of Hill, who stated (1995: 276) that 'an emphasis on the distance between owners and managers fails to capture the sense shared by all directors that they are in fact already running their companies in the interests of the shareholder and this is what legitimises their activities'. Admittedly these claims may well be merely directoral rhetoric, but increased shareholder activism, greater public interest in the activities of boards, and a desire for legitimatization on the part of directors, provide strong incentives to act as good stewards of the organization.

This may not be enough to satisfy agency and transaction-cost theorists. The evidence of boards' rather limited input into the strategic decision-making process makes it them prima facie rather inefficient mechanisms for reducing potential managerial opportunism. This view could be supported by the fact that information on strategic options is controlled via the executive committee, which may suggest that the board is a passive instrument. However, we found no evidence from executive directors that information was withheld from the board or that executives tried to steamroller non-executive directors over decisions. The effort in the executive committee was focused on gaining consensus over a decision and on bringing it to the board fully formed and coherently argued. This elimination of dissension was represented throughout the lower levels of the firm, as business, unit strategies came up through the organization. Much of it is due to the information-processing capacity of the board: the board cannot listen to every nuance of debate; it expects the strongest proposals to survive, and it expects a certain generalization of its presentation so that it does not get lost in the details. No evidence of manipulation was found. Like Hill (1995), this research continually encountered directors who sought to embody the idea of the 'professional director', with strong commitments to the success of the firm, and who saw their purpose as improving the value of the business within the targets and culture of the company. The ideas of stewardship theory thus gain backing from this data.

In terms of elites' theory, we have found that there are strong directors and weak directors—that is, directors who are members of an inner circle, and those who are outside, a division of power not co-terminus simply with the split between executive and non-executive director. Identifying elites with the board of directors is therefore conceptually inadequate. This finding is further reinforced by the fact that strategy is often developed by managers throughout the organizational hierarchy, which suggests that real power does not lie only at the top, but is dispersed throughout the firm. These conclusions mirror those of Pahl and Winkler, who also stated (1974: 120) that 'in our companies, however, membership in the cabal of controllers could not be given any consistent definition in terms of position'.

For resource-dependence theorists, there was evidence that non-executive directors did contribute to 'opening doors' for firms through use of contacts, so, in a rather indirect way, aiding the strategy process. We shall explore this issue further in Chapter 6.

In the next chapter, we examine the board's role in the control of the organization. Though this role has been treated as conceptually distinct from the strategic activity of the board, we shall see that, in several important respects, the board's use of certain organizational control systems can be highly proactive and form part of the scanning of the environment for future business opportunities and prospects for organizational renewal.

Appendix. Case illustrations

Business definition

In the four case companies, there was strong evidence that the corporate boards were actively involved in the strategic process, both in the design of explicit organizational definitions and in the choices made for the business portfolio and decisions made for acquisitions and divestments. Usually, of course, this is not a one-off event but an incremental process, and changes will be made gradually as the organization adjusts to its changing environment. We found that the board was an integral part of this continuing process.

The delineation of strategic boundaries is intended to focus opportunity-seeking behaviour to support organizational strategies (Burgelman 1991; Simons 1994). Before privatization, BAA's sole focus was the running of airports. The introduction of a strong retail price index formula following privatization prompted the need for a wider specification of strategic activity and increased search behaviour. The decision to diversify into four core businesses in the mid-1990s represented a major shift away from the existing corporate purpose, which was in essence to manage airports. The reconception of the mission and the scope of the business formed part of a continuing board-level debate over the merits of diversification:

> The board discusses all major decisions. Anything over £10 million goes to the board for debate. Most decisions are continuations of existing projects, but on huge issues like the Heathrow Express, we will have a meeting the day before, have dinner, and people connected with the plan will present. We never approve decisions of any kind until we show the non-executives. Everyone is up to speed. (BAA director)

At BAA, the mission statement provides a clear overview of the values and direction that employees are expected to embrace. The statement conveys information about how the organization creates value—'most successful airport company in the world'—the key priorities—'customer safety and security the highest priorities'—the strategy—'seeking continuous improvement in costs and quality of our services'—and the relationship with staff—'enabling employees to give of their best'. The board updates the mission statement every year in order to maintain its relevance. 'We decided in our mission statement that we had better move into four businesses. The proposal came forward—it was a shared view of strategy. We wanted to go into manufacturers' outlets. Our retailers thought it was retailing of the future. We partnered with a US leader' (BAA director).

Though diversification was supported by the management committee, and was particularly strongly championed by the chief executive, gaining agreement at board level was difficult. The non-executive directors were well aware that a previous diversification into hotels and property had failed, with a resulting condemnation by the City, and they were anxious to preserve shareholder value and ensure that the same mistakes did not happen again.

> The idea came into the strategy committee and was held there until we found a way to do it. The plan then went to the management committee. The company had diversified before and had failed. Once we decided to go, I told the board through my monthly report that we were working on it, so they were not surprised by it. We must go back to the board again and ask for another £10 million. I keep telling people through the Chief Executive's report. There was much debate as to whether we should diversify.   (BAA director)

> There are some issues where we might debate with the board 'what should we do'. Should we support DanAir at Gatwick? We took advice and soundings with the board. There is a huge public enquiry about Heathrow—we had to decide whether we could fund this. The more quality we have on the board, the better will be our decision-making.   (BAA director)

A major part of the corporate definition discussion for Securicor is the maintenance of the brand identity. The firm's reputation for integrity, reliability, and security has been the foundation for its growth, but all strategies, and, in particular, targets for acquisition, are assessed for their likely impact on the brand image. The preservation and enhancement of the brand as the key asset for Securicor were a principal role for the board, and were mentioned by all directors interviewed. For example:

> We inherited the Securicor brand name, which has strong implications for integrity and solidity. This is our most important asset. And the board has to recognize that. The board must bear in mind the brand name in all of its dealings. So the first job of the board is about protection and development of the brand name. All board members must understand this. Indeed, the strong name of Securicor is important in attracting non-executives, good quality non-executives.   (Securicor director)

It is the *board's* role, therefore, to act as guardian and enforcer of the corporate values and ensuring the maintenance of brand integrity. At Securicor, the board meets twice a year to discuss all issues concerning strategy and the focus of the business: 'We have, maybe twice a year, an away weekend from Friday evening to Monday morning. We will sit down and review the whole of the group's business and a strategic overview. We have an evaluation and planning exercise. We can be very critical of what has happened' (Securicor director).

As with Securicor, the board of Burmah Castrol is deemed to be responsible for ensuring the integrity of the brand: 'With a brand such as ours, there are so many opportunities open to us. Some of these are geographical, some technological, some marketing. It is the board's role to probe these opportunities and make sure that the value of the brand and the Castrol name are not endangered' (Burmah Castrol director).

At Burmah Castrol, the board is not the originator of strategy—it is the management committee that is responsible for the strategic management and policy direction of the company—but before the annual strategic plan is devised, the board will identify, with the chief executive, a number of principal issues that have to be included. This process 'provides an overlay to the strategic discussion'. Again, the strategy process is top down and bottom up—'the chief executive will say: these are the objectives, principally stated in terms of financial targets (growth in earnings). We invite you to make proposals to meet these targets. It is an iterative process.'

There is no formal mission statement published by Burmah Castrol, but, in interview, directors were forceful in stating that there are certain underlying values that are firmly in the domain of the board: 'We are the guardians of the values of the firm. It is up to us to maintain the integrity of the company' (Burmah Castrol director). The annual report states that the board is responsible for the development and implementation of strategy to provide for the company's commercial success. It was clear from the directors' interviews that the broad strategic direction—the business the company is in—is controlled by the main board. A key tenet of the firm is that 'diversification cannot take place from the bottom up', and the firm regularly reassess the business portfolio as part of the diagnosis and change process. This is crucial in a firm that has grown in part through a strategy of in-fill acquisitions: 'Every three years we go back to absolute basics and ask some fairly basic questions, for example, what are we doing in a particular business? A firm must continuously renew itself' (Burmah Castrol director).

At Allied Domecq, business definition is clearly part of the board's role:

Determining the business mix, which parts of the sector to back by allocation of resources and so on, is how the board adds value. This can only happen outside the operating businesses. (Allied Domecq director)

The board determines the shape of the business portfolio. (Allied Domecq director)

In an organization that has broad interests in retailing, spirits and beers, and food, and is highly diversified, maintaining the strategic boundaries and focus is very important. The group is seeking to concentrate on spirits and retailing in order to become an international player. In terms of the company's values, the board is responsible for ensuring a coherent and consistent value structure and culture throughout the organization: 'In a company such as ours, the board ensures that synergies in values are extracted and that the group as a whole develops a culture that is harmonious' (Allied Domecq director). The mission is to grow shareholder value by 'working together across the world in our chosen sector of drinks and hospitality. We enjoy providing the best in quality—reassured by brand performance and our customers' perceptions of what we offer' (Allied Domecq Annual Report 1995).

A major decision in the company was to dispose of its foods business in 1994. The food business was increasingly viewed by the board as not representing an 'area of strength in terms of management capabilities'. This decision was originally devised by the chief executive and chairman, who then called in the non-executives to discuss the idea on an informal basis. Once the logic of the decision was accepted, it was a question of convincing the executive directors. The chairman and chief executive called together the top 300 people in the company—'the guys who are responsible for us making the budget'—to explain the core idea of changing the company from a 'conglomerate to one which focuses on two sectors—retailing and spirits and wines'.

The non-executives were a key part of this. They helped the chief executive and the chairman with the executive members—they helped to push the idea. We used them like consultants. The board was involved all the way through. We also discussed at board level what we should accept, in terms of cash, for the businesses. The non-executives were helpful here too. (Allied Domecq director)

Gatekeeping

In each of the four case companies, it was clearly stated that the board was not responsible for the formulation or creation of strategy. Rather, at the heart of the strategic process was the executive committee, which took the lead in strategy discussion and which coordinated the strategy development process in business units and divisions. These committees were staffed with the heads of the major business units, functional chiefs, the chief executive, and the finance director. The role of the executive committee in acting as a strategic filter to the board is confirmed in the views of directors in the four companies. The executive committee develops strategic options and examines those of the management committees of business units or divisions. This forum meets on average once a week. The strategic *content* of the corporation is determined largely by this group. Strategy formulation is clearly left to those members of the company who have the best information and greatest understanding of the business. In the case of BAA, the executive committee is supported by a strategy team, comprising three people headed by a strategy director, who is not a main board director. The *modus operandi* of this unit is largely to *receive* ideas from the chief executive or other executive directors and to examine them for their potential—though, through the strategy unit's continuous monitoring of the environment, it will inevitably diagnose new opportunities.

Though the executive committee has the principal role of developing strategic options, it became clear that it is the board's role is to act as gatekeeper to strategic proposals:

Now we are much more geared to strategy confirmation. Strategy develops in the management committee. There is a debate with the board on possible options, both in pointers for the business and in financial terms.   (BAA director)

We have got an EDC [Executive Directors' Committee] which meets twice a month. The EDC would review the previous month's results and decide on acquisitions and disposals. The acquisitions would be ratified at EDC and then it would be put to group board. We have got a lot of wise men who would ask wise questions. There are 7 NEDs [non-executive directors] on the group board. Most have long experience in the business world. They ask searching questions.   (Securicor director)

In the gatekeeping process, a key normative constraint is that the strategic proposals are in line with the business definition of the company. Board members base their judgements on a number of criteria, including the track record of the proposer, the internal logic of the proposal, its strategic fit, the clarity of presentation, and so forth. The board, however, has the latitude to encourage proposals that do not immediately seem to fit the definition of the business as ordinarily understood. In other words, the board can encourage innovation and entrepreneurship. The gatekeeping function is normally associated, particularly in the sociological literature, with rewarding conformity. In some cases, however, gatekeeping can be relaxed, so that non-conformity will not be punished and may even be encouraged.

Non-executive directors play two roles in the process. First, they provide evaluative feedback on a proposal, which is essentially a critical role, examining the content of the proposal for rigour, value creation potential, and, importantly, its timing ('does it make sense to pursue this *now*?'). Secondly, the non-executive directors can bring their own ideas based on their experience with their own companies and contacts, which in a real sense forms a new stream of information on which to revise the original proposal. Such information—for example, 'when we [i.e. the non-executive's own company] wanted to dispose of a business, we sought out an alliance as an exit strategy'—is intended to point the proposal in a new direction. This new information can help to develop a submitted proposal, and this kind of information is greatly valued by executive directors.

At Burmah Castrol, the non-executive directors contribute to the 'macro-tactics' of the business: 'their role is to criticize the strategy constructively. They do not need to go into the details of the product market strategy—they need to see the big picture and give their advice' (Burmah Castrol director). An important decision taken by Burmah Castrol was to sell a significant part of their business portfolio—the fuels business (to the Frost Group in July 1995, for £89 million). The decision was placed in the strategic plan as an 'under-review' item (as opposed to a 'definite-decision' item). The executive team worked up the proposal and put it to the board meeting, arguing strongly for the sale on the grounds of focus and strategic logic and the financial impact the divestment would have: 'the board deliberated it, discussed timing and how much we could get for the sale and so forth. The logic was strong so it was passed' (Burmah Castrol director).

At Allied Domecq, the sector businesses manage their operations with the support of the executive committee, 'which provides direction and authority for the day-to-day control of the business' (Allied Domecq Annual Report 1995). The sectors and business units operate within a framework of delegated authorities and reserved powers that seeks to ensure that certain transactions, significant in terms of size of type, are undertaken only after careful corporate review. The two key strategy generators are the executive committee and the strategy committee, and so strategy formulation, in common with the other companies, does not take place at board level. However, 'the key strategies will come before the board and we will take decisions on them. So the non-executive director can bring a dimension to strategy' (Allied Domecq director).

Discipline

It was clear that, in all four case companies, the executive directors regarded their non-executive directors as people of considerable talent and standing and that developing proposals was a process that was strenuous because, as one BAA executive said, 'nobody wants to look ridiculous or lacking judgement at a board meeting'.

Because the board meeting is a major arena for executives to build their standing and gain resources from the company, they are highly conscious of the need for strong performances. Thus the proposer of a strategy needs to ensure that the proposal is sound and well developed first before it reaches the executive committee and, secondly, when it comes to the board. When asked what was the role of the board, a Securicor director said: 'It is a confidence. It adds confidence to decisions made by the EDC. It gives a seal of approval. You can't underestimate the importance of the check. You have to get things into shape before it goes to group board. It makes you do your homework.'

At Burmah Castrol, the appointment of strong non-executives is encouraged, for the quality of their insight and the capacity to raise the game of the executives: 'There is a particular breed of businessman who bullies too much, has an overbearing style. They do not want

strong people around them. But for us, we want strong non-executives—we want to be confident about our ideas, have them subjected to intelligent criticism' (Burmah Castrol director).
  At Allied Domecq:

> The executives and the non-executives do work quite closely, though there is a certain amount of tension. There is a certain amount of edge in bringing forward proposals. Executives know they will be questioned by non-executives. It's still a team—there's one character who is disliked—but the executives do feel nervous, particularly as they are performing in front of the chairman of the remuneration committee, who is a formidable figure. (Allied Domecq director)

Confidence-building

It has been seen that through this gatekeeping process, proposals, though rarely rejected, were submitted to criticism and, at times, suggestions for new direction. This review and revision activity is important, but it is not usually a discrete process; it is normally accompanied by the process of encouraging and reinforcing successful managerial behaviour. As stated earlier, in each company, strategy consisted of a top-down and bottom-up approach, with the board setting broad strategic parameters and business units developing strategies to fit in with the core business direction and overall financial aims. In its gatekeeper role, the board will ultimately have the final say in the shape and stretch of the strategic plans coming up from the business-unit heads and lower-level managers. Through the board's comments back to these managers, strong performance can be reinforced and strategic insight can be given: 'We know who is good. They are the people with good track records, who do it time and again. If these people come up with ideas, we will listen' (BAA director).
  At Securicor, this process of reinforcement and encouragement is made easier through the formal structure of the business. The corporate structure dictates that each executive director sits on a subsidiary board. This is an important avenue for lower-level managers to impress and for senior executives to give positive feedback and encouragement to able employees:

> Monitoring company health comes from my attendance of subsidiary board meetings. I wander along, 'walking the ship'. I talk to individuals, I get to branches when I can. I prioritize my involvement. It is very important that senior managers have contact. I could walk into any business in the organization and know it was well run and what the morale was like there.   (Securicor director)

> It is difficult, but you must do it. I talk to the grass roots. It is very important to tell people whether they are doing well or not. I expect my colleagues, both senior and junior, to do the same.   (Securicor director)

The clarity, originality and presentation of strategic ideas from business units during the strategic planning process are important to the Burmah Castrol scanning of managerial talent: 'We believe strongly in decentralization. We expect the heads of divisions to work hard and implement good strategies within the framework we set down. Four times a year management has to give a good account of themselves. The board assesses them. This is a strong opportunity to give feedback and a good chance for management to impress' (Burmah Castrol director).
  Allied Domecq underlined the importance of *informal* contact with managers in the confidence-building process: 'We look at the sector boards and below once a year in terms of man-

agement development. But a lot of work assessing and discussing with managers is done outside the formal board meeting' (Allied Domecq director).

Non-executives are also encouraged to meet with sector heads and key business managers, ostensibly to learn more about the business, but this process also presents an opportunity to assess the calibre of managers and to encourage their plans for the business.

5
The Control Role of the Board

The central challenge in the governance of organizations is how to balance the discretionary power of managers with accountability to the shareholders. The organization depends for its success on two distinct factors: the value-creating activities of management, who are responsible for the day-to-day running of the enterprise, and the capital provided by the owners of the firm. Because of the increased size of companies and the dispersed nature of ownership, it is costly for shareholders to monitor and control managerial actions, which leaves power in the hands of management, some of whom may abuse this in pursuing their own agenda, where this conflicts with the interests of shareholders (Ezzamel and Watson 1997). Several control mechanisms have been proposed to ensure alignment of managerial discretion with shareholder interests. The major external mechanism is the market for corporate control, in which the threat of takeover induces incumbent management to greater efficiency. Imperfections in the market and the wider effects of takeover bids, including excessive focus on short-term performance to keep the share price high in order to avoid the attention of bidders, suggest that this mode of control has limited effectiveness (Parkinson 1994; Ezzamel and Watson 1997). A great deal of attention has, therefore, focused on the chief internal mechanism for control: the board of directors. Berle and Means (1932) refer to the board specifically as a solution to the problems raised by separation of ownership and control, with the board posited as a control mechanism to protect shareholder wealth against managers abusing their discretionary powers. According to Herman (1981), because the legal power to control the running of the company rests with the board of directors, the board is key to an analysis of corporate control.

Two problems emerge with this view of the board's responsibilities. First, under the managerial-hegemony thesis, the board is perceived to be an ineffective control mechanism, because of the information asymmetry between executive and non-executive directors (Pettigrew 1992), the use of entrenchment strategies by executives (Walsh and Seward 1990), and the growing difficulty of controlling complex, often international businesses in turbulent environments (Bartlett and Ghoshal 1989, 1993). Secondly, the control role appears, prima facie, to conflict with the board's contribution to determining the strategic direction of the firm. If, as policy recommendations have made clear, non-executive directors are to act as independent monitors of the firm, how are they to fulfil their role of providing management expertise?

In this chapter, we shall argue that, contrary to the managerialist tradition, boards can exert control over the running of the organization through the use of management control systems, and through responsibility for assessing top management and determining their incentives and sanctions. We shall also argue that the seeming conflict between the board's strategic role and the control is more apparent than real, and, indeed, that the distinction between the two roles is blurred. We have already seen, in the discussion on the strategic role of the board, that two distinct forms of control are at work. These are, first, the framing of corporate values, or, to use Simons' phrase (1994), determining the belief systems of the organization, and, secondly, establishing the boundaries of strategic activity. These are central to the strategic process. A central theme of this chapter is that the board's role as a control mechanism is conceived by directors (in particular non-executive directors), not in terms of policing, typically on a management-by-exception basis, but rather in terms of diagnosis, using the control systems of the firm to set new strategic direction through a process of identifying trends and new opportunities, focusing organizational attention by setting new strategic targets and performance goals.

The chapter will begin with an overview of approaches to defining control, before examining the board's use of control systems, both operational and strategic, within organizations. The capacity of directors to focus organizational attention through conceptualizing control systems as diagnostic mechanisms is then discussed, and we conclude by exploring the board's other primary control function—the assessment of executives, including the use of incentives and sanctions.

Defining control

Berle and Means define control as the ability to determine the board of directors: 'control lies in the hands of the individual or group who have the actual power to select the board of directors' (1932: 4). This definition has been supported by Herman, who states that 'the basic question of establishing who has the power over key decisions, as a practical matter, revolves ultimately on determining who has the power to name the top executives of the corporation' (1981: 54). Fama and Jensen (1983) distinguish between 'decision management'—the initiation and implementation of decisions—and 'decision control'—the signing-off and monitoring of decisions. In widely owned firms, the authors argue, the two forms of decision should be taken by distinct groups. Management—the full-time officers of the firm—should undertake decision management because of their superior knowledge and expertise, and decision control should be undertaken by the board of directors. For this separation to be efficient, the board must be able to represent shareholder interests accurately and to be truly independent of management (Ezzamel and Watson 1997). But it remains widely recognized that the de facto control of companies may rest with the managers. For example, *The Economist* (1994) argues that:

In theory, company boards should improve the parts of corporate governance the stock market cannot reach. They hire the boss, fix his pay, monitor, correct and, if necessary, fire him. In principle, too, boards can function well without the active involvement of shareholders—who therefore avoid the risk of acquiring inside information that legally circumscribes their ability to trade shares. Yet in Britain, America, and Japan, boards have been mostly ineffective in corporate governance; and in Germany their record is mixed.

This has led to definitions of control centring on the power to determine the broad direction and policies of the organization. Control, on this view, is 'the power to decide upon the corporate strategy of the enterprise, where corporate strategy involves the "determination of the basic long-term goals and objectives of the enterprise and the adoption of courses of action and the allocation of resources necessary for carrying out these goals"' (Scott 1997, quoting Chandler 1962).

The board's legal obligations to the shareholders involve a fiduciary duty to supervise managers to ensure that they act in the best interests of shareholders. This involves an oversight function that, in the normative literature at least, implies some degree of confrontation (primarily between executive and non-executive directors). The board has been described as the shareholders' first line of defence against incompetent management (Weisbach 1988). Directors must satisfy minimum standards of diligence, care and skill, with diligence referring to 'the expected level of active engagement in company affairs' (Parkinson 1993: 98). Executive directors are required to give their full-time attention to company affairs, while non-executive directors, though the precise content of their duty is not clear, do have a 'duty of some sort in relation to the detection of management fraud', though 'whether non-executives have any responsibility for company performance in general, arising from a duty to supervise the quality of management decision-making, also awaits further litigation' (Parkinson 1993: 99).

Recent UK policies have argued for the non-executive directors to monitor the performance of the company, and that of management, through their formal position on the main board and also through board committees, in particular the audit and remuneration committees. The board as a whole is responsible for reporting on the company's system of internal control (Cadbury 1992; para 4.5), and the UK's Turnbull Report (1999) has gone further, requiring directors to identify and manage all risks associated with their organizations, over and above the purely financial.

The different theoretical perspectives on boards of directors support the view of the board as a control mechanism. According to agency theory, the board is an alternative monitoring device that controls the corporate agency problem by governing management's decisions and assessing their impact on shareholder wealth (Fama and Jensen 1983). In the TCE tradition, the board is primarily a 'governance structure safeguard between the firm and owners of equity capital and secondarily . . . a way to safeguard the contractual relation between the firm and its management' (Williamson 1985). Class-hegemony researchers stress the board as representing a power elite that can control the extent of management involvement. Resource-dependence theorists argue that boards can exercise a control function by being the source of key information, providing resources for operations and for ensuring favourable transactions between firms through the use of board interlocks (Zahra and Pearce 1989). The managerial-hegemony theory believes that boards should act as control mechanisms between shareholders and the actions of management, but argues that boards in fact fail to fulfil this role, owing to the power of chief executives, poor board processes, and inadequate information.

For boards of directors there are two board areas that constitute its control role:

the employment of internal control systems to monitor the operating divisions of the company, and assessing senior management (Walsh and Seward 1990). The internal control mechanisms at the board's disposal are, first, tailoring incentives to ensure alignment between shareholder and manager interests and, secondly, the dismissal of managers (Walsh and Seward 1990). We shall examine each in turn.

The board's use of control systems

A system of controls is 'the process which allows senior management to determine whether a business unit is performing satisfactorily, and which provides motivation for business unit management to see that it continues to do so' (Goold and Quinn 1990*b*: 21). The reasons for introducing such a system include the co-ordination of major elements of the organization, harmonizing employee and organizational goals through appropriate incentives, and identifying deviation from agreed targets (Goold and Quinn 1990*b*).

The presence of control systems within the organization is generally viewed as providing information feedback (Simons 1991), and such systems are considered essential to ensure that key aspects of organizational activity are properly planned and assessed (Goold and Quinn 1990*a*). There are two broad forms of control system: operational and strategic (Lorange *et al.* 1986; Goold and Quinn 1990*b*). Operational control 'tracks management performance against cost and revenue objectives' (Goold and Quinn 1990*b*: 345) and focuses on a twelve-month time span. The emphasis is strictly on financial objectives, and this form of control does not explicitly take into account long-term and non-financial aims. Strategic control, on the other hand, is 'the critical evaluation of plans, activities and results, thereby providing information for future action' (Schreyogg and Steinmann 1987: 91). Strategic control systems thus require a longer-term perspective and a focus on strategic progress.

Operational control

Budgetary and planning cycles
In the companies studied, which are structurally diversified, the planning process followed a bottom-up process, with the subsidiaries submitting plans followed by budgets as part of the annual planning cycle. Before the planning cycle begins, however, the corporate (or divisional) top team (or both of them) outlines the major objectives for the firm as a whole, presents the major product/service areas, and gives rough estimates of the kind of targets it expects to be achieving. This broad framework is sent to business units and serves as a template to appraise the submission of plans and budgets from the business units (see Bower 1970: 41–2).

The business unit prepares plans that detail, among other issues, product/service goals, estimates on product volume, new directions for the business, marketing strategies such as pricing and placement, and forecasts for market share and profit. To each of these are attached some measures of expected revenue, return on investment, and profit. There is also usually some description of staffing requirements forecast. But, at this stage, the focus is not on the numbers (save only for general estimates) but on the strength and coherence of the plan. This plan is then submitted to the division (or next level), and here, subject to revision and refinement, the plans from the various business units are collated and merged into the divisional plan. The next step is then for business units to provide a detailed budget for the coming year. This is much more focused on numbers, including hard financial forecasts.

The annual review of plans and budgets allows management to assess strategy and costs in the light of changed environmental circumstances (see Lorange *et al.* 1986). Though such reviews have been criticized on the grounds that they occur too infrequently, are too bureaucratic, and promote 'inward-looking' rather than externally focused mind-sets (Lorange 1989: 146–7), they nevertheless provide an important source of internal control and represent a useful lever for the board to understand the progress of the business. As individual business-unit plans and budgets are drafted, they will come before the board, which will determine whether the strategies are in line with overall company policy and whether the budgets are demanding enough and setting a reasonable level of return on capital, and of sales, profitability, and market share. The review of the operating companies' budgets provides a useful forum for monitoring the performance, both past and prospective, of the respective management teams.

In addition, once the planning process has been completed and the budgets set, the main board typically analyses the performance of the operating companies each month at the main board meeting. Performance against stated aim and against budgets is assessed, and it is not uncommon for the heads of operating companies to make presentations to the board (if they are not board members already). Scrutiny is also tight in preparation for the half-year and year-end reports to the public. There is, therefore, scope for monitoring the performance of the organization at this stage.

In large firms with wide spans of control, there is a large amount of data to be evaluated, which could not possibly be handled in depth at a board meeting. Boards therefore receive consolidated financial data (consolidated usually at divisional level). The board monitors the process and the performance of the divisions on a management-by-exception basis. The provision of financial data in the annual budgets makes the board's task in assessing the stretch and risk of the proposed plan and budget relatively simple: board members armed with records of performance from recent years are able to make comparisons relatively straight-forwardly. The amount of time given over to discussion of the figures tends to be minimal:

We take maybe fifteen minutes over the financials. In board meetings, we spend more time looking ahead, at growth opportunities, new directions. We get the numbers out of the way pretty quickly, unless there is a problem. (executive director)

We have limited time to get involved with the intricacies of the business but we can all understand a balance sheet. If the figures look wrong it is pretty apparent. (non-executive director)

Reserved powers

One clear method used in companies for operational control is to draw up formal statements of delegated powers, usually referred to as reserved-powers statements. Delegated powers, framed in statements of reserved powers (that is, powers or functions that are reserved to the board for decision), detail the thresholds of decision-making on a number of key issues. The thresholds are usually financial in nature, the most common example being capital expenditure. In one large multinational, any project that requires spending over £6 million has to come to the board for decision. Between £1 million and £6 million, the executive committee has power to decide. Below £1 million, and the decision rests with the operating subsidiary board. The level of detail, of course, will vary according to individual company norms and culture.

Such statements make the process of monitoring much easier, since it is relatively simple to discover whether any operating subsidiary is acting beyond its limits as set down by the main board. A number of interviewees stressed the importance of this issue—for example, 'Having reserved powers is vital, those powers which are not delegated but have to be decided by the board. Things happen between board meetings and there should be some written procedures to cover this' (chairman).

This determination of specific powers that a board does not delegate, and by extension, those that it does, forms part of the organizational planning, cost, and resource allocation control systems and is best described as a mechanism for management by exception. Reserved-powers statements are encouraged by Cadbury (1992). The reserved-powers statement provides a formal constraint on managerial action, and variances from subunits will be reported to the board for remedial action (Simons 1991).

Strategic control

The annual planning cycle deals with the short-term performance of businesses. An organization and its business units and divisions will also have long-term strategic goals. As Goold and Quinn (1990*b*: 44) state:

Budgetary control . . . stresses financial objectives, and usually concentrates on the coming twelve months. It does not deal with a company's progress relative to its competitors, it does not cover non-financial objectives that may be important to the eventual achievement of secure profitability and competitive strength: it pays no explicit attention to longer-term goals and objectives; it does not generally take account of social objectives such as health and safety, the physical environment, etc.

The existence of three-to-five year plans (in some cases longer) was commonplace in the organizations researched, and the annual planning cycle was used to assess progress on the path to achieving these targets. Thus the review of strategy in business units and the organization as a whole was made on a rolling year-by-year basis, with the board as the final judge on fit between organizational and business-unit goals and the level of budgetary targets.

Strategic objectives typically included qualitative and quantitative targets, and had strategic milestones for their achievement and a concern with competitive bench-marks, and with a focus on business-wide threats and opportunities, not just with financial performance measures.

The evidence from this study is that strategic control *as a whole* is largely an *informal* process, rather than a formal, itemized scrutiny suggested by the model of control outlined above. Data from interview responses are given in Table 5.1.

Strategy discussions
Strategic reviews take place usually once a year, sometimes off-site, and would consist of a thorough discussion of all strategic issues of the business, reviewing important concerns and identifying opportunities and threats. A broad review of progress of the various parts of the business would be included, at a general level, with presentations made by divisional (or in some cases business-unit) heads. However, the board as a whole would generally not attend. The executive committee will naturally form the core group in the strategic review, with perhaps some other functional and divisional heads, but the non-executive directors will normally not be there. One executive director said:

It may take three days and for much of that we will simply be throwing around ideas, a lot of which will be rejected. The non-executives cannot afford to give up that kind of time, and it would not represent the best use of their time. We provide a document for them stating what we have identified as useful ideas and we will discuss that at the next board meeting.

For some companies, non-executive directors will be invited to the review, typically for one day. Often this invitation will coincide with important presentations made by senior managers seeking to influence the top management team of the potential of a new plan or direction, or to see a manager tipped to be a future board member. But, formally, the board as a whole is not usually represented at these meetings.

The obvious opportunity for boards to monitor progress of strategic initiatives is through the board meeting. Usually held monthly, the board meeting will normally open with a review of progress of divisions and units by the chief executive. Board papers distributed beforehand will give directors a fuller picture and the chief execu-

TABLE 5.1. *Strategic control measures*

Measures	Frequency
Discussions of strategy at board meetings	24
Strategic reviews	9
Quality data/customer satisfaction data	9
Benchmarking progress against competitors	6
Conversations with shareholders/stakeholders	3
TOTAL	53

Note: Multiple responses allowed.
Source: Interviews (n=51).

tive will typically talk about a number of key points. If a new strategic proposal is to come before the board, the nominator will present the case, allowing the full board an opportunity to weigh its potential. The problem for the board is that checking the progress of strategy in various units may be difficult, owing to the possible complexity of that unit's strategy and the asymmetry of information that puts the board at a disadvantage. The result can be that the non-executive directors will emphasize financial controls in assessing a decision or strategy (which may produce an emphasis on short-term payback and an avoidance of high-risk-return strategies (see Baysinger and Hoskisson 1990)). It was certainly the case in interviews with non-executive directors that the chief source of information on which they based their judgements was financial data: 'You can see pretty quickly if the return on investment is not as good as it should be, or was forecast. If there are mitigating circumstances, that's fine, but they'll have to argue those very clearly' (non-executive director).

But other non-executives stressed features of the board meeting that allowed them to overcome adherence only to financial control. The quality of a director's presentation defending his or her choice of strategy, his or her response to questioning, the adaptation of a strategy in the light of changing environmental circumstances, and its continuing logic in the face of the changing corporate portfolio were all issues cited in the interviews. The responsibility for monitoring the performance of managers and the firm as a whole does not, of course, fall entirely on the shoulders of the non-executive directors. The executive directors also have an important role to play. The main complaint of non-executive directors, as we have noted, is that they lack the information (or the time and/or expertise fully to process information) on the performance of the chief executive. Because non-executive directors suffer a knowledge asymmetry with executive directors concerning the decision processes of the top management team, non-executives may rely on financial information to judge the performance of directors. Though this is an important yardstick, the link between director performance and firm performance is complex, and there are many intervening variables. As Eisenhardt (1985: 136) states, 'good outcomes can occur despite poor efforts and poor outcomes can occur despite good efforts'. The importance of executive directors in this regard is that they are privy to the internal decision-making process that the chief executive heads, and they are in a position to judge the competence of the chief executive's rationality and the choice of strategic and tactical initiatives, regardless of their outcomes (Baysinger and Hoskisson 1990). One executive director said: 'I see the chief executive every day, sometimes formally, sometimes informally. I know his style, his thought patterns, what he thinks about certain issues and what he would think about certain things. He always seems on top of everything and has a very good grasp of detail.' The role of the executive director in assessing the performance of the chief executive is explored later in the chapter.

Monitoring of the environment and benchmarking
The performance of the strategy (and that of the chief executive and other members of top management) must be viewed in the light of prevailing environmental

conditions, and the performance of competitors, if its contribution is to be fairly assessed. As Walsh and Seward (1990: 426) state: 'The board . . . might have a difficult time holding the manager responsible for poor organisational performance if its firm's product is a commodity sold in a low growth market marked by stable demand.'

The attribution of praise or blame concerning the performance of strategy (or particular units, or managers) is always difficult precisely because of the potential for managers to put poor performance at the door of adverse environmental circumstances, or to accept responsibility for success in the light of peculiarly favourable operating conditions in the external environment. The monitoring of the environment was a task that non-executive directors interviewed felt comfortable with, because the determination of what the constraints were could be assessed at a fairly high degree of generality. For example, a non-executive director of a major bank said: 'You can get very good information from the media and analysts' reports on the nature of the industry. There are some very large changes occurring but the general nature of how the industry is transforming is fairly clear, at least at this time.'

Comparative data on organizations in the same sector were readily available and were, on occasion, provided to the board prior to board meetings, according to the interview findings. This was mainly in the form of economic data—market share, growth figures—and financial data—revenues, turnover, financial ratios, and so forth. It was usually a board decision as to which companies would form the referent sample, and which position the company should aspire to in any league table: 'As a board we decided who we should be measuring ourselves against and on what criteria. So when we come to prepare board papers, we will have a page or two of graphs showing what our competitors are doing and how we stand against them' (chief executive). These comparator companies also formed, in some cases, the external parameter for pay decisions for executives.

Quality indices

Internal data on quality measures, most usually customer satisfaction, form useful benchmarks on progress towards various stated aims and values. Normally firms look for year-on-year improvement within the firm concerning quality goals, though there was evidence from this research that, on certain processes, external benchmarking was possible and actively encouraged. Another form of external validation, the achievement of quality awards, was being attempted by some companies—for example, the European Quality Award, BS5750, the Baldridge Award, and Investors in People. Employee satisfaction was also sought, and companies surveyed their workforce frequently to assess commitment, satisfaction, and morale. In some cases, indices for customer satisfaction, quality, and employee satisfaction were part of the performance-management goals for senior managers: 'Our bonuses are tied to how well we are looking after our customers and staff. So you can be sure that, if for no other reason, we are very committed to these issues' (executive director).

Conversations with stakeholders

Given that the evidence from this research points to the fact that board members are usually well connected and plugged into various networks of influence (see following chapter), directors are in a good position to learn of how others perceive the company and its strategy in meetings they have with shareholders, stakeholders, investors, and the media. Much of this information will be at a high level of generality, but doubts expressed by a large investor, for example, will be taken very seriously, and may serve to control the strategic direction of the firm. These conversations will be conducted both by executive directors and by non-executive directors either formally or informally and their findings may provide useful information for discussion for the board meeting (for further discussion of the nature of board dialogues with external constituencies, see Chapter 6).

The audit committee

An increasingly important device for board involvement in control is the audit committee. The Cadbury Report has argued for changes in the role and scope of the audit function: in particular, the report has emphasized the need for improved internal controls and has highlighted the place of audit committees in effecting greater accountability in companies. The Cadbury Code (section 4.5) states that: 'the directors should report on the effectiveness of the company's system of internal controls'. Though directors already have an implicit duty to ensure that this is done, the code urges directors to make a statement in the report and accounts as to the effectiveness of the company's internal controls.

The audit committee is intended to provide a link between the board and the auditor independent of the company's management, which is responsible for the accounting system (IOD 1995). The chief aims of an audit committee are to improve the quality of financial reporting, to reduce the potential for fraudulent practice, to provide authority for the non-executive director, to improve the channel of communication with the external auditor, and, perhaps most importantly, to review the adequacy of the company's *financial control systems*. The audit committee is not usually expected to have any responsibility for appraising executive decisions of monitoring the effectiveness of management; that is, they are not expected to have responsibility for strategic controls (Coopers & Lybrand 1986; ICAEW 1991; Parkinson 1993). The audit committee is an important vehicle for ensuring the supervision and accountability at board level (Tricker 1984). It can also serve to increase the legitimacy of a company and can reduce directors' exposure to liability (Harrison 1987).

The Cadbury Report has insisted that all listed companies should have an audit committee with a minimum of three members, with membership limited to non-executive directors. The external auditor, too, Cadbury recommends, should be present at meetings of the committee and there should be a meeting of the audit committee and the external auditor at least once a year without executive board members present (Cadbury 1992).

The companies in the sample had audit committees in place, composed exclusively of non-executive directors (mean of three members), though invitations to the meeting were usually extended to the finance director, in line with the Cadbury recommendations and, in some cases, the chief executive. The external auditor would also be present. The head of internal audit within companies liaised closely with the chairman of the audit committee but usually would not attend the meeting, which was held once, or in the case of a few firms, twice, a year. The benefits of the audit committee, according to the directors interviewed, were several. First, the delegation of audit issues to the audit committee means that the committee has more time to devote to these issues and can discuss their implications in greater depth than would be possible in regular board meetings. 'It is not a leisurely pace, but we can afford to dwell on a topic which is important and which we feel merits the time. Sometimes the board will specifically ask us to examine an issue in detail and report back. The audit committee gives us the flexibility to do this' (non-executive director).

Given that many non-executive directors had a financial background (or at least considerable financial acumen), allotting them the task of devoting their energies to scrutinizing the audit process represented a good use of their expertise. The converse of the former point is that a consequence of delegating audit issues to the audit committee is the freeing-up of board time to devote to other key concerns that may have received a cursory examination or been ousted altogether from the board agenda. Since board time is a valuable commodity, ways in which it can be best used are constantly sought. The committee structure is a primary means of effecting this: 'If we went into the minutiae of the audit, we wouldn't have time for anything else. Probably people would fall asleep, too. By farming it out, we can get them to tell us their findings in a brief fashion without getting bogged down in the detail' (executive director).

The audit committee as a forum for the exercise of non-executive control is very important. In the audit committee in particular, the non-executives can exercise their voice and be seen to make a valuable contribution, enhancing their credibility. The committee also offers an opportunity for the non-executive to bond as a team and create a collective identity. 'I get to spend more time with my non-executive colleagues and we discuss the business and other issues in the business environment. I can learn a great deal' (non-executive director).

The chief roles of the audit committee were to review the chief financial statements (the half-year and annual), and to review the company's statement on internal control systems delivered from the internal audit function, before they pass to the main board. The interviewees said that these documents would be subject to intense scrutiny in the same way that a main board proposal would receive detailed attention, with drafts often being amended or sent back for further clarification. Establishing a good working relationship with the external auditor, and clarifying the scope of his/her role was also considered by respondents to be an important task.

Focusing organizational attention: Control as diagnosis

The presence of control systems within an organization helps to monitor the progress of the business by providing tools to examine, for example, the accounting systems, the critical success factors of current strategies, budgetary and planning targets, and long-term strategic goals. The evidence of this study is that financial or operational control tends to be more formalized than strategic control, though there is a significant amount of activity in this area, particularly in the form of strategy reviews, quality measures, and monitoring of the environment. Most of this activity proceeds on a management-by-exception basis, with the board becoming proactive only in cases of shortfalls in realized outcomes against predicted targets, or as a result of major changes in the environment that prompt the revision of budgets and plans and performance targets.

Though management by exception is largely a reactive stance in terms of board involvement, and its prevalence in organizations has been used to support the managerialist hypothesis, the data revealed that the passivity of boards is more apparent than real. Just as the board provides the strategic context that determines which plans and proposals will be accepted and which will be rejected, so the board's choice of measures and control mechanisms will determine where organizational attention will be focused and which elements of performance will be incentivized and rewarded. The choice of controls, therefore, made by the board will form part of the strategic context determining process. Ideally, the control system and measures will be aligned with the strategic direction and values of the company. That is, the belief systems and the control systems will reinforce each other. In times of change, this may not always be possible, and mixed messages may occur: 'We want to encourage teamwork and innovation, but until we get our compensation and benefits plan in place, managers and their staff are still being rewarded on short-term individual contributions, which is the way it's always been. We have a long way to go' (executive director).

As Simons (1991: 61) states, 'organizational attention is limited and top managers must decide what to emphasise and what to de-emphasise'. In many of the companies, there have been clear moves away from hierarchical, individualistic, results-driven cultures, constrained by a focus on short-term profits generation, to cultures that emphasize flattened structures, team-based working, with greater focus on process improvement and innovation and a longer-term perspective to encourage the development of human capital. Boards have had to decide how best to encourage this shift; they have had to determine which control systems will best encourage the behaviours and outcomes the organization is seeking to foster. 'We want to push leadership right through the business. We can't have just ten or twelve people leading this firm, we need to have innovative ideas coming right the way through. We shall have to loosen the strictures on people, increase development and reward entrepreneurial thinking' (executive director).

The board of a fast-moving consumer goods company driven by strong short-term targets almost exclusively financial in nature was concerned that its highly individualistic culture and lack of innovative activity were eroding their long-term competitive advantage: 'We had to rethink. We knew there would come a time when our results would plateau. We are in a mature market and we have to be much cleverer about new ways of marketing and distributing our products. We cannot keep up this pace indefinitely' (executive director).

The control systems in place, if used in a management-by-exception approach, enable the identification of problems and misalignments between intention and reality in plans and budgets. But organizations are not static and nor are markets; there is a constant evolution of the business and organizational environment that entails that, if organizations are to compete successfully, their processes and measures and goals have to change over time to reflect new conditions and new challenges. The process of which controls to use and which incentives to implement will vary, therefore, according to context. The important implication of this line of argument is that it becomes a key board role to diagnose the potential for new markets, new opportunities, and shifts in direction. This process of diagnosis, intimately linked to the weighing of opportunity costs, was highlighted in Chapter 4. In terms of control systems, the gathering of information through these systems can enable the board to assess strategic uncertainties, discuss trends, and stimulate discussion about the likely outcomes of various strategic options or scenarios. In other words, control systems may be used proactively to foster discussion about new strategic direction, rather than just being used to keep a 'steady hand on the tiller'.

It is up to us to look at the broad trends. As directors, we have to take the helicopter view and this does not mean focusing just internally. There is a real danger that if you ignore the external environment, you will be left behind. It is our job to pick up the trends and say, should we get into that, or move this way?   (chairman)

The diagnosis of strategic uncertainties, and the attempt to make decisions based on opportunities and threats that arise from those uncertainties, are part of the scanning activity that boards regularly undertake. Conceptually, this is bound up with, first, the regular review of the corporate definition. At formal and informal meetings of the board, there is a good deal of attention paid to the continuing viability of the business the firm is currently operating in and the attractiveness (or not) of other markets or ventures that would take the firm in a new direction. As one executive director said:

We are constantly on the lookout for new opportunities. We are an acquisitive company and though we have guidelines on what a target should look like, if the target is outside those guidelines but sufficiently large and attractive, we can make that a new core business. We expect the non-execs to play a role in this, often checking out informally the reputation of the target firm with their contacts, telling us if they've heard anything on the grapevine.

Discussions, too, take place in the monitoring of strategies, to understand whether there are any major obstacles on the path to their achievement. Detailed reviews of progress and strong attention to information flows increase the possibility of finding unanticipated opportunities and also marked deviations in performance among operating units. In one company, a mobile phone operator, the chairman said:

We meet as an executive team every Monday morning, where we discuss every piece of information, and pore over what the competition are doing. Once a month the board meets and we talk to them about all the information. and news we have gathered. This kind of stuff reveals the weak points and the areas of potential.

This approach is to be expected in large firms where bottom-up strategy-making is the norm. Lower-level managers are encouraged to develop strategies in line with the corporate definition and strategic framework. But innovative and entrepreneurial behaviour is also encouraged to varying degrees. This 'autonomous' behaviour (in Burgelman's terminology) is important to organizational learning and for developing change initiatives. Managing this process will be the responsibility of managers throughout the organization, but responsibility rests with the board, which, as gatekeeper and also in its role as confidence-builder, will determine which options will be chosen.

Assessment of senior managers

The foregoing discussion has centred on the board's use of control systems to shape and monitor organizational effort. A further critical element in the control of the company is the monitoring of the performance of the chief executive officer and other executives. Finkelstein and D'Aveni state that 'boards of directors are charged with ensuring that chief executive officers carry out their duties in a way that serves the best interests of the shareholders' (1994: 1079). According to Lorsch and MacIver, the chief executive is 'the acknowledged expert. Outside directors are part-timers, while the chief executive not only spends most of the time leading the company, he or she has usually been involved with it for his or her whole career' (1989: 80). As the best-informed person on the board and in the company as a whole, the chief executive is in the best position to take an integrative view of the organization. This means that the chief executive is the linchpin of the strategic process. In addition, successful chief executives are often invited onto the boards of other companies, which increases their prestige, contacts, and knowledge, and so gives them increased power within their own company and encourages chief executive entrenchment.

The chief executive is usually the principal mover in the recruitment of directors. The chief executive is also the chief disseminator of information to the board (Zahra and Pearce 1989). One of the major problems facing boards attempting to assess the contribution of the chief executive (and other members of top management) is to determine the extent to which he or she is responsible for the factors that affect organizational performance, or whether it is environmental or situational forces that shape the current position (Walsh and Seward 1990). The board needs, therefore, to conduct an assessment of top management as well as an assessment of the environment.

The main area for the board to analyse and make a judgement upon the performance of the chief executive and other executives is at the board meeting. Chief executives normally make a presentation at the beginning of a board meeting, outlining company progress, including financial results, the state of strategic initiatives, and any opportunities and threats that are on the horizon (or even closer). The judgement of the board is, therefore, dependent on the quality of the information the chief executive wishes to reveal and the amount of questioning the board member is encouraged to pursue. That the information provided by the chief executive is accurate and not lacking in any important regard is something non-executive directors, indeed the whole board, have to take on trust. The amount and nature of questioning allowed to take place within the boardroom are the responsibility of the chairman. The chairman controls the vocalization of opinion in the boardroom. He or she sets the tone and has the responsibility to ensure that all opinions are heard. This becomes problematic, however, when the chairman is also the chief executive (that is, in cases of chief executive duality).

The performance of managers can be based either on their behaviour—for example, in the decision-making process—or on its outcomes—for example, the tangible results of the decision-making (Baysinger and Hoskisson 1990). For the first type, labelled strategic control, managers are appraised largely on subjective criteria—for example, their reasons for adopting the direction proposed, the quality of debate, the desirability of the strategy before implementation, and so forth. For the second type, labelled financial control, managers are judged against their performance in meeting targets and delivering measurable financial performance to the company (Baysinger and Hoskisson 1990). The important point that Baysinger and Hoskisson make is that non-executive directors, because of their limited knowledge of the decision-making processes within the organization and the asymmetry of information between executives and themselves, must rely almost exclusively on financial controls to judge the performance of executives: 'While relations between inside directors and top management may be open and subjective (strategic control emphasis), relations between (truly) independent outside directors may be more objective and formulaic (financial-control emphasis)' (1990: 79).

But it is not only non-executives who can check the performance of the chief executive. Executive directors also have a very important role to play in this process. The main complaint of non-executive directors, as we have noted, is that they lack the information (or the time and/or expertise fully to process the information) on the performance of the chief executive. Executive directors are in a much closer position to judge the performance of the chief executive. Their presence on the executive committee with the chief executive, as well as a wide range of other formal and informal interactions, gives them increased potential for assessment. But a key theme that emerged from the interview data was that the chief executive was considered to be very influential in terms of contributing to business performance and was held to possess the most detailed knowledge of the company, and, when directors talked about poor chief-executive performance, it usually concerned experiences of former incumbents who had long since left the respective companies. The belief in the abilities of the chief executive usually entails that only in the most adverse of circumstances are chief executives ousted from their position: 'It would have to be something very drastic for us to remove the chief executive. He would have to be cracking up or actually found with his hand in the till for it to happen' (non-executive).

This was an often repeated sentiment. The chief executive's influence over the executives' remuneration and selection tends to prohibit them from making direct criticism of the top officer. To do so would be viewed as dangerously confrontational and certainly would provoke the chief executive to entrench his or her position further. The main route for executives who do have doubts over the competence or moral probity of the chief executive is to have informal talks with either a non-executive director or, more usually, the chairman (should the role be distinct from the chief executive).

Compensation arrangements: The remuneration committee

The non-executive element on the board is intended, in part, to set compensation incentives in order to align the interests of executives with those of shareholders. Stock option plans, pay for performance, and share ownership provide the executive directors with incentives to maximize company performance and firm value. The setting of rewards by the non-executives also has the result of avoiding the invidious position of executives determining their own pay rises, with the obvious threat of excessive pay increases.

The role of the non-executive director in the setting of executive compensation is formalized in the mechanism of the remuneration committee (Conyon 1997). The remit of the remuneration committee is to 'recommend to the board the remuneration of the executive directors in all its forms, drawing on outside advice as necessary. Executive directors' should play no part in decisions on their own remuneration' (Cadbury 1992: para 4.42). The Greenbury Committee Report on directors' remuneration (Greenbury 1995a) endorsed both the need for companies to set up remuneration committees and for such committees to be comprised solely of non-executive directors, as well as underlining the desirability of support structures to such committees, primarily in the form of outside consultancy advice.

Exclusive non-executive membership is the norm in the UK, with a median of three non-executives on committees, though there is still evidence that executive director presence continues in some boards (Conyon 1997). The relationship between remuneration committees and executive pay was examined by Main and Johnson (1992), who found in a survey of 220 UK corporations in 1990 a positive correlation between director compensation and the existence of a remuneration committee, suggesting that remuneration committees produce a racheting effect on pay levels. A negative association was found by Benito and Conyon (1995) in a panel study of 200 firms between 1986 and 1994, indicating that more research is required to examine the precise nature of this relationship.

The companies in the present sample had all established remuneration committees, in the main meeting annually, and comprised solely of non-executive directors (mean membership of three). The evidence of this study was that decisions on pay are determined using a matrix of measures, including performance against targets, external pay comparators, and organizational performance, measured against financial and market factors. This matrix was considered necessary to reflect the complex forces that may affect pay calculations. Tying executive pay to absolute firm performance does not reveal how executives are performing with respect to an external reference group (Kerr and

Kren 1992); therefore, it was not only firm performance that was measured, but performance against competitors (relative performance) and market relative performance.

Market factors were very important in determining executive pay. Comparisons with other executives in relevant industry labour markets were a central factor in retention and motivation. Remuneration consultants were used extensively for this purpose, not only in terms of design of reward structures but also in conducting pay surveys benchmarking key referent organizations. The complexity of the company—size, scope, degree of change—was also important, as these factors affected the contribution of executives and the degree of their discretion. Reliance on internal company research for information, particularly from the personnel department for legal and tax issues, was also common.

Though the remuneration committees in the sample were composed entirely of non-executive directors, and therefore were chaired by non-executives, some organizations did invite the chief executive to attend meetings to discuss the performance of members of his or her executive team. Some said that the chief executive took a back seat in discussions, while others stated that the chief executive took a full and active part in the debate, save for when his or her own pay was to be dealt with.

Pay for performance is the normal means by which the board seeks to align managerial effort with organizational goals. Empirical research on the link between pay and performance has produced mixed results. Some researchers have found a positive association between company performance and pay (Coughlan and Schmidt 1985; Murphy 1985), two studies showed no support (Redling 1981; Kerr and Bettis 1987), and, while most showed significant relationships (Tosi and Gomez-Mejia 1989), 'less than 10% of the variance in change in executive compensation was explained by the combination of firm performance and size in each' (Gomez-Mejia and Balkin 1992: 194). Despite the equivocal results, the assumption that executives are highly motivated by pay remains tenacious. However, contra the arguments of agency theory, pay was not viewed in terms of motivation for directors, and the incentive effects of performance pay were thought to be overstated. If pay was considered important, it was for 'keeping score' rather than amassing large bonuses *per se*: 'I don't need to have an incentive to do well. I want to achieve the best possible performance and money is only a way of keeping count of my progress. Of course it is important that I am well paid, but that doesn't *drive* me. My motivation is to do a fantastic job' (executive director).

This view of motivation was repeated consistently. The need for achievement and the intrinsic challenging nature of the job and a desire to appear successful, both inside and outside the firm, suggest that pay as a motivator may be overemphasized at this level. The motivational power of pay may rest therefore in its role as a symbolic reward (Finkelstein and Hambrick 1988; Lawler 1987). The idea of keeping score nevertheless put a high premium on the accuracy of measuring performance, and the importance of the board in monitoring the effort of individual directors.

The non-executives' role in setting executive pay through the mechanism of the remuneration committee is potentially the most problematic in terms of the relationship between executives and non-executives. Controlling pay is a sensitive issue but executives stated that the fairness and transparency of the process were crucial, as well as the belief that the non-executives understood the elements of their performance. If directors are motivated by the intrinsic satisfaction their work provides, rather than by extrinsic rewards, then it may be that the chief motivating force of the board in general and of the remuneration committee in particular lies not in increasing financial compensation but in the setting of stretching goals.

Disciplining directors

If executives underperform, the board has two choices: to revise their incentive structure or to dismiss them. Demotion or reassignment are also possible options, but 'senior managers are typically dismissed in these circumstances' (Walsh and Seward 1990: 429). Tracking whether the executive turnover is voluntary or involuntary is difficult given that departures at this level are typically stage managed to maintain the reputation of the organization and the outgoing executive.

Consistently poor individual performance, the continued underperformance of the individual's division, function, or department, or malfeasance were the three main issues cited by interviewees that lead to dismissal. For boards to be in a position to evaluate an executive, the attribution of the responsibility for the underperformance has to be placed with the individual, rather than with environmental causes. In the case of executives, their knowledge of one another through close contacts in the day-to-day running of the business makes this process relatively open. In most cases there was a recognition that the recruitment process had not been full enough and that the elevation of the manager to the board was misjudged. A sense that the director was out of his depth, rather than self-seeking or morally questionable, was the chief reason for prompting discussion over dismissal.

The robustness of most selection processes ensured that incompetence or poor fit with the organization and the board was unlikely. The problem remains, however, that judging whether an individual is capable of operating effectively on a board can really be only assessed when that individual is actually promoted: 'We hired a guy with impeccable credentials from the outside. He had even been earmarked for the chief executive position, and I think he came with that expectation. But he just never performed outstandingly. He also had that touch of arrogance that meant he wouldn't call for help. He left to join another firm as their CEO. I don't know how they are doing since he joined them.'

The inability of some executives to cope with changing circumstances, or to develop new ways of thinking about the organization to promote continued competitive advantage, is also a key reason for the decision to dismiss.

We had a strong charismatic chief executive who strategically acquired a Dutch company. He persuaded us this was the right move with a brilliant presentation, stressing the synergies we would gain. But the success didn't happen. But instead of cutting our losses, the chief executive became determined that it should not be considered a failure. Great tensions developed in the boardroom. The problem was that not enough information was coming to the board that did not flow through the chief executive. So we didn't know that he was going off the rails. Finally, when the true extent of the damage became known, we fired the chief executive and sold the acquired company—but it was like a fire sale, we got virtually nothing for it. (executive director)

In the case of the dismissal of the chief executive, we found, in common with Mace (1971) and Lorsch and MacIver (1989), that this occurred only under the most drastic of circumstances. A good deal of literature has focused on the difficulty of removing a chief executive, since many on the board will owe their position to the chief executive and so may be unwilling to voice concerns about him or her. However, the notion of the liability of directors for underperformance ensured a more pragmatic stance: 'The Chief Executive is like the captain of the team. When you are winning, he takes the credit. When you start to lose, you look for reasons. If the captain is in charge of team selection and strategy and tactics, he must also be responsible for his team. If someone isn't playing well, he must motivate them or drop them. If you continue to lose, you may have to drop the captain.'

It is clear from the interviews that the process of dismissing executives in general, and the chief executive in particular, is one that does not take place through formal channels. The chairman's role is crucial here. He or she has to identify the danger signs, according to the interviewees.'Companies are not static and the chairman has to recognize whether the board is equipped for change or not. For example, a chief executive who has built a firm up may not have the relevant skills to cope with that change. The chairman must make sure the board reacts in order to ensure the company's survival' (chairman).

This points up the fact that awareness of the chief executive's performance and his or her team is under constant scrutiny in most organizations and that any decision to eject the incumbent will typically not be a sudden one, or, for the other executives, an altogether surprising one. This may reflect an unwillingness to face conflict openly, or it may reflect the need to smooth the breaking of an intense relationship, which, if badly managed, could have serious implications for the health and reputation of the company. The turnover of a chief executive (and other members of the top management team) is a major control option the board has at its disposal. The fact that it is not used often does not detract from the fact that the latent power this option gives the board acts as an important discipline to top management.

Discussion and conclusions

This chapter has been concerned with the role of the board in the control of the organization. From recent discussion in both the academic and the practitioner literatures, it is clear that the board's role as an internal control mechanism is prominent, both normatively and conceptually (Johnson *et al.* 1996). Common across the theories of boards of directors is the view that an efficient undertaking of the control role by the board will align the interests of managers and shareholders and so lead to greater organizational effectiveness.

Contrasted with this view of the board as an important control mechanism is the managerialist belief that boards *in practice* are ineffective in the control of firms because of CEO entrenchment, information asymmetry between the executive and non-executive directors, and lack of independence, and so a lack of contestability, on the part of the non-executive directors. Bound up with this characterization of boards is the notion that there is an apparently irreconcilable conflict between the board's role in the strategy process and the board's role in monitoring and controlling the organization, which reduces the efficiency of board working.

We have sought to clarify how boards, in reality, do function in their control role and also determine the activities that constitute that role. From the analysis of the board's role in strategy, it was apparent that the board has the capacity to set or control the boundaries of strategic decision-making and also can determine, to a large extent, the belief system of the organization. The board, therefore, can control the strategic context of the organization (Bower 1970; Burgelman 1989). Regarding the implementation of strategy, the board has regular opportunities to appraise the plans and budgets of individual operating units and major functions of the organization through the annual planning cycle. Importantly, the board may revise the plans and budgets put before it, usually on the grounds that the strategies are not in line with the overall company direction or because the budgetary forecast is insufficiently stretching. The long-term targets of the organization and its business units are also subject to scrutiny from the board. This reinforces the contribution of the board to context setting and discipline, activities that undermine the managerialist thesis, and serve to break down the distinction between the board's strategic and control roles.

This blurring of the boundaries between the two roles is accentuated by the board use of control systems as tools for diagnosis. Boards, through the monitoring of the environment and through the application of individual directors' business experience, are able not only to discern external norms of performance that can be used to gauge effort in the focal company, but also to *look forward*, through a process of diagnosis, picking out trends and opportunities for the business to move into, and even redefining the strategic context. The non-executive directors are particularly helpful in this regard, bringing their knowledge of wider business practice to inform debate. Consistent with this theme is our finding that boards may actively help companies to unlearn organizational practices that have become dysfunctional (Nystrom and Starbuck 1984). That is, boards may diagnose new opportunities, select new performance measures, and emphasize certain control systems at the expense of others, in order to bring the organization to a new focus.

The role of the non-executive directors on board committees also served to reinforce their status as valued members of the organization. But concerns about the nature of board committees represent in microcosm doubts about the board as a whole: the lack of complete information for the non-executive to make judgements, the process of selection that can compromise the monitoring function, the potential conflict of interest that arises if close social ties exist between non-executives and executives.

The findings of this research have shown that boards engage in both strategic process and monitoring activity in the organization. The development of social ties through the advice and counsel-giving process highlighted in the discussion of strategy built trust between members of boards and increased the sense of common purpose. These social ties may be thought to reduce the vigilance of the non-executive directors and so reduce the effectiveness of the board as a mechanism of control. But in this chapter, the value of the control levers is to contribute directly to the strategy process. Identifying and pursuing trends and opportunities from the monitoring of the organization requires collaboration and cooperation between the executives and non-executive directors. Such collaboration, and the receptiveness of the executives to receive advice, are enhanced by the degree of interpersonal trust. Balancing trust and control is a necessary requirement, given the structure of the unitary board. Trust and control are not polar opposites: they have to coexist: excessive trust leads to an unchallenging board or to the dangers of groupthink, while excessive control can create division within the board and encourage strategies of entrenchment and the inhibition of information flows. These chapters have shown directors engaged in combining cooperation and control. In the next chapter, we shall see how these two factors combine in the board's other major function: managing the institutional role.

Appendix. Case illustrations

Monitoring the operating divisions of the company: The use of control systems

The strategic process begins in the four companies by the issuing of planning guidelines that are sent to the business units. The business units then devise strategic plans in line with the guidelines and submit them for examination to the executive committee. These plans include analysis of current attractiveness of the market, the potential of existing and future products and services, the nature of environmental circumstances and the likelihood of change in terms of competition, technology, and political and social contingencies. The plans of the various business units are collated by the executive team and are either accepted are sent back for further detail or amendment. In Securicor, Burmah Castrol, and Allied Domecq, business units are required to produce five-year plans that are sent to the corporate centre. These plans are revised annually, as part of a rolling process. For BAA, the business units are required to construct five- and fifteen-year plans.

The guidelines from the executive committee are in the form of financial targets (return on capital, return on investment, and so on) and commercial (for example, quality and customer satisfaction indices). But the business units at this stage are not required to give detailed financial breakdowns of the strategic plans—just broad figures to accompany the strategic aims. Once the strategic aims are agreed, detailed budgets are demanded by the executive committee for the forthcoming year.

> The individual firms work out their budgets—then they go to the divisional level, the divisional Financial Director. The budgets are then put in a pack. The four divisional budgets are collated. That is presented to the EDC, who go through and question the divisional CEO. The revised budget is put to the group board. We ask them to note it. We seek formal approval at the next board meeting. We look at the trading budget (P&L), Capital Expenditure/Cash Flow.   (Securicor director)

In Securicor, there is a rolling three-year plan for each of the individual trading subsidiaries (over fifty businesses). The plan is revised annually (from January to March). The business plan is not a budget; no detailed figures are expected. The emphasis is on the income streams, competitor analysis, product analysis, and political, economic, social, and technological factors. At this stage, the businesses are deciding: 'What it is we are trying to do. We hang around this human resource policies, operational policies, sales plans and so forth.'

The financials are discussed in macro-terms, with broad estimates of the anticipated sales figures, profit numbers, number of assets employed, return on capital numbers, and the expected cash flow 'pencilled in'. Individual firms look at the plans in the period between January and March, after which they go up to the divisional boards and reviews are made to fall in with divisional plans. By mid-to-end February, each division presents a divisional plan and puts this up to the EDC for examination and comment. The EDC then prioritizes the plans and resources are provisionally allocated. At this stage, any completely new proposal, for example, an acquisition, may be factored in. By early April, the business plans are finalized and reviewed by the board. The board is given divisional consolidated summaries and has at least two weeks to look at them. A 'meaningful' board meeting follows, which sets an overall plan for the group. The plan is reviewed annually, in the same timescale (January–March). It is amended to take into account any changes.

There is also the annual budget process. This is very much a numbers exercise. The budgets are built up in trading subsidiaries into a financial budget. This occurs in the summer (June–August). They are expected to approximate to year 2 of the business plan approved in April, but in much more detail. It starts at the bottom ('you know what your overall plan is, now give us your budget') and goes up through all levels, sifting and refining, an iterative process, through branch, subsidiary, division, EDC, board. By the September board meeting, the overall trading capital expenditure and cash-flow budgets are presented to the board for approval. So, by the beginning of the first week in October, there are detailed budgets for the year.

In BAA, annual budgets and medium-term business plans are reviewed by the board before being adopted formally. Revised estimates for the annual out-turn are prepared monthly and analysed in detail on a quarterly basis. Monthly management accounts analyse variance and report on key performance indicators. As befits a company managing large-scale projects, there is a strong emphasis on the group's capital investment programme. This is subject to detailed process analysis, together with approval and monitoring of expenditure. Post-completion reviews are conducted on a systematic basis and significant overruns are investigated and reported back to the board.

The companies' focus on customer satisfaction also reveals itself in the objective setting and monitoring processes with a heavy emphasis on quality indicators, measured mainly through customer satisfaction surveys. 'Managers' incentives are tied directly into these indices, so there is great focus on getting them right' (BAA director).

In Burmah Castrol, broad objectives, largely in terms of financial targets, are given at the beginning of the year. There is a five-year strategic plan, which is updated every year. The updating begins in the first half of the year and climaxes in the July board meeting. Each division revises its own plan each year. The chief executive meets with each head of division at the beginning of the year to discuss the strategic plan and to agree on some issues. The revised divisional plans are then sent to the chief executive, who 'makes sure that the issues discussed are covered in the plan'. This document deals 'with how the head of division sees things, has some numbers—but we don't do five-year numbers. We debate this in committee, the CEO and his advisers, and the head of division and his committee. The CEO therefore has the opportunity to see the shape' (Burmah Castrol director).

At Allied Domecq, the process is broadly similar, with 'strategy in the broad sense' articulated by the board and bottom-up proposals presented by the operating businesses, though, 'as we get more focused, the strategy-making will interfere more with the operating strategies'. There is an annual budget process as well as forecasts for the following three years. These business projections are consolidated and presented to the board and actions are agreed, or revised and resubmitted.

Focusing organizational attention: Control as diagnosis

The boards of the four companies monitor the performance of the various business units and business streams at executive committee meetings (usually weekly) and at board meetings (usually monthly). In both cases the reviews are concerned primarily with examining the financial data and analysing progress against strategic initiatives. Some non-financial targets will also be reviewed monthly, as in the case of BAA, which reports on quality and customer satisfaction data at each board meeting.

At the board level, the financial performance against budget of the major divisions or business units will be assessed. At Securicor, for example, the board looks at performance against budget and against the prior year, and examines the cumulative budget against the prior year. Cash flow is also scrutinized. 'This would take three–four hours. This will be items 3 or 4 at every board meeting. Another important activity is the CAPEX review, where we review our capital expenditure projects' (Securicor director).

The emphasis for the board in each of the four companies was to focus on deviance from the plan, and exceptions. The board meetings are held each month and directors receive a good deal of information concerning the financial figures, though this is usually consolidated at the divisional or large business-unit level.

The main performance review is the annual budget discussion, where the previous year's results are analysed and set the standard for the coming year. The heads of the principal divisions and the chief executive make presentations to the board as a whole, beginning with progress against strategic objectives and then examining the state of play against budget targets. At Securicor, for example, at the annual review, 'The board would look at PEST factors. We circulate figures, simple summaries of the fifty companies. We consider any approvals. Each CEO makes a report on his division. All papers are circulated beforehand. We look at matters relating to employees—unions, pensions, etc.' (Securicor director).

Time spent reviewing past figures would be relatively brief, except for cases where there was deviance from forecasts or other major problems. Discussion would normally centre on prospects for the current strategies and income streams and future projects and initiatives. Here the emphasis is obviously on development of the particular businesses. However, it was claimed that, at BAA, with regard to elements of strategic control, matters were less well developed:

We are at a low stage of understanding. The board would look at the financials—the one-year budget, the five- and fifteen-year plan. In relation to the 5th terminal, they will get various aspects relating to it, 1 or 2 financial projects, projected out-turn, rates of return, architectural concept, reports on planning engineering; once we start building, we get a quarterly review on spend. Where we are less clear (haven't worked out how it should be done) is how to describe the longer term. This is less financially tangible. How can this be monitored? For example, customer service, report every month from surveys with passengers. It is a complex document. As a board, we should stand back and say of the 120 items we survey, only a proportion of which are controllable, 'Which are inadequate and which demand more attention.' We should prioritize security queuing and check-in queuing. We should encourage the board to encourage us to create priorities. (BAA director)

The concern is therefore for the board to emphasize some control processes in order to enhance organizational attention and to develop action plans. According to one BAA executive director, the role of the board is 'to develop these priorities to maximize returns'. For a company such as BAA, which places strong reliance on the management of large-scale projects, post-expenditure audits are important control indicators, monitoring the performance of major projects, particularly when issues of overspend are involved. 'There is continuous assessment. Even the performance of auditors. We get these results every month. Performance is measured in terms of productivity, quality. We have the normal system of budgetary control' (BAA director).

Burmah Castrol has monthly reviews of the performance of the divisions, the chief executive meets with the heads of the divisions, and 'all the results are shown and matched against budget. It's a two-hour meeting if things are going well, a four-hour one if they are not!' (Burmah Castrol director). The chief executive will always have the finance director with him at these meetings, and sometimes will include the group HR director, or corporate development director, or others 'maybe for an item'. Following this meeting, the chief executive and the executive team 'will review the whole picture, and then we will go to the board'. The chief executive reports the distillation of findings of these meeting in his review at the monthly board meeting. The detail for the non-executive directors is far less than would be required for the chief executive's meeting or executive committee: 'We have a general drive to reduce the amount of detail, spurred by the non-executives. Thirty-two pages on capital expenditure are reduced to three. Information on our factory rationalization comes to three pages of text and three pages of figures' (Burmah Castrol director).

For both Burmah Castrol and Securicor, monitoring of the brand is extremely important, since the brand is regarded as perhaps the key asset in each organization. Data on brand value, penetration levels, and other marketing research are therefore major pieces of information that are analysed by the boards of these companies. Decisions, too, on how best to utilize the brands—through entry into new markets or through new product development—are also taken at board level.

At Allied Domecq, too, brand management control is a vital monitoring process—brand performance and customer perception of quality are the two vital indicators of company health. In times of low inflation, price rises were difficult to achieve for the company, and so there was a consequent emphasis on innovation and a step-up in investment on brands. For Allied Domecq, the foreign-exchange disaster that brought the company almost to its knees in 1991 has resulted in strengthened controls and monitoring processes: 'The internal audit and taxation processes have been greatly enhanced. So too is the quality of management information' (Allied Domecq director). Group and sector management are all responsible for the identification and evaluation of key risks applicable to their parts of their business. Overall responsibility for internal control rests with the directors to safeguard the group's assets. A treasury committee was set up after the foreign-exchange incident to set policies for foreign currency management, monitor currency exposure, and ensure strict definition and control of instruments used. A code of conduct was also issued by the board in 1995.

Once a quarter the finance directors of the sectors and major businesses meet and figures and issues are discussed, while 'we have a whole load of chaps in Burton to count the beans'. A sophisticated management information system allows almost immediate inspection of data from around the group. A detailed list of delegated powers is strictly adhered to. The chairman and chief executive meet frequently on an informal basis to discuss broad issues, to monitor key trends both inside and outside the business and to diagnose new opportunities—for example, the divestment of the foods business, and the acquisition of Domecq. Though in this case the chief executive and chairman were responsible for the feedforward analysis, the initial idea was quickly shared with the rest of the board, who were invited to comment.

Audit committees

Performance is also monitored on a formal basis by the audit committee. The four companies each had an audit committee, comprised solely of non-executive directors. At Securicor, the internal audit department reports to the board audit committee, with the chief internal auditor attending the committee meeting. Though formally comprised of non-executive directors, the finance director also attends, as does the company secretary, and the head of external audit. The group internal audit team has sixteen people. They are responsible for auditing to a prepared programme (set out annually in advance, agreed by all chief executives) auditing all fifty firms in the group. The head of internal audit reports to the finance director, and has direct access to chief executive and the board audit committee. For many years, Securicor operated without an audit committee,

> but the advent of Cadbury and the size of the company gave birth to the need for a committee. To do things properly, it needed a sensing process before things got to the board. So there was both push and pull in relation to the audit committee. It now performs a useful function and avoids the board skimming across certain issues. It adds some formal processes and formal discipline. Previously, it was left up to the finance director or the CEO to do things in a moral, ethical way.   (Securicor director)

At BAA, the audit committee is a 'key area where performance is monitored' (BAA director). It meets at least once a quarter to receive reports from the internal and external auditors and to assess the impact of any control issues arising.

At Allied Domecq, the audit committee meets four times a year and includes a review of the effectiveness of the group's system of internal control. This committee receives reports on the state of control from the group internal control function and from the external auditors and from management. The latter is based on a 'letter of assurance' in which the sectors confirm the adequacy of their system of internal control and their compliance with group policies. It also requires the reporting of any significant control issues that have emerged so that areas of group concern can be identified and experience shared.

Burmah Castrol's audit committee reviews the internal audit programme and 'ensures co-ordination between internal and external auditors' (Burmah Castrol Annual Report 1995). It monitors the effectiveness of the internal control systems and reviews the half-year and annual financial statements before they are submitted to the board. It can also make recommendations on the appointment of external auditors, with whom it discusses the nature and scope of the audit.

Informal reviews

In addition to the regular quarterly, monthly, and annual performance reviews (with the group boards involved in the latter two on primarily a control-by-exception basis), the executive committees will have informal conversations and contacts with business heads throughout the organization. These discussions help to flesh out the picture given in formal review, which tends to focus on financials and a rather 'headline' approach to the strategic progress.

The four companies also hold periodic strategy review days, where a group of executives and business-unit managers will meet, perhaps for a full day, to discuss current issues, the state of business progress, and the need to revise targets in the light of changing environmental circumstances. At BAA, such meetings are often held to discuss major projects—for example, the Heathrow Terminal 5 proposal. The board as a whole will not usually be involved in these meetings but will be kept informed by memorandum, or through informal discussions between key executives and the chairman and non-executives.

Regular meetings with customers and important clients by members of the executive team also help to gain useful data on the progress of the firm, its quality and reputation, and delivery of service: 'You have to meet with customers regularly, for example I met recently with the chief executive of NatWest. At that level, you get good feedback from customers. We have a partnership relationship with Midland Bank—if they are doing something, they tell us, we advise and vice versa' (Securicor director). Burmah Castrol holds a regular away-day meeting, usually in February each year. The executive team meet at a country house for dinner in the evening and the following day will discuss about six key issues. What emerges from this meeting is then discussed with the non-executives at the next board meting, and also informally through telephone calls and *ad hoc* meetings.

In addition to the regular monitoring process, the Burmah Castrol chairman and chief executive meet every week on a formal basis, though without a fixed agenda: 'the content of the meeting will vary, from discussing last month's results, to appointments the CEO is proposing to make, to proposals for sponsorship' (Burmah Castrol director). This meeting, which enables the chairman to raise key points and allows him clear insight into the firm's strategy and intentions, also provides a major opportunity to gauge the performance of the chief executive: 'I can see the chief executive in action on a number of occasions in different forms. One is in the board, one is in this meeting. I also see him in the public domain when we present to shareholders—the chief executive has a major role here. People will say to me "Isn't he doing well?"' (Burmah Castrol director). The chairman meets with the other non-executive directors twice a year in an informal manner to discuss the performance of the chief executive.

Rewards and sanctions

Executive remuneration at the four companies was fairly standard, with packages including salary, bonuses, and long-term incentives. Each firm has a remuneration committee, composed of non-executive directors, with the finance director and chief executive usually invited to attend. Remuneration is tied to a matrix that includes overall firm performance, individual contributions against personal objectives, and external comparators.

Interviews revealed that pay was not a major motivator; directors instead mentioned external equity, social comparison, and keeping score as important requirements of pay.

Discussion of dismissal as the ultimate sanction against underperformance was limited, as this is a highly sensitive area. Hypothetical instances that were described confirmed the view that no direct confrontation with the executive concerned would be undertaken in the boardroom: instead, informal soundings would be taken among board members, and, if action was deemed necessary, the chairman would try to arrange a face-saving arrangement for the executive to leave the company.

6
The Institutional Role of the Board

The board of directors functions at the 'institutional' level of the firm (Provan 1980; Perrow 1986). The board's position at the apex of the company, monitoring and counselling management and bearing a fiduciary relationship to the shareholders of the company, ensures that directors have constituencies both internal and external to the organization and face contingencies from both domains (Perrow 1986). Indeed, Mintzberg (1983) called the board the mediator between internal and external coalitions.

There is a strong theoretical tradition concerning the board's role in helping to acquire critical resources and serving as a legitimating function for organizations. A major part of the board's work is to respond to, or anticipate, environmental forces and their impact on the organization. Reducing environmental uncertainty has been viewed, by resource-dependence theorists in particular, as a key element in board endeavour. The sources of uncertainty are many and varied—turbulence, lack of information, poor forecasting, and so forth. The use of the board as a co-optative mechanism reflects the potential of the board in fostering long-term relationships with key external constituencies to increase information and so improve knowledge about external forces (Pearce and Zahra 1992). As Provan (1980: 222) argues, 'boards of directors have been studied from essentially two functional perspectives: the internal control function of boards and the external function of co-opting important elements of the organization's environment'.

Under co-optation theory, non-executive directors derive a large part of their value through acting as links to other organizations or constituencies that are important in terms of resource acquisition or enabling the conduct of business. The most obvious example would be the board-level appointment of a member of a financial institution in order to gain better access to funding (Provan 1980). The more uncertain the environment, the more the board will focus on its external role, with an increase in board diversity to maintain links with the external environment (Pfeffer 1972, 1973; Pfeffer and Salancik 1978; Provan 1980). Board interlocks are a prevalent phenomenon in organizational boundary spanning as 'firms strengthen their boards by inviting acknowledged leaders in different sectors of the firm's environment to serve on the board' (Pearce and Zahra 1992: 412).[1] A consequence of such appointments is mooted to be the increase in prestige of the host organization and, strong messages are sent to stakeholders concerning the quality of the firm and its ability to attract high-calibre personnel.

---

[1] The literature on board interlocks is large and an examination of this phenomenon was beyond the scope of this study. For interested readers, see the discussions by Pennings (1980), Burt (1983), Johnson *et al.* (1996), and Scott (1997).

In addition to the board performing a resource-dependence role, theorists have also emphasized the board's role as the primary signalling source of the organization's intentions and purpose. Bower writes: 'instinctively, when an organisation succeeds or fails, we turn to the top to see who is responsible and to ask what sort of person led this organisation to its present state' (Bower and Weinberg 1988: 42). The board is the ultimate source of power in an organization (Bazerman and Schoorman 1983), and, since it is the board that has formal control of the organization, its statements and behaviour have the power to confer legitimacy and authority upon the firm. Though we have seen that this de jure power may be usurped by management, which may lead to the legitimacy of the company depending on one person—usually the chief executive—or a dominant coalition, nevertheless, the board, in many cases, assumes leadership of the firm and presents the organization to its external constituencies.

The major resource that boards facilitate access to is capital. The securing and maintenance of investment to the organization are highly important for the survival and competitiveness of the firm. In this chapter, we shall explore the board's relationships with shareholders, both institutional and private, followed by an examination of the relationship boards have with stakeholder groups, and also how the institutional investors themselves conceive of the relationship. We then turn to the role of non-executive directors and how their contacts and boundary-spanning can feed into the strategic process.

Relationships with shareholders

Most normative studies put the board's relationship with shareholders as vital to the effective running of the company. The Cadbury Report urges boards to ensure greater accountability to shareholders and to provide useful and timely information to them. The requirement to satisfy the interests of shareholders is not a simple one, since investors differ as to their objectives and their investment horizons. Some institutions favour wide diversification in their portfolio make-up, with small stakes in each and frequent dealing. In such cases, contact with portfolio companies is minimal. Others choose to hold fewer stocks with larger stakes, and look to establish close relationships with their portfolio companies. Their larger holdings in the companies means less frequent dealings in their shares (Charkham 1994*a*). Scepticism about the role of the board in ensuring corporate accountability, together with a loss of faith in accounting and auditing practices, have brought calls for greater shareholder intervention in the running of organizations (Gilson and Kraakman 1991; Pound 1992; Useem 1993; Useem *et al.* 1993). Broadly speaking, there are two types of shareholders: institutional and private; we shall examine each in turn.

Institutional shareholders

The role of institutional shareholders in exercising good corporate governance has long been recognized and in recent years the concentration of ownership in the

hands of a small number of large institutional investors has brought about the potential for greater monitoring of management. The change has been dramatic. In 1970
private investors owned two-thirds of public companies, whereas the figure in 1998
was less than one-fifth (Charkham and Simpson 1998). And, within the fund management industry, there have been further consolidation and concentration of assets
under management.

The growth in institutional shareholders is due chiefly to the growth in pension
funds and, to a lesser extent, insurance funds (Short and Keasey 1997). The increase
in occupational pension schemes and other forms of long-term insurance or assurance plans has seen both groups of funds grow significantly. Tax advantages of this
form of private retirement saving, compared to personal equity holdings, ensure the
development in the popularity of these forms of personal savings (Short and Keasey
1997).

Institutions do not own shares themselves; they hold them on behalf of their
clients, the trustees. The fiduciary duty of institutional investors is, therefore, not
to exercise governance over a portfolio company, but to act in the best interests of
their trustees. This fiduciary duty entails that institutional investors cannot continue to invest in companies if that is against the interests of the beneficiaries,
which undermines to an extent the role envisaged for them as long-term governors
of British industry. Trustees have a fiduciary duty to maximize the benefits of their
members, and ideally they do this by instructing the institutional fund manager
what to do on their behalf. It is directors who have a fiduciary duty to the *company*
and so have the duty to exercise governance over industry. Untangling the nature
of fiduciary duties helps make it clear why calls for institutional shareholders to
become more involved in monitoring companies may not be easy to fulfil. It is
trustees, rather than institutional investors, who should be under scrutiny, since
they are the real owners.

A number of other issues may explain why institutional investors do not want to
become more actively involved in corporate governance. One concerns potential
conflicts of interest. If investors have other business interests with the organization,
they may be less likely to question management in case they put those other interests
in danger (Short and Keasey 1997). For example, some fund-management organizations are part of investment banks, which act as advisers on investment to companies. The free-rider problem also acts as a disincentive. If institutions collectively
seek to monitor the management of portfolio companies, they bear the costs of
attempting to improve the performance of those firms. But it is open to individual
institutions to free-ride on this collective action, to reap the benefit on improved governance without bearing any of the costs. A third problem concerns the issue of
inside information. If institutions do become involved in the management of their
portfolio companies, they become privy to insider information and so unable to
trade in those shares, which may increase the losses they incur (Short and Keasey
1997). The incentive to raise the quality of corporate governance therefore seems to
be small.

However, there are a number of reasons why the view that institutional shareholders should exercise greater responsibility has become a dominant theme in the corporate governance debate. First, though trustees own the shares, their control over them in terms of instructions to institutional fund managers is often more apparent than real. Trustees often lack specialized knowledge of companies and are content to delegate full responsibility for investment to the fund manager. Secondly, in recent years, the concentration of ownership in the hands of a small number of large institutional investors has brought the potential for greater monitoring and influence in the management of companies. Thirdly, there have been a number of high-profile examples of institutional investors flexing their muscles and removing underperforming managers.

Dissatisfaction at the performance of portfolio companies usually triggers an exit strategy. But, as institutional holdings have increased, exit has become problematic; selling would only depress the market, making exit costly. Moreover, given ownership concentration, they would be selling mainly to one another. The alternative is for institutions to use their 'voice' and investors now have greater incentive to seek relationships with portfolio companies and develop their influence.

Private shareholders

There were an estimated 16 million private investors in the UK in 1997 (ProShare 1998). The demutualizations which took place, when five mutual societies—the Alliance and Leicester, the Halifax, Norwich Union, Northern Rock, and Woolwich—converted to plcs, gave nearly one in three of the UK's adult population shares, and augmented the privatization programme of the 1980s, where the number of individual shareholders in the UK rose from around 3 million to a peak of 11 million. Although such privatization initiatives have increased the overall number of individual shareholders, the proportion of shares held by the personal sector is declining. However, it must be borne in mind that although institutional investors held 85 per cent of the value of the UK stockmarket by 1998, much of this represents activity by pension funds or insurance companies investing money on behalf of individual savers, so the indirect stake that individuals have in the stock market is considerable. Individual investors therefore represent a key stakeholder group. Private shareholders, in common with institutional investors, principally want two things from companies: a good share price and good dividends. Though there has been a great deal of prescription on increasing the quantity of reports and other information to investors in the name of greater transparency, the evidence suggests that private shareholders do not want a great deal of information. Certainly, only a small minority actually want to read the annual report and accounts, let alone demand supplements to it, such as environmental and community reports. Most prefer simple, user-friendly information, 'which can fit on two sides of A4 and can be read in a few minutes' (ProShare 1998). Indeed, private shareholders can be quite vociferous about glossy reports, arguing that they reduce the dividend. The solution, in the case of many large companies, is to send out a short-form annual report and request shareholders to tick a box if they want the full report. Those who are interested in the full report from companies (ProShare estimates this to be at most 100,000 private investors in the country) can ask for the detailed information—information that is legally required. For smaller companies, the costs of producing reports, particularly adding a further short-form report, can be astronomic.

The importance of strong relationships

The interview data from this research show that boards place a strong emphasis on maintaining good communications and relationships with investors, both institutional and private. Naturally, however, in terms of directors' time, it is meetings with the large institutions that dominate. Meetings with fund managers and the senior management of institutions tended to be formal, while informal meetings characterized the relationship between the board and indirect conduits of information to shareholders and stakeholders, investment analysts, and financial journalists. There was wide variance on the frequency of these meetings—some are held twice a year (close to the interim and year-end reports) and, in the case of one very large public company, contact with analysts and fund managers could be up to two or three times a week, usually by telephone.

According to Marston's (1993) study of the top 550 UK businesses, 84 per cent of chief executives attend company meetings with analysts and fund managers, and 96 per cent of finance directors are present (quoted in Charkham 1994*a*). The interview data from this research show that analysts, fund managers, and large institutional investors will typically ask to see the chief executive and finance director and, often, the chairman. In addition, analysts and fund managers may also like to see a functional director (for example, the marketing director) for further information. For any company, there is a hierarchy of investors and, to some extent, analysts, in terms of size and influence. The largest investors can usually ask to see any of the company directors they choose, and nearly always the chief executive, chairman, and finance director will be present. Such meetings are taken very seriously—for example, 'We pull out all the stops, we wine and dine them, and give them our full attention' (chairman). For smaller investors, the chairman or finance director alone may meet them, or smaller investors may be grouped together and be given a presentation. For the smallest investors, telephone contact may be the preferred means of contact by the company.

The reasons behind the board establishing regular contact with investors and other constituencies are several. First is building corporate legitimacy and confidence in top management: 'Meeting with large investors and analysts is an essential part of a director's business. Keeping people well informed brings confidence in the company. Even if you have a problem, it is better to discuss it so you can show you are on top of it and are doing something about it' (executive director). Secondly, access to scarce resources is thought to be smoothed by a close relationship with key external constituencies:

We used to be a fairly secretive company, primarily because we are operating in a very competitive market. But we realized that we were treated with something like suspicion in the City. We wanted to raise money to fund an acquisition and we knew that if we didn't open up more, we would have trouble finding capital easily. We arranged a series of meetings, with share-holders, analysts, journalists, to describe our strategy, and how we do things. It went down very well, and meetings are now much more regular, either over lunch or at set-piece occasions. (chief executive)

Establishing the calibre of the board and senior management and the soundness of the strategic direction of the organization is crucial to impressing investors and commentators. Boards felt that allowing external constituencies an inside glimpse of the intentions of the firm also provided a third benefit—namely that, in the event of a takeover bid, shareholders might look upon the incumbent management more favourably, having been 'locked in', so to speak, to the strategy the firm had chosen. This outcome is linked to a fourth: that the better the relationship between the board and external constituencies, the more likely it will be that the shareholders and stakeholders will take a longer-term view of the company.

The content of discussions in meetings with investors and other groups was obviously dependent on the nature of the group concerned. The general rule is that, the more powerful and influential the constituency, the more detail they will receive about the firm's intentions. In broad terms, the board, or whatever grouping of directors is thought useful for the purpose, will talk to large investors about strategy, progress towards stated objectives, the capital structure of the firm and any plans to change that structure, board remuneration, and managerial succession. Fund managers and analysts would be given detailed short- and medium-term forecasts. Smaller investors might have to settle for information contained in the company publications, though board directors said that they would field calls from individual investors if the matter was particularly pressing, though, in the normal course of events, such individuals would be dealt with by the corporate affairs or public relations department.

Such meetings can also act as an opportunity for directors to take soundings on any proposed change of strategy or major initiative. Directors said that, as a matter of course, investors would be consulted if changes were being considered to the strategy, capital structure, or management succession. Again, the board coalition would be responsible for this, and discussions might be formal or informal, depending on circumstances. Such soundings were considered very important to get buy-in for proposed strategies or changes in capital structuring.

We wanted to acquire a business, a very large one. We had tried acquisitions ten years ago and it had been a disaster. So we consulted with the shareholders. We knew if they didn't see the logic of our plans they would think 'they're going down the same route again' and we would lose their confidence. So we told them our ideas and invited them to sit in at a board meeting when the ideas were being presented. Though at the end they still had doubts, we were able to take those on board and I think they were happy eventually. (executive director)

Though most companies take heed if shareholder opinion is against a particular proposal and either revise or reject the plan or initiative, nevertheless, directors said that, in some circumstances, the board must take a tough decision and act contrary to prevailing opinion in the long-term interests of the company:

Some shareholders want a return, usually in the short term. They are concerned by the dividend. Sometimes, we have to do things which will safeguard our future but will lead to a dilution in earnings. In such cases we have to try and win the shareholders over. But if we can't we have to go ahead and hope they will see the wisdom of the action later. This is what management is about; making tough judgements.   (executive director)

The institutional investors canvassed in this research said they did not want to become actively involved in the running of a company. They were concerned about possible conflicts of interest. First, there was the problem of receiving price-sensitive information: a company providing an investor with information that is not generally available will make the investor effectively an 'insider'. Secondly, institutional investors said that placing a nominee on the board presents the problem of the nominee being co-opted by the board, again effectively rendering the nominee an insider and reducing the degree of independence he or she wishes to enjoy. The difficulty and costs associated with closely monitoring every company in which the investor has interests would also be too great, it was said. The strategy of meeting with senior board members of companies was considered to provide good information, and, though some concealment could take place, 'in the end people get found out. You can't hide the signs forever and remember, you are getting information from different sources and you hear the rumours' (institutional investor). The meetings with boards therefore allow a window onto the company for the institutional investor and also provide a discipline for boards and management; any proposals have to be coherent and logical, with all the bases covered. The second means for investors to maintain strong lines of communication and accountability has been through the appointment of non-executive directors. Some investors are pro-active in this area: 'If we think a board needs strengthening, we may say "we know so and so is available, he would be useful to you as a non-executive". We try to influence their choice in this way. We would never demand the appointment of a specific person, but we often give a steer' (institutional investor). The Cadbury Report has given strong impetus to the appointment of non-executive directors to boards, and this development receives support from investors: 'The non-executive is our eyes and ears in the firm. They are essential in maintaining a check and balance to the executive directors' (institutional investor).

The annual general meeting

Though much of the dialogue between board and shareholders and other external constituencies takes place in various formal and informal meetings, there is, of course, the set piece of the annual general meeting, which is nominally the main forum for shareholders to meet with the directors of a company (though there is no obligation on all the board to attend or for the chairman of the meeting to answer questions) (Charkham 1994a). But the idea of the AGM as an instrument of shareholder voice has been dismissed by numerous scholars. Charkham (1994a: 294) is partly dismissive of the AGM:

To the general observer, the AGM is on the surface a non-event. In normal circumstances they are poorly attended. Penetrating questions are seldom put. Institutional shareholders prefer to ask quietly on another occasion rather than give an appearance of public confrontation; besides, if they have fastened on to an interesting point they may not wish to reveal it to their competitors. Private shareholders are more likely to be concerned with peripheral social issues or with their own experience as customers.

However, Charkham does say that, 'despite all this, many chairman I have questioned are far more sensitive to the potential problems of an AGM than their shareholders might imagine; it concentrates their minds far more than might possibly be supposed' (1994*a*: 295).

There was evidence from the interviews in this research to support this claim— that, the annual general meeting was taken very seriously indeed by many companies:

We prepare very hard for it. It is the one set-piece occasion where shareholders can meet us and ask us questions, any conceivable questions. You can't go in underprepared, otherwise you might end up looking ridiculous. (chairman)

It's inevitable that most shareholders will not turn up—it's just as well because we would need a very large hall indeed to accommodate them all! But that doesn't mean it's not an important affair. It's a legal requirement and you have to be professional and credible, open and forthcoming. (chief executive)

We have to get away from stultifying AGMs. We have to show a more positive and friendly face to the shareholder. (executive director)

One executive director recalled an annual general meeting where the board members, who had expected a routine meeting, were confronted by a number of angry shareholders concerned about the environmental problems caused by an small overseas subsidiary. 'We weren't really prepared—the unit in question was tiny and we certainly weren't expecting questions on it. But they did ask and we didn't have the information they wanted at our fingertips. We learnt an important lesson.'

Institutional investors who were interviewed attended annual general meetings. All but one of the investors have voting policies, many introduced after the Greenbury Report (1995). There have been numerous calls by bodies such as PIRC, the ABI, NAPF for institutions to use their votes on major issues. Cadbury, too, is clear on this issue: 'Voting rights can be regarded as an asset, and the use or otherwise of those rights by institutional shareholders is a subject of legitimate interest to those on whose behalf they invest' (1992: 6.12). In addition, institutions have been urged to disclose their policies on the use of voting rights. Moves to make such courses of action mandatory have been mooted (Company Law Review 1998). But in practice, institutions did not use their voting rights as a matter of routine. Voting with management was the norm, and abstaining in problematic circumstances. 'If we are dissatisfied with a company's performance, we would seek to have meetings with them. If we oppose management at the AGM, it would cause too many waves and attract publicity. It's not the way to change things, because management may become defensive after that' (institutional investor). Nevertheless, on certain issues, if soundings had been ignored, or there were clear breaches of codes of conduct, then institutional investors would resort to either abstaining, or in the extreme case, voting against management. 'In cases where there are proposals that are contentious, for example on directors' remuneration, which do not conform to the Greenbury code, we will abstain or in some cases vote against' (institutional investor).

The high levels of non-participation in the annual general meeting by institutional investors, together with the high levels of support for board resolutions for those that do vote, indicate that private rather than public pressure was certainly the preferred means for influencing organizations.

The AGM is a major forum for private shareholders to gather information, but in reality this set-piece occasion is dominated by the large institutions and analysts. Simpler procedures for private shareholders to table resolutions would help, and, as PIRC argue, 'those private investors who have formed a group should be entitled to a meeting with management, in the same way that institutions do' (PIRC 1997: 21). The key point is that many private shareholders do not attend AGMs because of cost or time constraints, and the notion of a single forum for companies that have perhaps a million shareholders is looking distinctly outdated. With modern electronic communication, there exists the capability for AGMs to take place interactively across the world through video-conferencing and for important announcements to take place via e-mail and Internet throughout the year, and not just at the AGM.

The annual general meeting is a useful forum, but, in reality, the opportunity to question directors and get them to reveal information that is not statutorily necessary is minimal. For large shareholders and analysts in particular, there is a need for more detailed information, and greater opportunities to discuss substantive issues of direction and financial performance with members of the board.

Financial reporting

The first point of access for most shareholders in terms of information about a company is the annual report and accounts. Under positive accounting theory, 'the role of financial reporting theory is to supply a monitoring device to reduce information asymmetry between the principals (i.e. the investors) and the agents (i.e. the management) and thereby reduce agency cost' (Courtis 1993: 18). The annual report, and the six-monthly report, are statutory requirements for public companies, and, for the main report, the format is usually fairly consistent across different organizations—chairman's statement, chief executive's statement, highlights of the year, the balance sheet, and the profit and loss account. The annual report is the vehicle for the company both to sell itself to prospective shareholders and to encourage existing shareholders to maintain (and perhaps increase) their stake in the company. As well as doing this, the annual report also has to present a 'true and fair' picture of the company's performance. The tension between the demands to deliver an accurate depiction of the firm's performance and to present the company in the best possible light to prospective and current investors can be considerable, particularly if the company is experiencing difficulties. Doubts about this issue, as well as concern over the standard of auditing, fuelled by cases such as Polly Peck, Coloroll, and British and Commonwealth, large organizations that collapsed shortly after their accounts had been duly audited, brought the subject of disclosure of information to the fore. As Parkinson (1993: 136) says: 'The availability of accurate and up-to-date information on company performance is of fundamental importance. In the absence of reliable accounting data, effective supervision of management is impossible, as is the accurate pricing of shares which is crucial to the market modes of control.'

The Cadbury Committee was set up in part because of 'a perceived low level of confidence both in financial reporting and in the ability of auditors to provide the safeguards which the users of company reports sought and expected' (Cadbury 1992). Although it is probably too much to hope for to expect improvements in governance to eliminate cases of fraud and failure altogether, nevertheless, raising standards, it is argued, may reduce the incidence of such cases and improve confidence in the system generally. A number of interviewees stated that raising the quality of financial reporting was essential in order to improve corporate credibility. One finance director said: 'A key process of the board is in the provision of reports. How the board presents itself to the outside world is crucial, so anything the board produces should be clear, truthful, and stimulating.'

Whilst the annual report remains the primary medium for conveying financial performance, there are other ways of communication that are widely used. In fact, with the rise in power of institutional shareholders, the annual report and accounts have been supplemented by other means concerned with conveying the long-term potential of the company. As might be expected, there was wide variance in the provision of information in the annual report. Many directors were concerned with the cost of providing additional information for the report. They believed that, for small shareholders, the information contained in a standard annual report was adequate. Other directors said their firms produced a number of published information sheets on a variety of issues for larger shareholders and stakeholders.

A key theme of interviewee responses was that the use of electronic media can improve information flows between company and investor and significantly reduce the costs associated with traditional methods. Specifically, the Internet is now available for disseminating a good deal of company information quickly and efficiently. However, a note of caution should be introduced concerning such initiatives as the short form. While the annual report and accounts must be signed off by the auditors, there is no such independent sign-off for this document.

In addition to simple, easy-to-access information, private shareholders want *equality* of information, particularly that which will affect the share price. An important block to share ownership is the 'them-and-us' attitude—the idea that analysts can be given a briefing and private shareholders cannot causes unease. Analysts are given information that does not make them insiders. If they are given presentations private investors want the same. With electronic media the scenario of companies providing information in this way to private investors is becoming an economic reality.

Good communications and relationships between the board and external constituencies can achieve a number of aims, including an increase in corporate legitimacy, greater trust and confidence in senior management, potential support in a takeover situation, and an increase in the potential to secure scarce resources. We have examined the nature of board dialogues with investors. Another major source of information about the external environment and potentially a large factor in obtaining resources is through the boundary-spanning activity of directors themselves, both through their contacts and through their being placed on the boards of other institutions or organizations.

Boards and stakeholders

With fifty of the world's largest economies being companies, and the 500 largest corporations controlling 25 per cent of the world's economic output (Goldenberg 1998), the impact that businesses have over a wide area of society is immense. It has been argued that it is through the company's wider network of relationships that corporate performance is sustained (Freeman 1984; Deakin and Hughes 1997*a*). The American Law Institute report *Principles of Corporate Governance*, argued that 'the modern corporation by its nature creates interdependencies with a variety of groups with whom the corporation has a legitimate concern, such as employees, customers, suppliers and members of the communities in which it operates' (ALI 1992: 78), while the RSA's *Tomorrow's Company* inquiry report concludes that 'only through relationships with—and between—employers, customers, suppliers, investors and the community will companies anticipate, innovate and adapt fast enough, while maintaining public confidence' (1995: 1).

There are two theories on the role of stakeholders in the organization, one weak, the other strong. The weak version states that shareholders' interests cannot be served unless the company takes into account its other key constituencies. According to this weak theory, the shareholder remains the primary focus, but regards satisfying stakeholders as essential in ensuring shareholder value. The strong version dislodges shareholders from their primary position and argues that companies are responsible to the community in the widest sense and 'if they fail to discharge that responsibility, they have no moral right to exist' (Jackson 1998). The findings from the interviews show that the weak version is primary. Though in law managers are accountable only to shareholders, they have obligations to stakeholders, and fairness and balance in the handling of stakeholder groups are necessary to ensure the firm remains effective.

The recognition that organizations should move from a shareholder to a stakeholder perspective is the central tenet of stakeholder theory. A stakeholder is defined as 'any group or individual who can affect or is affected by the achievement of the firm's objectives' (Freeman 1984: 25). These stakeholders are: owners, consumer advocates, customers, competitors, media, employees, environmentalists, suppliers, governments, and local community organizations. These groups or individuals all have, according to the theory, a legitimate stake in the organization and are in a position to affect organizational outcomes (Wang and Dewhirst 1992). There has been disagreement over who should be included among the stakeholders and whether it is sensible to assign priorities to certain groups. But, as Hosmer (1995) points out, in order to count as a stakeholder, the issue is 'whether or not (a) group at some point in the future can affect the achievement of the objectives of the firm'.

The problems for stakeholder theory are several. First, the decision-making process may become lengthy if all competing claims of stakeholders have to be considered. Secondly, there seems to be no clear decision rule when attempting to adjudicate between rival claims of stakeholders. Thirdly, if other stakeholders are put before shareholders, this may reduce share values and may bring less willingness to invest (*The Economist* 1994: 5). Tricker argues against the stakeholder model by stating that stakeholder groups are not discrete but in practice interact and that the groups are not homogeneous (see Tricker 1984). The lack of research on how decisions at board level are taken when a stakeholder orientation is adopted has further limited the acceptance of the model.

The term 'stakeholder' was one that gave interviewees considerable problems in terms of definition. Many interviewees were unsure as to whom to include in any putative list of stakeholders. Some believed that only the shareholders should have a legitimate claim on the company:

In law, the directors' duty is really only to the shareholder. A director has a fiduciary duty to look after the shareholders' interests. If a director has to start looking after the interests of others, then this may divert attention away from shareholders. (executive director)

Every list of stakeholders you see has different constituencies. Do we, for example, include competitors in a list of stakeholders? Or the media? The concept is too broad. (executive director)

A number of directors stressed the impossibility of keeping every party with an interest in the company happy. For example: 'If you paid attention to every group and their claims, nothing would ever get done. Imagine what it would be like if you had representatives of each group on the board—how would you ever make a decision?' (executive director).

The interests of some groups work against the interests of others, according to a number of directors, and this would entail trade-offs that would greatly increase the complexity of board decision-making. For example, the desire of employees to earn bigger salaries would work against the wishes of the shareholders to keep costs down and also against customers, who would inevitably see a rise in prices as the result of any successful wage claim. But the number of directors who viewed their allegiance solely to shareholders was relatively small. Many directors were sympathetic to the concept of stakeholders, asserting that the argument for profit maximization, which holds that any form of social activism represents a divergence from the drive for profits and ultimate shareholder value, is one that does not apply in its crudest form:

In business you have to make profits, but that is not all there is to it. You have responsibilities to other people, people you employ, people you buy from, people you sell to and so on. In any business you enter into relationships with people, and if you pay no attention to those relationships, you will quickly see your profits drying up.

This argument, one that was repeated by several directors, is a call for enlightened self-interest. Another director put the matter this way: 'We first and foremost concern ourselves with enhancing shareholder value. But the way we do this is to make sure that we are well regarded and keep everyone who deals with us happy. If your employees, customers, suppliers, creditors and others are happy, then you must be succeeding as a business.'

Customers, employees, suppliers, creditors and lenders were seen as comprising the heart of any list of stakeholders. The choice of these groups was made on the basis that they form some kind of 'contractual' relationship with the company. Other constituencies mentioned included pressure groups, the media, competitors, the government, and the community as a whole. These were considered by some to form a 'second tier' of stakeholders, to be given less priority that the groups first mentioned.

Though most directors said their organizations did not have representatives of stakeholder groups on their boards, most companies had processes by which the interests of stakeholders could be regularly aired. Examples include human resource directors on the main board, key account managers for large customers, and quality initiatives and long-term relationships with both large suppliers and customers, environmental subcommittees of the board, frequent contact with the press through press offices and public relations departments, and so on.

The public relations benefits of ensuring harmonious relationships with stakeholders were thought to be considerable. But a number of directors stressed that their companies had no hidden agenda behind many of their good works, simply the desire to be seen as a 'good corporate citizen'. 'We have been in the area for many years and we feel we have a special relationship with the town. We are the largest employer and we feel a special obligation to maintain our reputation and put something back into the area, like sponsoring the arts festival, or the football club and so on' (executive director).

When asked how deliberations on stakeholders were factored into the decision-making of the board, interviewees were less than clear. There seemed to be no formal process for discussing stakeholder concerns specifically, but, if significant issues arose, they would be dealt with on a case-by-case basis. Regarding the development of strategy, directors said considerations of stakeholders would become prominent only if there would be a large adverse effect on any group as a result of a decision— for example, a large plant closure, or possible environmental damage. On this view, stakeholders seem to be accorded a 'management-by-exception' approach, the only realistic way, according to many directors, that it is possible, given the time constraints on board decision-making.

Establishing contacts with the external environment

Non-executives drew considerable influence from their political and personal networks, according to directors interviewed. Some chief executives were non-executive directors on other company boards and some had affiliations with large charities and academic institutions (for example, on boards of governors). Such appointments served to increase the prestige of the company and the external reputation of the chief executive him or herself. One chief executive said: 'Sitting as a non-executive on another board is a good learning opportunity. You can see how other boards conduct themselves, what processes they have, how they deal with issues. You also get to meet some very clever people, not wholly connected with your own business, which is good as you tend to get very focused on your own concerns.'

The non-executive directors interviewed expressed the view that their contacts in the external environment were an important element in their added value to the board. Few executives said that non-executive directors were chosen specifically for the strength of their contacts. Nevertheless, they believed such contacts were useful and could possibly give a firm an edge in a market. For example, one executive director said: 'The non-executives we have bring a lot to the company, not only in terms of their contributions to the board either. They have a wider set of relationships outside the firm which can be beneficial to us.'

All signs from the interviews suggest that the knowledge transferred to the boardroom from encounters with external parties is weighed along with everything else. Because the sources of this knowledge are privileged and valuable, the information derived is deemed important and represents new strategic information.

It was clear from the interview data that maintaining good contacts with shareholders and other stakeholder groups was crucial, a finding that supports the conclusions of Hill (1995) and undermines, to an extent, the managerialist thesis and adds to the empirical evidence for resource-dependence theory. The building of contacts with shareholders helps to bring corporate legitimacy and confidence in top management access to scarce resources and may prevent the threat of takeover. In some cases, this relationship may also enable investors to take a longer-term view of the firm.

> We select non-executives to fill a gap we may have in terms of expertise. For example, a growing part of our business is overseas and we needed someone with good contacts and reputation to advance our interests abroad. We appointed a former member of the diplomatic service who has served in embassies throughout the world and is well known for his integrity. He knows many foreign government officials and has saved us a great deal of time cutting through red tape and getting us to meet the right people. (executive director)

The non-executive director was also an important conduit for conversations with key investors. On some occasions, non-executives will be consulted by investors over concerns over some aspect of the company strategy and performance, if other avenues of debate, primarily with the executives, have been exhausted.

It is not only the non-executive directors who were responsible in building contacts with external constituencies: executives claimed to have extensive contacts in their particular area of influence, often with competitors, and some information was formally shared between competing firms, notably in benchmarking exercises (the sharing of remuneration data between personnel directors is a well-attested example). Executive directors said that they knew who the key players were in their respective stakeholder groups and aimed to ensure good relations with them. 'I meet competitors all the time. We all know each other. We discuss trends, difficulties, products. It's pretty macro-stuff but it's important to do it' (executive director).

Discussion and conclusions

This chapter has been concerned with the institutional role of the board, in particular its relationships with shareholders and stakeholders. The interviews revealed that companies devoted much time and energy to building strong working relationships with their major shareholders. Of central importance to this relationship are the formal meetings, typically held twice a year, between senior company management and the fund managers, where companies discuss their performance and their plans. Both companies and fund managers appear to perceive these meetings to be an effective means of ensuring that investment decisions are fully informed. Such meetings increase the 'personification' of investors. Greater contact between managers and shareholders increases peer pressure on management, and enhances the relationship between the two groups, bringing their interests closer together. Such a relationship could improve performance. As Roe (1994) argues, managers used to owe a fiduciary duty to a faceless group of shareholders. If the 'personification' of this relationship is realized, loyalty to real people would replace mere legal responsibility as a motivating force. This improved relationship reduces misinformation and bias and improves decision-making through building better information networks.

Improving information flows into the firm through direct and frequent contact with shareholders means that the present conceptualization of the relationship—the shareholder as monitor, the manager as the watched—can be redrawn as a partnership bringing mutual gains and enhanced performance. However, directors still expressed concerns over the need to deliver high-quality performance year on year and harboured a sense of the short-term nature of some investors, a sense reinforced by the short-term incentive structure of fund managers themselves.

Direct intervention in problem companies tends to be of a covert informal nature, usually with the implicit threat that the institution will publicly voice its concerns. Persuasion and influence are the principal approaches. Instances of institutions actually going public and voicing their dissatisfaction were rare, usually because such a decision would affect the share price of the offending company significantly and also its reputation. Offloading the shares thus becomes problematic, and other investors within the company may not be overly happy that one institution has chosen to devalue its stake in the company. The ousting of directors from a problem company suffers from similar drawbacks, and is used only in extremis.

One issue seldom addressed is who monitors the monitors; in other words, to what extent are institutional investors themselves accountable? The institutions stressed that, in a highly competitive field with performance measured on a quarterly basis and comparisons across funds publicly available, accountability and performance are readily seen. But the conflict of interest that some institutions face when dealing with portfolio companies—investing in the firm while taking other business from them—and deciding whether institutional investors are genuinely accountable to their beneficiaries shows that the institutions face corporate governance issues themselves (Short and Keasey 1997).

The findings on attitudes to stakeholding suggest that boards consider the embracing of the idea of stakeholders as one of enlightened self-interest, rather than adopting a stronger version of the principle. Details of how the boards factored in stakeholders to decision-making remained hazy, leaving a sense of *ad hoc*, case-by-case assessment, rather than any considered approach to stakeholder groups.

The impact of shareholder and stakeholders on the behaviour of board members is considerable. The expectations of external constituencies quickly become internalized and their presence in the minds of board members can have a strong controlling effect. Like the impact of non-executive directors on the executives, key external groups act as a discipline to the board, and this too constitutes an argument against managerialism (Hill 1995). Developing realistic expectations between the board and shareholder and stakeholder groups is a matter of building open and trusting relationships. The benefits to all groups in terms of improved corporate governance are likely to be high.

The non-executives' role in providing knowledge and contacts to help the strategy process and to enhance legitimacy was supported by this research. For such a role to be effective, collaboration between the non-executive and executive cadres is needed to ensure the motivation of the non-executives to share their capabilities and knowledge and to be confident that their advice and counsel will be valued. Non-executives typically offered opinions about the external environment, over and above simply providing information about it. In a board characterized by low trust, such behaviour would be rare, and a key element in the strategy process would minimized.

Appendix. Case illustrations

Developing relationships with external constituencies

From the interview data, it is clear that the four companies strongly value good relations with shareholders. All four companies had investor relations departments, which were responsible for maintaining links and ensuring good communication with existing and potential investors. The importance of maintaining a healthy dialogue with shareholders is shown at Securicor, where changes to the board structure and a drive for transparency were reactions to what was perceived to be a negative impression of the company held in the City.

For Securicor, these changes were necessary for two reasons: first, to increase the share price of the company, to fall in line with the main company aim of increasing shareholder value, and secondly, to enhance the company reputation: 'I did believe the Group was at a cross-roads. The Group was coming into profit with Cellnet and we thought that the City would take an interest in us and scrutinize us more closely' (Securicor director). A third reason for maintaining good links with shareholders emerged from Allied Domecq: a high share price and confidence in the company from the City provide a defence against the threat of takeover. 'We are constantly being talked of as a potential takeover target. We need to ensure that we have some shareholder loyalty and adequate defences against predators' (Allied Domecq director).

The chief focus in all the companies, as expected, was with institutional investors. They received the most attention from the companies in terms of information and time given by board members. The main activity in investor relations occurs twice yearly, at the interim and full-year results:

> When we announce our results in June, we give presentations to analysts and shareholders. This happens twice a year. There are more on an *ad hoc* basis. The meetings with shareholders are mostly attended by the finance director and the group treasurer. Also we have contact with institutional investors just before we go into our close season, to give them an update. For larger ones, they can have interviews, they can come to us. There are usually two people present at the time. For smaller ones, we have a meeting in London or wherever. (Securicor director)

Discussions with shareholders would, in broad outline, cover progress in major businesses, developments in strategic plans, growth forecasts, and responses to industry and sector trends. The same process would be conducted with analysts (though after the close season). Though the intention prima facie is to share information with institutional investors, the meetings are also a key opportunity to increase confidence in the company, both in terms of the strategic directions and financial forecasts, but also in terms of the quality of the board and management. The meetings present, further, a chance to gather information from shareholders and analysts, and so may form part of the environmental scanning process.

In circumstances concerning a major change in strategy, the companies would tend to consult with institutional investors to gain some view of possible reactions to the new move. This happens informally, with usually only the most senior board members present—the chairman and chief executive and often the finance director. But though these soundings are important in 'testing the water' for a new idea, an adverse reaction on the part of the shareholders may not be enough to deter the new direction. At BAA, for example, a proposed diversification that was coolly received in informal meetings with institutions was nevertheless pursued, the reasoning being that there only needed to be 'more persuasion of our case'. According to one director: 'Shareholders are not uppermost in my mind. Before, my predecessors went into the hotel business, but there was not much money in it. We were certain to lose money. If manufacturing outlets work, it could be profitable. I talked to various people. We meet with institutional investors twice a year. They are not keen, but we've made the decision' (BAA director).

Burmah Castrol also places great store on its relationship with shareholders. In the annual report, the board is held responsible for 'the achievement of a proper balance between the interests of all who have a stake in the company's prosperity'. The aim is to establish a commonality of interests of shareholders and employees. 'We try to keep in particularly close contact with the top fifty of our institutional shareholders together with those who are not but should be. If this is done well, the firm is perceived well. The main thing is no shock' (Burmah Castrol director).

As this statement illustrates, institutional investors form the top of the hierarchy of investors, and so relations with these groups is considered to be very important. At Allied Domecq, a change in the incentive scheme for executives was sent in draft to thirty institutions—'We asked them: "is this a good idea?" ' So the opinion of key investors is important. But this is not to underestimate the importance of small shareholders: 'The board regard it as very important to meet the "average" shareholder. The AGM is the natural forum to do this and the psychology is very important. It is the only occasion that the board is exposed in an uncontrolled way. Anything could come out. In terms of preparation, therefore, it is very thorough' (Allied Domecq director).

Analysts are met regularly, too. At Allied Domecq, there are twice-yearly meetings with groups of analysts (for the discussion of annual and half-yearly figures) and 'approximately thirty meetings a year on a one-on-one basis'. These meetings are usually attended by the finance director and the company secretary. 'There are also dozens of phone calls during the year. We either make a major presentation or speak to them locally.'

Stakeholding

All four companies expressed a desire to operate in ways that are congenial not only to shareholders but also to other stakeholders, in particular customers and employees. The most general formal used by the firms was that of a virtuous circle: if customers and employees are delighted by the firm, this will result in an organization that will achieve its aims, thereby enhancing shareholder value. Despite this rhetoric, however, a number of directors stated that trade-offs were inevitable: 'We operate on fairly low margins—we have to be tight and efficient. We wouldn't achieve shareholder value otherwise. But our shareholders and employees are at opposite ends of the spectrum. So we have to try to make a balance. Balance is what it is all about' (Securicor director).

Nevertheless, commitment to the stakeholder concept is strong: 'The board has to operate within the Companies Act and has to take on not just looking at shareholders' interests, but also the interests of employees, customers and suppliers' (Securicor director). At Burmah Castrol, the board is intended to show responsibility to: 'other interest groups as well as shareholders. We have to provide a healthy work environment for our employees, give stability of employment and also give our trading partners a good and honest service. A board is the moral conscience of the firm and has to ensure the code of ethics is observed' (Burmah Castrol director). Operating in an environmentally sensitive business has made such a stance imperative. The organization has now set up an environmental committee.

At Allied Domecq, though strategic emphasis for the board is firmly on ensuring shareholder value, nevertheless 'we recognize that we have other stakeholders, particularly employees and customers and suppliers' (executive director). The company has a strong focus on environmental protection, with a main board director given responsibility for reviewing policy and implementation and reporting annually to the board. Sponsorship of the arts and education and membership of the Portman Group promoting sensible drinking are further organizational activities.

BAA's commitment to the stakeholder ideal is considerable, given the pressing concerns over airport safety and security and the issue of aircraft noise and pollution. The company has published environmental reports since 1993, which set out policies for noise and exhaust emissions, air and water purity, wildlife conservation, the nature of building design and materials, energy use, and waste management (Annual Report 1994). Employees are offered profit-sharing and are frequently canvassed for their views on the company and management.

Boundary-spanning

Few directors said that non-executive directors were chosen *specifically* for the strength of their contacts; other qualities, particularly their experience, independence, and objectivity, were thought to be more important. Nevertheless, it is clear that the non-executive selection process does involve an examination of the external environment and an assessment of which particular areas the company should access through bringing someone to the board. At Securicor, the board is detailed to look at 'PEST' factors—political, economic, social, and technological issues—and is structured accordingly:

> Our board is structured to look at PEST. We have a financial City man; a commercial/ politician; and a moral/humanist. When we choose non-executives, we look at the political, economic, and social factors. They are specifically chosen. They provide a balance. We do not expect them to furnish us with contacts, not very much. As well as being common-sense people, if they disagree with something, they will say so. They have that strength of personality. We don't want a 'yes-man' board—that's a waste of time.   (Securicor director)

At BAA, too, with its aim of international growth, the choice of non-executive was obvious: 'NEDs are of very high quality—we have to defend our proposals strongly. The non-executives all expect high performance. [Non-executive 1] will be very helpful as we expand overseas' (BAA director). At Burmah Castrol, non-executive directors are encouraged to sit on external committees or to use their influence with third parties to gain important strategic insights: 'The non-executives can use their position and strength, for example, to sit on committees, to be members of effective bodies or assisting the company in an indirect way to achieve its strategy, such as where one non-executive's experience of India is giving us insight into possible expansion there' (Burmah Castrol director).

The introduction of a number of powerful non-executive directors was intended not only to bring new expertise and objectivity to the board, but also to signal that the company was indeed focused on the external marketplace. A further consideration to Allied Domecq was the need to be seen to be complying with best practice following the foreign-exchange loss of £150m. in 1991: 'It is very important to be seen to have heavyweight non-executive directors. For us, there is added importance because of the currency loss. We needed to be seen to have strong non-execs. We have had a history of developing our own internal management, but the shareholders needed to be reassured that we had proper controls in place' (Allied Domecq director). Operating in the sensitive drinks market, lobbying in Government circles is considered important:

> our industry is of major economic importance. In the UK we are leading employers and exporters, We generate total tax revenues estimated at £15 billion. In addition, the spirits industry sources most of its requirements domestically while exporting most of its outputs. This further enhances our total contribution to the economy. In seeking to persuade the

government of the importance of policies, which help rather the drinks industry, we are therefore pursuing wider interests than the simple protection of our shareholders' investments. (Annual Report 1995)

Allied Domecq also encourages its executives and senior managers to become non-executive directors at other companies (though not to take more than two such directorships).

7
The Dynamics of Board Process

The degree of involvement of boards and directors in the processes of strategy, control, and the institutional function is subject to considerable variation, with some boards more active than others in their engagement with, and influence in, these roles. The traditional view of boards is characterized by a non-executive cadre monitoring executives to reduce agency costs, their value stemming from the independence they enjoy from the full-time members of the executive. Collaboration between the two groups is problematic, on this model, since it may give rise to a reduction in vigilance and compromise the independence of the non-executives. However, during the course of this research, we have seen that, in the three major roles of the board, collaboration is important for their effective undertaking. Normative theory in corporate governance, informed by the independent board model, has focused on issues of board structure and composition. Neglected in this approach has been scrutiny of the relationships within and outside the board, and how the interpersonal dynamics affect the culture and cohesion of the board.

As Pettigrew and McNulty (1995) argue, structure does not simply determine, but also enables. Following Giddens (1979), structure and agency are inextricably linked, and that action both constitutes and is constituted by structure. The importance of relationships is therefore central to understanding the enabling and constraining factors that have influence within the board. Because the board in UK public companies is internally differentiated, a number of key relationships have to be managed. These relationships tend to be ill-defined in formal terms and are negotiated over time in varying ways in different organizations.

The conditions that encourage greater involvement and the development of relationships, implicit in the discussion so far, will be explored explicitly in this chapter. The key elements in this explanation revolve around the relationships between board members, the interplay of power, influence, knowledge, and information among them, and the processes of negotiation and accommodation that they construct with one another. We will concentrate on the dynamics of boards to understand the nature of board involvement, and the enabling and constraining conditions of such involvement.

In this chapter, we shall examine first the key relationships within the board: between chairman and chief executive, between executives and non-executives, and in particular the role of the chairman in managing these relationships and promoting teamwork. The role of trust in developing board cohesiveness is then explored.

Relationships within the board

The chairman and chief executive

The relationship between the chairman and chief executive is of crucial importance since it 'lies at the heart of a network of other associations. Its quality has knock-on consequences, affecting relationships with other board members and the executive team' (Roberts 1998: 13). In the organizations we studied, all but one had split the roles of chairman and chief executive (and the exception was planning to split the roles within two years), many in response to the Cadbury recommendations, which stressed the benefits of such a division in terms of balancing power and authority at the head of a company.

Difficulty arises in achieving balance, since the roles are ambiguous and tend to overlap. In some cases, the two individuals attempt to formalize the relationship through written schedules of roles and responsibilities. Several boards constructed formulas such as the chairman being responsible for the board with the chief executive responsible for the day-to-day operations of the firm and for managing the performance of the executives. One problematic issue is that such is the complexity and uncertainty of much that comes before the board that responsibility for particular actions will frequently not be clear-cut. In practice, there is a constant process of negotiation between the two individuals over time. In the early stages of the relationship, this process is particularly delicate, as each attempts to understand the other and to seek out ways of working together. If this negotiation is not handled well, if there is defensiveness or mutual suspicion, then there is strong potential for the two individuals to slip into a struggle for power (Roberts 1998). The importance of creating trust and an openness to the relationship is, therefore, essential: 'nothing should be hidden from one another. That is absolutely destructive. Regular meetings, where everything is up for discussion, is the key.' If this trust is achieved, the chief executive gains a valuable source of advice and counsel in the chairman. A number of chief executives in the sample mentioned their sense of isolation at the head of a large organization, particularly in the early months when anxiety is high and there is considerable uncertainty. Having a sounding board in the chairman, a colleague with whom sharing problems and concerns about the company can be undertaken, was mentioned by a number of chief executives as being extremely helpful.

The negotiation process is influenced by the respective profiles of the two individuals. If the chairman is the former chief executive of the company, then seeking a balance between the two roles can be problematic. The chairman may continue to cast a long shadow over the organization, and should he or she not withdraw sufficiently from his or her former role, the new chief executive may find little space for his or her own thoughts and plans. A sensitive issue in such circumstances is the desire of the new chief executive to begin to stamp his or her own mark on the organization, through reviewing and changing strategy and structure or ways of working, since these interventions may be interpreted as implicit criticism of the former regime. The loss of power felt by the chairman may be considerable, with the result that his or her withdrawal from contacts with executives and ceasing to be the focus of operational issues may be resisted. This may be particularly so where the incoming chief executive is relatively inexperienced in the role or new to the sector.

In newly formed relationships, there is often defensiveness on both sides. In what is hidden from the other, there is space to create false pictures and false expectations may be fostered. A new chief executive is looking to prove him or herself and may have an interest in criticizing the past, a past in which others have invested heavily. There is also the pressure to act quickly on the part of the new chief executive.

A good deal depends on whether the new chief executive is an insider—that is, whether he or she has risen through the organization—or an outsider—chosen from the external labour market. Insiders are closely involved with the business and have an intimate knowledge of its workings. The learning curve for such individuals is obviously less than for outsiders and their understanding of the power relationships and culture of the organization is potentially strongly advantageous. The insider, with greater firm-specific knowledge, tends to place less reliance on the chair as a source of information. However, such socialization within the organization may hamper efforts for change.

The development of a positive relationship was held by interviewees to depend on a mutual respect for one another's competence and a lack of doubt about whether the one will intrude on the other's domain. Over time, a deepening sense of the other's working style and idiosyncrasies will emerge, and, if so, then the relationship can develop into a positive force for the organization and enable the board to foster a supportive, open culture. Interviewees highlighted the concept of complementarity between the two individuals, the dovetailing of two persons' knowledge and experience that balances and completes the gaps in capabilities and style of the other.

The relationship between executives and non-executives

The unitary board's mix of executive directors and non-executives has the potential for both creativity and conflict. The executive group varies in composition, sometimes including the heads of all major businesses or departments, or functions, or, in other cases, a subset of these—for example—the finance director and the marketing director. These executives will be part of the top management team, the level below the board and usually the body that is changed with strategy formation. The executives combine organization and function-specific knowledge with a capacity (with varied instantiation) for the prized characteristic of 'helicopter thinking' or strategic thinking, and the ability to think outside business unit or functional or departmental concerns to address the wider interests of the organization.

The executives on the board are powerful individuals who represent a key source of knowledge and expertise for the organization as a whole. The individuals have varying reasons for being on the board and some may covet the chief executive's role. Though many executives interviewed expressed loyalty to their chief executive, this certainly was not blind loyalty, contra much managerialist thinking. Directors expressed the view that the chief executive's ideas or plans were discussed on a case-by-case basis and that there would not be a blanket approval for any idea coming from this source. However, a number of interviewees said that, in some cases, executives would follow the plans of chief executives, even if privately they did not agree with them, in order to find favour with the chief executive and to further their own ambitions of rising to the top job.

Coalitions were common among executives, but these seem not to have been fixed. They would break down along the lines of particular issues. Depending on the particular issue involved, the coalitions would shift. There were examples of coalitions involving individuals on the basis of friendship and tenure within the firm, which meant more permanent coalitions, but this was rare.

Executives met frequently both formally and informally and would have developed notions about one another's competence and contribution to the executive team and the board. Some formed part of the chief executive's 'in-group'—chosen on a varying basis of personal characteristics, general agreement with the chief executive, and track record, while others were conspicuously part of the 'out-group'. This tended to foster resentments on the part of the out-group.

The executives' attitude to non-executives ranged from suspicion that they were simply policemen on the board who served to provide little in the way of added value, to the perception that they provided a valuable service in terms of advice and counsel as well as contacts and sources of external influence. Such perceptions were obviously influenced by the status of the non-executive directors. This has an internal and an external aspect. High status is important not only internally, in terms of establishing credibility with senior executives, but also externally, in enhancing the credibility and legitimacy of the board with external constituencies. Status can derive from a number of sources: first, from the personal characteristics of the director, his or her experience, track record, professionalism, character, integrity, wisdom, assertiveness—and also from his or her contacts and linkage to a wider business network; and from his or her ability to contribute meaningfully to board discussion. 'When we talk about strategy, I give opportunities for the non-executives to pick up on issues. If they don't take them, then they are foolish' (chief executive).

Here, too, the concept of complementarity is important; there is a requirement for the non-executives to bring a wider perspective to the board discussion: 'The executives know the business better than anyone. I don't need non-executives to talk about that. I need them to give me input on strategic matters, the big picture' (chief executive).

Status is also derived from the non-executives' membership of the various board committees. The carrying-out of routine work in these committees can establish the profile of the non-executives and helps to convince the executives of the value of the non-executives to the organization. The receptiveness of the executives to the non-executives is, of course, dependent on the ability of the non-executive. 'I don't see them as a resource really. I inherited this group and they haven't really impressed me. We were discussing remuneration and one non-executive, who is a university professor, said: "I've never had a bonus in my life. I don't see why others should want them either" ' (chief executive).

The Dynamics of Board Process

Tied to this was the complexity of the business, a factor that can make it particularly difficult for the non-executives to understand the details of the workings of the organization and, as a result, to make useful contributions: 'They want me to contribute top strategy, but I don't know if this particular compound is going to make a saleable drug, or whether investing in biotechnology will make the projected returns' (non-executive).

A circumstance where the non-executive cadre became highly influential was when the organization was facing a crisis. In common with Mace (1971), Lorsch and MacIver (1989), Demb and Neubauer (1992), and Pettigrew and McNulty (1995), we found that non-executives can exercise greater influence in times of high turbulence. In such conditions, the weighing of options and the need for objective, detached opinion becomes essential: 'If you are facing a crisis, you don't necessarily want the discussions to be dominated by the people who put you in the crisis in the first place. The non-executives can stand back and assess things coolly, without the emotional commitment that an executive may have to a particular course of action' (executive director). The picture of non-executive directors acting as checks and balances to the executive group, and the adversarial nature of the relationship, was not borne out in the interviews (see Table 7.1). The discipline effect, where the executives were trying to raise their game in putting forward proposals before the board, clearly takes the form of a check to managerial initiative, but the majority of executive directors saw this as a useful way of improving proposals. Most stressed the important contribution non-executives make to the strategy process and their involvement in monitoring the performance of the firm. The dynamics of the relationship between executives and non-executives will echo that between the chairman and chief executives. Both groups are involved in a negotiation and clarification of involvement and the mutual judgements of respective abilities.

The ratio of executives to non-executives will have some bearing on how well the two cadres operate: a critical mass of non-executives is important. The issue of how large the board should be is a difficult one. Large boards bring greater diversity and bring greater knowledge and information to board discussion. On the other hand, large boards make coordination difficult and may reduce interpersonal relationship-

TABLE 7.1. *Qualities brought by non-executives*

Qualities	Stated by non-executives(n=21)	Stated by executives(n=30)
Objectivity/independence	15	20
Advice to the board	12	8
Knowledge of external environment/ wider experience	8	4
Check and balance to power of executives	6	12
Confer legitimacy	3	5
Contacts	5	7

building and make cohesiveness more unlikely. The average size of the companies studied was eight, with a clean split of four executives (including the chief executive) and four non-executives (including the chairman).

Managing the relationships: The role of the chairman

There are a number of different models for the role of chairman. Some chairmen were content just to run the board meeting and have formal contact with the chief executive, while others saw for themselves a more developed role, including advising the chief executive, attending top management team meetings, visiting different business units/departments, and taking part in meetings with key external constituencies. Though some chairmen were formerly the chief executive of the organization, this was seen as a potentially difficult arrangement, given the potential for the chairman to continue to exert a formidable influence and to encroach too much into the newcomer's space. Much more common was the elevation of a non-executive to the chairman's role. This entails the chairman having a less deep knowledge of the firm, and the degree to which he or she does become actively involved with the firm will depend on the individual's experience base and how his or her knowledge of the organization develops as he or she moves into the role. Further, their willingness to expend the effort to learn about the company and invest in building relationships over and above a minimal obligation is also a crucial determinant of their involvement.

The chairmen interviewed saw themselves as acting both to complement the chief executive and to build a harmonious board environment where the free flow of knowledge, information, and debate makes possible a strong relationship between the executive and non-executive cadres.

Non-executives are in a dependent relationship to the executive team because of the asymmetry in knowledge and power (Roberts 1998). They are also at a disadvantage in terms of the time they can give to the organization. There is little that can be done to remedy the lack of time that non-executives can give to the organization, but certainly the difference in power and knowledge between executives and non-executives could be eased by the action and style of the chairman.

The chairman ensures that a climate of openness exists, and that all directors are encouraged to give their views. Comments from the more thoughtful and less extrovert members are important to gather, and the number and length of interventions from dominant members must be curbed. 'I have to encourage the non-executives and some executives to contribute. I have to make sure that all views are heard and that no opinions are being suppressed. Often I will ask each member in turn for their views if an important decision is being taken. Normally I will sum up at the end of each agenda item, to make sure we are all agreed on what we are doing' (non-executive director).

Important to the quality of the board meeting is the nature of the information given to directors prior to the meeting. The preparatory papers that detail the key elements of the agenda are a vital element in ensuring that non-executives have as much opportunity to contribute as possible. Given the time scarcity that the majority of non-executives are under, their preference was for detailed summaries of major issues: 'I want easily digestible pieces, not huge swathes of paper that I couldn't possibly read. Two sides of A4 for each issue is enough.' Much depends here on the service given by the company secretary, who will prepare board papers and distribute them prior to the meeting. The setting of the agenda is also a key element of board preparation. In the main, the board agenda is set by the chairman and chief executive, aided by the company secretary. In most cases, other members of the board are able to table items for consideration in the agenda. The frequency of board meetings is usually fixed, typically for once a month, but a new chairman can opt to change the style, timing, and location of board meetings: 'Board meetings used to last almost all day, what with lunch and catching up with gossip. I introduced a sharp morning meeting and be in and out in two hours.'

Some chairmen would insist on holding board meetings occasionally at key sites of the business, away from headquarters. On some occasions these would be held abroad. This would increase to some extent the knowledge that the non-executives have of the organization and also help the confidence–building process of directors as they meet the personnel in the operational sites.

A key point raised by a number of non-executive directors was the propensity of the chairman to ensure that the board meeting remained focused on strategic, rather than operational, issues. 'We discuss largely the nitty-gritty of the business. That, in my opinion, is not what the board meeting is all about, and it is a waste of board resources. The board should be about strategic issues, not about how many nuts and bolts are produced on a certain afternoon. The non-executives are excluded from much of the discussion.'

As Cadbury (1990: 21) states, the job of the chairman is to 'arrive at the best outcome in respect of each deliberative item on the agenda and to do so by drawing on the collective wisdom of those sitting round the board table'. Once issues are open to debate, the chairman's role is to keep the discussion on track and not to foreclose contributions too early.

The focus on strategic issues is aided by the presence of board subcommittees of audit, remuneration, and nomination (and, in some companies, environmental and health and safety committees). As we have stated earlier, these committees enable key issues such as internal control and executive pay to be discussed outside the main board meeting, so allowing more time to be freed up for focusing on strategic initiatives. In addition, board committees serve to increase the influence and credibility of non-executive directors and add weight to the executives' view of the board as an important strategic mechanism.

Creating the right climate for board discussion also rested on small points of details, such as the degree of formality with which the board meeting is conducted, with, at one level, a strongly formal almost ceremonial aspect to the running of the meeting, and, at the other, a lighter, informal feel, where questions do not have to go through the chair at all times, for instance, and where humour is present in the proceedings. Choices as to the layout of the boardroom, lighting and heating and so forth, were also held to have an impact on the quality of board meetings.

Teamworking

Developing a sense of team within the board is problematic, since the role of the non-executive director is both to advise the executives and also to monitor their performance. Given that the board meets infrequently, the likelihood of a team developing within the board is small. The chairman does try to create some kind of building of team spirit, usually though holding informal meetings with the chief executive and the non-executives and through the pre- and post-main board meeting lunch or dinner. But, on the whole, few directors considered the board as a team: 'The board gets together too infrequently to become a team. We all know each other, but not really well, not like all the executives know each other. The non-executives will always be at a disadvantage, and if they are seen as policemen, the problem will be exacerbated' (executive director). In many respects, teamwork was not seen as desirable for the board: 'teamwork is not important. Indeed, in my company; there is a natural and desirable conflict of interest between the executives and non-executive directors' (chief executive).

This tension between the groups was seen as healthy, in order to prevent the 'cosy-club' scenario that would result in much decision-making going through 'on the nod'. Directors, however, were anxious to prevent an 'us-and-them' atmosphere between the executives and non-executives pervading the boardroom. An unwritten rule for organizations was that the non-executives should not meet as a team outside the board meeting, in case the executives imagined a conspiracy against them. The idea was 'to have a board who know each other and the company well but are not afraid to speak up on any issue' (executive director).

Creative conflict is, therefore, regarded as healthy: here the combination of trust and control that is essential for the working of the board comes into play. The board is looking for consensus and the elimination of dissension, but through a process of robust questioning of proposals and plans, rather than through a forced absence of dialogue.

The role of trust

In the relationships between members of the board, the development of trust is crucial. We have seen that the roles of the key players are not capable of exhaustive description and that there is considerable overlap and ambiguity within the board as to role and responsibilities. Domains of responsibility are, therefore, negotiated over time, and, because boards deal with decision-making at the highest level, usually in conditions of uncertainty, the potential for roles to develop and change and for there to be shifting and fluid perceptions of what constitutes a particular role is high. How is trust developed in such conditions?

The non-executives are in a dependent relationship to the executives in terms of knowledge and power. When groups are unsure of one another, personal interests may be protected by information being filtered or withheld, if there is any uncertainty as to how the other party will use it. In a trusting relationship, however, there will be little doubt as to others' intentions and information will be used to the greater good of the firm.

Trust is built not only around a feeling of competence in the other person or group, but also in a number of other salient factors. First would be a perception of high confidence in others, due to shared values and to belief in the ultimate intentions and aims of others. Trust in a highly political board is therefore difficult, with suspicion of individuals' motives or ultimate objectives being called into question (for example, an executive who desires the chief executive's role showing unquestioned acceptance of the incumbent's every word). In such cases, individuals become guarded and information can be filtered or withheld, depending on instrumental calculations concerning individual gain or loss.

Secondly, a major element of the trust-building process is the free flow of information and knowledge throughout the board. Open communication was viewed as essential. Contact between the key role-holders was characterized chiefly as trying to be clear and sufficiently open to ensure that misinterpretations did not occur or that feelings did not develop that political games were being played or that information was being withheld owing to suspicion or defensiveness. For the chairman and chief executive, regular and frequent interaction forms the basis of trust, since this form of interaction brings attachment based upon reciprocal interpersonal care and attention (McAllister 1995). The same principle holds for interactions between the executives and non-executives more broadly. The rule of 'no surprises' concerning proposals that come to the board emphasizes the importance of regular timely information reaching non-executives.

Thirdly, the degree to which the board members do not pursue their own personal objectives but subjugate their own needs and aims to the goals of the organization will influence the formation of trust between board members. The notion of doing what is best for the business rather than for personal or sectional interests was reflected in a number of interviews.

How the board defines its own purpose is an important element for the level of participation it engenders and for its propensity for trust development. The board as a group will have shared beliefs about what the board is for its particular organization. These beliefs or norms will have developed over time and so are path dependent, linked to previous incarnations, ways of working, and cultural factors. These norms constitute, in effect, the rules of the game for board activity. In some high-technology boards, for example, the board is decidedly minimal in its activity and the expectations of board members as to the level of effort required is not particularly high. On the other hand, a board with group norms of strong involvement and a history of objective, independent board activity will require different levels of effort from directors.

Though all boards differ in terms of their dynamics, nevertheless a number of

board norms emerged that were common across companies, that were seen to facilitate cohesion in the board. Three in particular are noteworthy. First, open criticism
of individual directors was beyond the pale:

If one had any doubts about the performance of the chief executive, the board meeting would
be the last place to air them . . . you would try to sound people out in an informal way. Almost
certainly, the chairman would know that something was amiss and he would approach you for
your opinion. If enough were of that opinion he might take the chief executive into his room
and tell him quietly that he had lost the confidence of the board. The parting need not be acri-
monious if it is done right.   (non-executive)

A small number of directors reported that their chief executives were bullying and at
times abusive in the board towards them. These extreme circumstances highlight the
dangers in overt criticism: introducing defensiveness and resentment, increasing
power differentials, and reducing cohesiveness.

A second norm is the 'no-surprises' rule, already mentioned, which holds that the
board should be made aware of important initiatives well before they come to the
board for formal discussion. This is to increase the sense of inclusion of the non-
executive directors and to allow them to make informed judgements when such initiatives are finally tabled. The third norm concerns voting. As one chief executive
said: 'If there is a need to vote on an issue, something is seriously wrong.' Boards seek
unanimity and to take the decision to vote on an issue means that the presentation
of the issue and the approach to it have not been wholly convincing in their logic or
their timing.

Conclusions

This chapter has described the nature of relationships within and around the board.
It has sought to build on the views of directors as they attempt to make sense of their
roles in large complex organizations. We also highlighted some of the key contextual
and structural features of boards that can affect the involvement of the board in the
running of the company. These included the status, credibility, and assertiveness of
the non-executive directors, the relationship between the chief executive and the
chairman, the effectiveness of the chairman in developing a receptive boardroom climate, the presence of board coalitions, the use of informal communications and
decision-making processes, and the influence of board norms in constraining boardroom debate.

Within the board, therefore, there are both strong positive and negative potentials
in terms of involvement and relationship-building. In minimalist boards, which do
not seek the wider participation of all board members, and tend to be dominated by
a particular individual or coterie of individuals, the presence of contestabilty and
dialogue is effectively minimized. In maximalist boards, the recognition that all
members have a part to play in the development of strategy and the monitoring of
organizational outcomes and processes moves the board beyond the concerns of

individualism and reinforces the collective rather than atomized view of board endeavour, synthesizing the interplay of individual difference (Roberts 1998).

What is increasingly important in judging board effectiveness are the capabilities and organizational resources available to the board. This is not just the obvious point that the board should have the best people possible as its members; the relationships between the board members and their relationship with internal and external constituencies are also crucial. The degree of cohesion of a board is an important factor in its operation. The evidence of the care taken in selecting directors in the case companies supports this view: candidates were chosen on the basis not only of their track record and experience, but also on their ability to fit into a team environment and to be compatible with other members of the board. On more than one occasion in the case interviews, board directors stated that a perceived lack of ability to 'get on' with others was the prime reason for failure to be promoted to the board. The cohesion of the board will also affect the information flows between directors. In the case companies we saw an emphasis not only on formal communication channels but also on informal discussions and the development and maintenance of networks. The nature of the relationships both within the board and between the board and other stakeholders can be an important source of competitive advantage.

These relationships and working patterns support the resource-based view of the firm (Barney 1991), which argues that the firm's internal strengths and weaknesses, just as much as its strategy and structure, are crucial in determining performance. To a large extent, the way the board members interact represents what Strauss (1978) has called a negotiated order, with individual directors establishing roles, rights and obligations through interactions over time. These interactions are unique to the firm and its board and are difficult to imitate and in this way represent potentially valuable differentiators over competitors. In terms of research on boards in general, normative theories of board structure may be helpful only up to a point: what really matters is the intangible asset of board cohesion.

8
Conclusions

Boards of directors in large UK public companies inhabit a rarefied world of power, influence, and responsibility. Directors enjoy the privileges of status and reputation and are, on the whole, well paid for their services. But there is also a weight of expectation on them, both internally from managers and employees and externally from shareholders and stakeholders, concerning their performance. This book has been concerned with how directors perceive their roles and responsibilities. A common theme that has run throughout this book has concerned whether management controls the board or vice versa. The issue of managerialism is central to the debate on boards of directors and addresses directly the issue of whether the board is a useful mechanism not only for determining that the interests of managers and shareholders are aligned but also for increasing the competitiveness of the firm.

Many studies have advocated that boards of directors become more involved with the running of the firm. The central issue of this research is to examine the extent to which boards *do* become involved in the running of their organizations, the modes of this involvement, and the constraining and enabling factors that influence the degree of this activity. The literature review shows few in-depth studies of directors' perceptions of their role, and Pettigrew (1992) and Tricker (1995) among others have advocated the pressing need for strong grounded research on directors' attitudes. This research has attempted to fill this gap and presents a model for the role of boards of directors that has emerged from the reports of directors themselves.

The picture that has emerged highlights the multi-functional nature of board activity, the internal differentiation between executive and non-executive directors, between the chief executive and other executive directors, and between the chief executive and chairman and the rest of the board. These internal dynamics shape individual boards and have a large influence on their effectiveness and harmony. This chapter sums up the major findings from the research and ends by suggesting some directions for future research.

Building relationships within and around the board

Much of the recent and continuing work in corporate governance has been concerned with changes in board structure and composition that have sought to increase the board's ability to exercise control. These changes include introducing a non-executive cadre, separating the roles of chairman and chief executive, and establishing committees of the board. The underlying assumption of such an approach is rooted in agency theory and in a structuralist view of power and control (Westphal

1996). Boards structurally independent from management are able to rein back managerial interests and align them with the interests of shareholders. The board as independent controller of management activity has become a dominant theme in corporate governance.

The results of this study suggest that such assumptions are warranted only in extreme conditions. In the main, the building of relationships within and around the board can enhance board effectiveness. An important aspect of the continuing negotiation of order in the boardroom concerns the development of trust between board members, and between the board and shareholders and stakeholder groups. The building of trust within the board entails a rejection of the adversarial model of board behaviour in favour of a view of boards that stresses the potential for interpersonal cooperation and teamwork. This can be encouraged by greater participation and an openness that encourages creativity and enhanced decision-making. Trust at the level of the board also entails a move away from the traditional agency view of individual self-interest and instrumentalism in the pursuit of power and influence. If the board is conceptualized by members as a hierarchy, then those members may characterize their behaviour in terms of an individual project competing with others, intent on becoming a 'success' to the exclusion of others, developing 'illusions of autonomy' (Roberts 1998).

A less hierarchical view of the board, and a greater awareness of the collective potential of the group's role in leadership, will promote trust and effectiveness in organizing concerted action, allowing the leveraging of the diversity in the group while not falling prey to destructive dynamics of factionalism and distrust of values and preferences different from the prevailing norms of the organization. This is not to say that boards should always strive to be collaborative and that the monitoring function is insignificant. Clearly, there is a threshold level of monitoring that needs to be in place to ensure that errors are caught, deviancies are corrected, and diagnosis can be carried out, a function that, as we have suggested, is vital in the strategic decision-making of the organization. But once this baseline has been established, board involvement can be characterized as a cooperative relational process enhanced by the development of trust-based relationships between board members. The coexistence of trust and control in the boardroom is essential for its effective working.

The development of trust also extends importantly to the relationship between the board and shareholder/stakeholder groups. We saw in the discussion of the institutional role for the board that the development of 'strong–weak' ties between boards and investor groups through what has become known as relationship investing has encouraged greater transparency and ultimately legitimacy of organizations and increased confidence in the governance system in general. The personification of the investor through frequent face-to-face meetings and the gradual development of mutual understanding reduce defensiveness on the part of the organization, produce a heightened awareness of the complexities of organizational activity on the part of investor groups (discouraging a reliance on the rather blunt accounting indices), and support a socializing process of accountability (Roberts 1998).

The board's strategic role

The role of the board in the strategy process has been a central feature of much pre-scriptive literature. The data from this study show that boards are not involved to any great extent in the strategy *formulation* process, but rather set the *parameters* within which strategic discussion takes place. This is achieved first through determining and maintaining (and adjusting) the corporate definition (what businesses we are in; criteria for acquisition and divestment). In large diversified organizations, the need for clear corporate definitions is essential (Hamel and Prahalad 1994), not only to those within the organization, but also to provide a clear signal to external constituencies (Finkelstein and D'Aveni 1994). The concept that the board sets the corporate defini-tion has obvious affinities with the Bower–Burgelman model of the strategic process (see Bower 1970; Burgelman 1991; Noda and Bower 1996), but in this study the role of the board in this process is emphasized. Similarly, Mizruchi's (1983) theoretical account of board power, which focused explicitly on the board's latent power in dis-missing the chief executive, is here extended and given empirical grounding. Import-ant, too, is the board's role as guardian of the corporate values, which determine the belief system of the organization (Simons 1994). From the case-study analysis, main-taining the integrity of the brands represents a crucial part of this process.

The board's engagement in gatekeeping activity, screening strategic options and revising and in some cases rejecting strategic proposals, provides a strong means to shape the direction of the organization. Though research has identified the board's role in reviewing and assessing proposals as an important element in adding value to the organization (Pettigrew 1992; Ferlie *et al.* 1996), the lack of evidence for boards overturning proposals has been used to support the managerialist claim. However, in teasing out the detail of this process, it is clear that boards set standards for the qual-ity and nature of proposals that are eventually presented before it; they set the boundaries of what is acceptable in a proposal and what is not. This is intimately bound up with the discipline function of the board, one of the few board roles that Mace found in his seminal 1971 study. Executives stated that presenting to the board required a great deal of preparation and was a test of their powers of logic and influ-encing ability. The board's flexibility in setting these standards, either allowing only proposals that fit strongly within existing strategic boundaries or permitting propos-als to succeed that are in important respects new departures, will determine in large part the ability of the firm to learn and renew itself. The gatekeeping process is repeated throughout the different levels of the firm, and it can be argued that the gatekeeping of the chief executive at the executive-committee level ensures contra-dictory information does not reach the board and so constitutes a manipulative activity that leaves the board without an opportunity for serious discussion of any-thing (Pahl and Winkler 1974). Though the executive committee does effectively fil-ter out many proposals, nevertheless, the presence of the board acts as a strong incentive for managers to perform as well as they can and this research confirms Mace's (1971) finding that the obligation to make presentations or reports to a for-mal authority acts as a driver to efficiency (see also Parkinson 1993: 197).

Thirdly, the board's confidence-building of managers at lower levels encourages managers with ability to develop a strategy that will increase the performance of the firm. Evidence from the case-study analysis suggests that this is a largely informal process, but taken very seriously by directors. This is a neglected area of board activity, but it supports the work of Noda and Bower (1996) on strategic resource allocation.

Fourthly, the selection process allows the board to determine the mix of personalities and abilities and so represents a signalling process, both internally to the firm and externally about the kind of board the company has and which managers are elected to director status. The selection process is dominated, in the case of executive selection, by the chief executive, and, in the case of the non-executives, by the chairman. The consent of all the board is required, however, and this consensus is considered important if the board is to work effectively. In the case of the chief executive, the chairman is usually responsible for the process of hiring and firing the top person, usually in conjunction with all board members and major investors. This confirms the findings of Hill (1995), but, in the case of voluntary turnover of the chief executive, the outgoing chief executive's recommendation is typically the person chosen, which could be interpreted as support either for the managerialist thesis, or for common sense, with the chief executive being in the best position to judge the merits of his immediate team.

The board's control role

The findings from the strategic role of the board included two major responsibilities that overlap with its control role. Defining the corporate purpose enables the board to control the boundaries of the firm, and its guardianship of the corporate values allows the board to be the arbiter of the belief systems of the organization. In the strategic planning and budgeting process, the board has the potential to exercise judgement on the quality and appropriateness of business-unit targets and strategies.

Through the medium of the board meeting, directors are presented with financial and strategic information concerning the business operations of the firm. This is monitored on a control-by-exception basis, with directors really exercising their influence only when confronted by major concerns over shortfall in meeting targets or deviance from strategic objectives. Discussion of past performance, therefore, tends to be brief if the firm is on track with its objectives. The focus is on future prospects for the organization. Here directors, through the monitoring of external environment, can use control systems as feedforward devices to identify or diagnose new opportunities, a role that has obvious overlap with the board's strategic role. The reassessment of priorities and control targets makes possible organizational renewal and learning (Simons 1994).

We have seen that it is the board that is responsible for allocative control for large investments or decisions through the powers reserved to it formally. This type of control is obviously different from the day-to-day operational control of resources, but, as Pahl and Winkler (1974) state, control over resource allocation constitutes effective economic control.

After the publication of the Cadbury Report non-executive directors were cast by commentators in the role of corporate 'policemen'. Though their importance as checks and balances in the boardroom was acknowledged, the finding from this research was that they were valued for their expertise, their contacts, and their 'outside' view. They were important in the process, too, of weeding out underperforming directors. Executives with concerns about a colleague tended to approach an individual trusted non-executive to make their feelings known. The process of dismissing directors, including the chief executive, is a largely informal affair, with much activity taking place outside the boardroom; individual directors meet and gradually a picture emerges of the person in question. The responsibility for the *coup de grâce* rests with the chairman, though much effort is given to face saving, not only to assuage the feelings of the outgoing director, but also to maintain a confident and united front to investor groups.

This evidence demonstrates that it is not just the non-executives who are responsible for monitoring the performance of the chief executive; the executives, who often have day-to-day contact with the chief executives, are in an ideal position to identify strengths and weaknesses and the followthrough on strategy implementation.

Dismissal of directors was rare, particularly so in the case of chief executives. A second theoretical avenue open to boards is to adjust remuneration to align the effort of directors to the interests of shareholders. The evidence of this study was that incentives either in the form of money or as share options helped retention but did not figure as strong motivators; pay was a way of 'keeping score'. Pay was largely determined on the basis of external comparisons, with social capital an active ingredient through status comparisons. This finding supports a social-influence perspective on director compensation (Belliveau *et al.* 1995).

The board's institutional role

There were four key findings from this study concerning the board's institutional role. First, non-executive directors did provide good links with external constituencies and, contrary to the managerialist theory, the information derived from these contacts was perceived as giving influence to the non-executive director. Knowledge gained from this source frequently fed into strategic discussion and had the potential to increase organizational learning. But it was not only non-executive directors who were expected to contribute to boundary-spanning activity: executive directors were also urged to develop contacts outside the company, a finding that supports the conclusions of Bower and Doz (1979) and Pearce (1983).

Secondly, maintaining good contacts with owners was seen as highly important. Institutional support and developing a strong reputation for good management and accountability were seen as crucial in enhancing business performance. The nature of a board's contacts with shareholders will influence its credibility and legitimacy and will send positive signals to the market that the board is both effective and vigilant.

Thirdly, we found little evidence that shareholders put direct pressure on boards to improve performance. Shareholders would typically be sounded out for their views on major strategic initiatives and there are regular meetings to discuss performance and future plans. But, in the case of underperforming management, shareholders would tend to have an informal discussion with either the chairman or a senior non-executive director, which was deemed sufficient to send a signal to the entire board.

Fourthly, the chairman's role in balancing the internal constituencies in the board-room was seen as crucial. For a board meeting to be effective, no one person should dominate the discussion and all members should feel comfortable enough, and have the opportunity, to contribute to the debate. With the presence of inner circles, and in the negotiation for resource allocation, these norms may often be subverted. But we found that most directors wanted to show their professionalism by ensuring all plans and objectives were discussed fully, with all views being heard.

Theoretical debates

This study has attempted to illustrate the nature of board involvement in the running of corporations. We studied actual board involvement primarily through extensive field interviews. Research has recommended direct study of board roles. This book has responded to that recommendation and provided some direct evidence about board roles in three key areas—strategic, control, and institutional roles. Previous studies on board involvement have looked at structural features such as board com-position (in particular insider representation), or examined specific decisions for which boards are responsible, for example, greenmail or poison pills (Judge and Zeithaml 1992), using data that are either secondary or based on large-scale ques-tionnaire studies. This research offers a different approach to examining board involvement.

A number of broad theoretical issues emerged from the research. First, the struc-ture of boards of directors—notably the split between executive and non-executive, and between the chief executive and chairman—is obviously intended to reflect agency concerns, and to a great extent the assumptions of both agency theory and transaction-cost theory underpin the control role of the board. We found that, in periods of difficulty for the organization, or in the monitoring of plans and budgets, the board's role is indeed to ensure that the causes of poor performance are identi-fied and dealt with, and that the targets submitted by management in the planning cycle are stretching and in line with the broad direction of the company. Similarly with the review and analysis of reports and proposals that come to the board for decision-making—ensuring that these plans are aligned with the main purpose of the firm and the interests of the shareholders.

Consistent with this theme, however, is the finding that boards may actively help companies to unlearn organizational practices that have become dysfunctional

(Nystrom and Starbuck 1984). That is, boards may diagnose new opportunities, select new performance measures, and emphasize certain control systems at the expense of others, in order to bring the organization to a new focus. This supports the stewardship theory of board activity and suggests that, in certain circumstances, both organizational economics and stewardship theories may be complementary. The combining of what Tricker (1994) calls the conformance and performance roles suggests that multiple theoretical lenses are appropriate. Reinforcing the case for complementary theoretical perspectives is the evidence of boundary-spanning activity on the part not only of non-executive directors but also of the executive directors, providing support for the resource-dependence view of board activity.

Concerning the managerial-hegemony theory, directors set the boundaries of decision-making and act as gatekeepers for proposals that will have major implications for their organizations. Together with the discipline function and the guardianship of the corporate values, such boundary control has a significant constraining effect on managerial opportunism. Directors themselves claimed that they acted in the interests of shareholders and had strong belief in the need for professionalism in their work. The board norm of liaising with owners on issues of strategic moment also presents an important check to managerial domination and potential deviance from shareholders' interests.

Our approach is, therefore, in line with greater calls for reconciliation between economic and organizational perspectives (Kosnik 1987; Eisenhardt 1989*a*; Judge and Zeithaml 1992) and shows that seemingly contradictory approaches can coexist as theoretical explanations. In particular, researchers in corporate governance should recognize that chief executives and boards, or shareholders and managers, do not always have different interests. Policy considerations in the field of corporate governance have been dominated by an underlying concern over agency costs. The findings of this study suggest that this may be an overly narrow view of board activity.

In broad terms, what we have seen through the empirical data is a view of boards whose members, through a complex interplay of context, individual abilities, and structural conditions, actively negotiate over time their respective roles and the social order of the board as a whole. With the legal duties of the board underdescribing the de facto operations of board running, and regulations and codes of practice covering only part of board endeavour, ultimately the board's mandate will mean different things to different people, and 'negotiation is needed to achieve order in the context of change' (Hosking 1996: 342). This has obvious affinities with Giddens's structuration theory, which argues for the interdependence of structure and action. As Pettigrew and McNulty (1995: 13) argue: 'the mobilisation and skilful use of power sources may change the rules of the game and provide a new context for subsequent influence attempts.'

Underpinning the discussion has been the central role of trust in enhancing both board task performance and board cohesiveness. The model of trust argued for has not been the traditional one of trust and control conceptualized as opposite ends of a continuum. Rather, trust and control are interdependent. Because the board operates in complex and uncertain conditions and is often characterized by role conflict, the potential for both trust and control to coexist is apparent. Control mechanisms serve to focus members' attention on organizational goals, while trust mechanisms promote decision-making and enhance cohesiveness.

One further theoretical dimension that deserves mention concerns the value of the board to the firm in terms of the human capital it comprises; the capabilities of its members and their commitment, which are key components of the value creation process (Snell and Dean 1992). The importance of human capital has long been recognized as critical in securing competitive advantage, and the resource-based view of the firm (Barney 1991) argues that bundles of capabilities and working practices and routines can directly influence organizational performance (Pfeffer 1994; Huselid 1995). This study has shown that boards can become involved in the running of the organization, and through their three key roles affect the shape and direction of the company. The human capital present on the board can therefore represent a major source of competitive advantage, not only through the individual capabilities and skills of individual directors, but also through the unique interrelationships and set of routines that form the dynamics of the board.

Practical implications

Though we are mindful of the dangers of succumbing to normative statements in this already overly prescriptive field, nevertheless a few statements are ventured to show what directors might infer from the study.

1. Although it is unrealistic to expect the board to be involved in strategy formulation, its role in determining the parameters of strategic activity is crucial. Strategy-making takes place at multiple levels within the firm—the board should attempt to guide the actions of lower-level managers to reflect their strategic intents; their actions define the organizational context in which lower-level managers identity opportunities and solve problems in the product market (Noda and Bower 1996). The more clearly such parameters are spelt out, through the use of reserved-powers statements mission and values statements and a transparent organizational portfolio and structure, the better placed the board will be to align the firm with the interests of shareholders.

2. The importance of board vision is not to be underestimated. By choosing what to emphasize and de-emphasize in the use of control systems, the board can signal attention and learning can be focused (Simons 1994). The diagnosis of the possibilities for new opportunities and changing direction is a key element of the board's role. Having a vision of where the company should be headed is vital if this activity is to be effective.

3. Boards have to track important changes in the environment, but this should not mean just the careful monitoring of commercially significant events. Effective directors go beyond this, developing and cultivating contacts with a wide range of both internal and external constituencies (see Bower and Weinberg

1988). The establishment and maintenance of such contacts are, therefore, an essential requirement for directors, both executive and non-executive.

4. The board has a major role to play in reviewing and approving strategic plans. Non-executive directors must be forceful and able enough to participate in discussions. For this purpose, adequate and timely information must be provided and allow them to have a fair view of the plans that come before the board. The board cannot rely solely on management to recommend the information requirements of the board—the board must determine these for themselves and insist upon them.

5. The signals sent out by directors concerning the climate and culture of the firm, its willingness to tolerate ambiguity and to encourage creativity and innovation, are extremely important. The nature of communication with managers is a vital element in the confidence-building process and the bringing-on of new talent. The clarity and saliency of messages, the choice of communication media, and the incentive structure should all reinforce the board's strategic intents.

6. At board meetings, directors should not be surprised by any item that is raised. All items that come before the board should have been circulated to directors well before the meeting. Further, all voices should be heard in the board meeting and no one voice should dominate.

7. Research shows that organizational effectiveness depends in part on achieving a match between control strategies and the strategic context of the firm (Gupta and Govindarajan 1984). We have argued for the positive use of control systems as a means for the board to effect change and learning. Ensuring alignment, therefore, between the control strategy and the strategic context is crucial.

8. There is a need for an explicit strategy of board development. The board should appraise itself regularly, taking into consideration such issues as the appropriate criteria for director selection, reviewing committees, decision-making styles, evaluating meetings, and the quality and quantity of information.

9. The director selection process is an important means by which the board can alter the skill mix and balance of its members. It is important that this process be as open and objective as possible. Appointing directors solely on the basis of the chief-executive's recommendation, or simply because the candidate has performed well as a senior manager, may give rise to problems following the appointment. If the new director is perceived to the 'chief executive's man' this may reduce his or her potential for questioning the chief executive, diminishing the control role of the board. Appointing solely on the basis of track record may not uncover whether the candidate will be able to operate as a director, nor whether he or she will be able to fit in with other board members.

10. Board norms in particular companies should be reassessed and, if necessary, jettisoned. The development of a norm that restricts the open questioning of proposals or performance in the boardroom restricts the potential influence

of board members. Restrictions on questioning the premisses of the company's operations, too, are detrimental to the effectiveness of the board and should be removed.

11. To conclude, with the increased scrutiny on matters of corporate governance, boards can no longer play just a legitimizing role, but must become more active and involved in the three key areas described in this study.

Implications for policy-makers

The field of corporate governance has been inundated with policy recommendations, as governments and institutional bodies seek ways to make companies more accountable and, ultimately, more effective in an increasingly competitive environment. Many policy prescriptions have had an implicit reliance on agency-theory assumptions. These assumptions centre on the nature of managerial motivation, which, it is claimed, rests on opportunism and self-seeking behaviour. The results of this study show that such assumptions may be misplaced, and the dominant trend to see corporate governance in general, and the role of the board in particular, as requiring shoring up in terms of sanctions and controls has been to the detriment of the performance characteristics of boards. In this respect, the Hampel Report (Hampnel 1998) represents a step forward, giving a governance framework based on guidelines and principles rather than prescriptive rules. Certainly, chairmen and non-executive directors did not see their roles primarily as restricting the power of executives and the chief executive, but as providing advice and ideas.

A second implication for policy-makers is that, though structure is an important element in determining the workings of the board, the real difference is made by the calibre of the board members and the nature of the dynamics of their working. The process by which boards operate is hard to legislate for. Much policy work has culminated in the development of standards that ultimately promote a 'tick-box' approach to corporate governance compliance. Though certain structures may be seen as comprising best practice and even laying down a necessary condition for the carrying-out of board activity, nevertheless, the real key to the working of the board lies in the development of relationships, not only within the boardroom but also externally with major constituencies.

A third implication is that there seems little enthusiasm for moving towards a German/Japanese model of governance. The findings from the data reveal that the unitary board and current institutional arrangements are viewed as a given, and enthusiasm for two-tier boards was distinctly absent. Reform in the boardroom was seen as unnecessary. All that was required, according to the interview data, was greater vigilance and a raising of the standards of professionalism. However, this did not extend unanimously to the idea of professional qualification for directors, without which a director could not operate.

Fourthly, one area that appears to be in need of attention is the influence of investors in ensuring good governance. Though the activity of investor groups was not the focus of this study, we saw that contact with investors was at a largely informal level, and would intensify only in times of poor performance or crisis. It may be that the power of the larger investors is not being used to its full effect, not only in terms of monitoring the performance of companies but also in giving advice on changes in management policy or personnel.

Enhancing accountability

A major criticism of boards of directors is that their form and structure have remained essentially the same under corporate law for over a century. As the Department of Trade and Industry's (DTI) review of company law states: 'The structure of company law is not just outdated: it can also contribute to problems and costs for business' (DTI 1998: 6). The proliferation of corporations and their increasing complexity have brought this issue to prominence. The greatest challenges that government and policy-makers face concern the area of increasing accountability and the performance of boards of directors.

We have focused in this book on the internal dynamics of boards and how the processes of the board affect the undertaking of its major roles. But boards are also subject to accountability from external constituencies. We have seen that organizations place great store by their investor relations. The need for consistency, predictability and transparency in managing the relationship with external constituencies is important to generate confidence in the organization and reduce the risk of shocks that could undermine trust in the ability of the board.

There are problems in the nature of the relationship between institutional investors and management. For example, the Myners Report (Myners 1995: 21) argued that 'some managers see their institutional investors as arrogant and consider themselves to be on the wrong end of an unequal relationship'. On the other hand, fund managers often accuse management of being secretive. Managers may also resist greater intervention on the part of the institutional investors on the grounds that institutional shareholders lack knowledge of an organization's operating procedures and specific context, and are perhaps not entrepreneurial enough for many firms. Most importantly, there is a concern that investors who develop a close relationship with firms may be given to price-sensitive information, which will prevent them from trading in the shares of that company. Greater personification of the relationship should help in these matters and in terms of insider information, our experience can be captured neatly by the PIRC's argument: 'companies in our experience do not feel inhibited in their discussions. If they consider the meeting requires the institution to become "an insider" they will ask permission beforehand. Certain institutions have let it be known that they are prepared to consider such requests positively, and in one case have established formal procedures for handling the situation. This should be encouraged.'

The trend for relationship investing will grow as more and more equity holdings end up in the hands of fewer and fewer institutions. The response of boards to this phenomenon will, to a large extent, determine the success of organizations. Transparency and honesty in the relationship between board and investor, together with the delivery of good returns and an appropriate balance between short-term results and long-term aspirations, bring strong demands for board endeavour.

Much attention has been paid to the issue of board composition, but much less to the related issue of board representation, the extent to which women, ethnic minorities, and foreign nationals are found in the boardroom. Women are underrepresented not only at board level but also in senior managerial positions. As Pettigrew writes, 'it is difficult to see greater female representation without increased representation of women in the business community as a whole' (1992: 18). With increasing globalization, and a growing interconnection of markets and corporations, organizations need to have experience of international markets and individual country cultures and contexts. Very little attention has been paid to the role of the board in managing across borders. The major route to increasing the international awareness of boards is to appoint foreign nationals, usually as non-executive directors. A foreign director can bring wide experience of local country conditions and broaden awareness of international issues in general. Increasing incidence of foreign director appointments will be a feature of enlightened board representation.

A number of prescriptive texts have highlighted the issue of board evaluation of its own performance as a major omission in board scrutiny, arguing that, without critical self-analysis, problems can occur in the dynamics and performance of the board that may make its role suboptimal. Companies that do undergo such a process usually admit that they do not employ any 'hard' metrics by which to gauge the effectiveness of the board and its processes, but instead have a number of informal barometers to measure the health of the board. From our examination of the case companies, we saw a number of techniques in play. At one firm, there is an annual review of board processes and practices, which is conducted by a leading non-executive, who interviews all board members individually and relatively informally to ask whether there is any area that can be improved. At another, a chairman's advisory committee examines the performance of the board and its committees overall. The clarification of accountabilities and the enhanced assessment of directors' contributions increase the board's evaluation and control role and also allow prevalent board norms to be uncovered and examined. They also provides a further opportunity to analyse the skill mix and size of the board and determine whether any new directors need be selected (or whether any incumbents need be released). For both individual directors, and the board as a whole, this mechanism was thought to be very important.

The issue of board self-assessment is linked to the issue of director training. There have been a number of studies that have documented the low level of take-up of director courses in the UK, reasons for which range from the unattractiveness of the content (or, at the least, the framing of the course), the unwillingness of directors to admit to needing training, and the lack of time directors have to take up training offers. Nevertheless, it is surprising, given recent managerial emphasis on continuous transformation and the learning organization, that many directors consider themselves exempt from this process. The main training and development opportunities continue to be business school courses, but greater emphasis is now being placed on coaching and mentoring of directors as a more effective way of increasing capability.

Increasing use of information technology in the boardroom may help to reduce the information asymmetry between executives and non-executives and speed the flow of knowledge throughout the board. With the rapid development of the Internet signalling changes in the way organizations are structured, more and more companies will become global and appoint board members from around the world. Video-conferencing technology is already established, enabling virtual meetings to take place and allowing the possibility of inexpensive link-ups to overseas heads/directors. The use of information technology would also help to increase the communication flow between board and shareholders/stakeholders, particularly small shareholders, who could access information about the company relatively cheaply. A virtual AGM would also represent a large step forward in increasing the attendance at that much-maligned event.

With organizations becoming more complex and the business environment unpredictable, the role of the board will come under greater scrutiny. With its position at the apex of the organization, the responsibility for the direction, values, and ethics of the organization, and ultimately its legitimacy and credibility, rest squarely with the board. Structure and composition of the board count for much in terms of how boards are run, but at the heart of the board's effectiveness is the calibre of its members, their willingness to participate, and the quality of relationships between them.

Appendix A
Empirical support for theories of boards of directors

Agency and transaction-cost theories

Work on boards of directors based on agency theory and transaction-cost economics is a relatively recent phenomenon (Kosnik 1987), but 'in the last ten years, a considerable amount of evidence has documented the prevalence of managerial behaviour that does not serve the interests of investors, particularly shareholders' (Schleifer and Vishny 1997: 746). The majority of empirical studies have tended to focus upon the link between board composition and financial performance, generally testing the hypothesis that, the more outside directors there are on the board, the better will shareholders' interests be served. The results overall have been equivocal. Baysinger and Butler (1985) was among the first studies; they compared the financial performance of 266 major US businesses over a ten-year period and found that the relative independence of boards, measured by the proportion of outside directors, had a positive yet lagged effect on the firms' average return on equity, relative to the industry's average return. Kesner (1987), in a sample of Fortune 500 firms, found that shareholder returns were enhanced by having a greater proportion of executives on the board, and Pearce and Zahra (1992) also reported that greater non-executive presence had a positive effect on company performance. Ezzamel and Watson (1993) found support for agency theory in a sample of UK companies that showed a positive relationship between independent non-executive directors and profit growth. Hermalin and Weisbach (1991), however, found that board composition had no impact on corporate performance in their sample of 142 NYSE firms. Pearce (1983) also found no relationship, as too did Chaganti *et al.* (1985) in their study of board composition and bankruptcy.

A problem with establishing the relationship between board composition and financial performance is that there are 'inherent difficulties in separating out the multitude of endogenous and exogenous factors that influence company performance, (which) make the assumed effects of board demographic characteristics on board effectiveness very difficult to establish' (Pettigrew 1992: 170). Other links have therefore attracted the attention of agency research. Greenmail has been used as a proxy for board ineffectiveness. Greenmail is what Monks and Minow (1995: 212) called 'possibly the most unconscionable way of avoiding takeover', where the board of a company subjected to a takeover threat offers to buy out the prospective raider at a substantial premium to the market price of the shares. The unconscionable aspect derives from the fact that the raider does not even have to make a bid for the company; the threat is enough. They receive a large cash payment for little risk, and the fact that a large payment is made to stave off a potential bidder may adversely affect the market price of the shares, thus reducing the wealth of existing shareholders. Kosnik (1987), in a study based on predictions from agency theory and managerial-hegemony theory, compared the board structure of fifty-three companies that paid greenmail and fifty-seven companies that resisted greenmail payment. She found that boards that effectively resisted paying greenmail were found to have more outside directors, as predicted by agency theory. The effective boards also had a higher proportion of outsider directors with executive experience.

Two other defences against takeover, the 'poison pill' and the 'golden parachute', have also been used to test the link between board composition and performance. Poison pills are rights issued to shareholders 'that are worthless unless triggered by a hostile acquisition attempt. If triggered, pills give shareholders the ability to purchase shares from, or sell shares back to, the target company (the "flip-in pill") and/or the potential acquirer (the "flip-over" pill)' (Monks and Minow 1995: 213). A bid that is beneficial to the shareholders of the targeted company can therefore be effectively vetoed by the board. G. F. Davis (1991) found that a greater proportion of insiders on the board had no relationship with the adoption of poison pills. However, Mallette and Fowler (1992) examined the relationship between board composition and stock ownership and poison-pill provisions and found that poison-pill adoption depends on the proportion of independent directors and that, the lower the equity holdings of inside direct-ors, and the higher the equity holdings of institutional investors, the more likely companies are to pass poison-pill provisions.

The golden parachute is a payment that is guaranteed to be paid to the executives of a tar-geted company should their firm be taken over (Knoeber 1986). As such, it represents a diminution of shareholder wealth and a reflection of 'entrenched executives arranging a large consolation prize for themselves' (Donaldson and Davies 1994: 154). Singh and Harianto (1989) examined the use of golden parachutes in a matched sample of eighty-four Fortune 500 companies, using variables from both agency and managerial-hegemony theory. They found that, contrary to expectations, the likelihood of having golden parachutes was associated with having more outsiders on the board. Research by Cochran, Wood, and Jones (1985) confirmed this finding, showing that the presence of outsider directors did not provide a defence against the use of golden parachutes.

Corporate breaches of fiduciary responsibility and illegal activity have also been used as sur-rogates of board ineffectiveness (Donaldson and Davies 1994). Kesner and Johnson (1990) studied the relationship between board composition and shareholder suits in 112 matched cases in Delaware. The analysis showed that boards sued tended to have a greater percentage of inside directors than those not sued, the relationship being even stronger in cases where the chief executive was also the chairman. This lends support to the agency thesis. However, in actual rulings against boards, the authors reported that there was no difference in board com-position for the two groups, though the research method employed entailed cutting the sam-ple in half for testing suit outcomes, which may have affected the result. Jones (1986) also looked at the effectiveness of board monitoring through the proxy of shareholder suits. In a sample of seventy-eight Fortune 500 companies over an eight-year period from 1970 to 1977, the author found that boards of medium size (more than twelve but less than seventeen mem-bers) and boards with 60 per cent or more outside directors were linked to a lower incidence of shareholder suits.

Kesner, Victor, and Lamont (1986) examined 384 Fortune 500 firms between 1980 and 1984 across a range of illegal activities and found that adding outsiders to corporate boards is unlikely to lessen a firm's involvement in illegal activities. In addition, those firms that have chief-executive duality are no more likely to be involved in illegal acts than those where the roles of chairman and chief executive are split. The study of Gautschi and Jones (1987) even found a negative relationship between outsider representation and the commission of illegal acts.

Instances of bankruptcy have also been examined as an implication of the effectiveness of board monitoring (Daily 1994). Daily and Dalton (1994a) found that firms with lower pro-portions of independent directors and chief-executive duality were associated with bank-ruptcy. Daily and Dalton (1994b) also found that higher proportions of affiliated (non-independent) directors have also been associated with a bankruptcy filing. Daily's (1996) study showed no association, however, between the composition of audit committees (outsiders versus affiliates) and the incidence of bankruptcy.

A narrower test of independence than the presence of non-executive directors on the board is whether the board has split the role of chief executive and chairman, with the chairman as non-executive director. Rechner and Dalton (1991) examined the financial implications of the choice firms take between separating the roles of chief executive and chairman and combining them. Taking data from 141 companies over a six-year period between 1978 and 1983, the authors found that firms with 'independent leadership' consistently outperformed those depending on the combination of the roles, on the measures of profit margin, return on equity (ROE), and return on investment. Chaganti *et al.* (1985) found that centralizing power in the hands of the chief executive is not likely to make a difference to the chances of failure. Donaldson and Davies (1991), in a convenience sample of 339 Standard and Poor's companies, found that shareholder returns (ROE) were superior where there was chief-executive duality in firms, so there was a negative relationship between the presence of a non-executive chairman and company performance.

Stewardship theory

Empirical evidence of stewardship's theory is slight. Donaldson and Davis (1991) examined the effects of chief-executive duality on shareholder returns, controlling for the industry effect and for size (both known influences on organizational performance). Using a convenience sample of 339 US corporations, with 76 per cent having chief-executive duality, the authors found that shareholder returns, in terms of ROI, were superior in the cases of CEO duality. Fox and Hamilton (1994) examined the reasons for diversification of 103 New Zealand firms and found, contrary to agency theory, that executives were motivated by a desire to maximize firm performance, rather than for self-serving ends. Hill (1995), in a study of 42 directors from 11 large UK firms, concluded that:

> the point to note is that these directors believe that they are working for their shareholders and that their own interests and those of their shareholders are congruent. When one adds the influence that major shareholders can bring to bear on a board when they choose to, and their willingness to activate their power if necessary, then the view that managers have distinctively different interests from shareholders and the freedom to pursue these essentially unconstrained is not tenable.

Donaldson and Davis (1991) also claim support from Vance (1983) and Sullivan (1988), whose studies showed that greater proportions of executive directors led to higher corporate performance. The failure of some studies to support agency theory (e.g. Cochran *et al.* 1985; Gautschi and Jones 1987; Kesner 1987; Rechner and Dalton 1991; Singh and Harianto 1989) also lends indirect backing to stewardship theory.

Resource-dependence theory

The results of Pfeffer's two major studies in the early 1970s provided strong empirical support to the resource-dependence theory. His 1972 study of eighty non-financial institutions showed that elements of board size and composition were positively correlated with the organization's needs to co-opt sectors of the environment. A further study in 1973, looking at the functions of boards of directors in hospitals, resulted in similar conclusions: the environmental linkage function of hospital boards was significant for hospitals dependent on the community for support (Pfeffer 1973; Provan 1980).

Provan (1980) examined the impact of an externally powerful board on the effectiveness of forty-six non-profit human service agencies (providing health, social welfare, and recreational services) concerning their ability to attract scarce funds. The author found that agencies that could attract or co-opt prominent members of the community and its power structure to serve on their board were better placed to attract sources of funds. Zald's (1967) study of the Chicago area YMCAs found that the percentage of business leaders on the board was positively correlated with financial contributions.

Boyd (1990) examined whether corporate boards respond to different types of environmental uncertainty. The evidence from 147 firms in nine industry groups found that boards tended to be smaller in a more uncertain environment, though they had an increased number of interlocks, a relationship that was stronger in high-performing firms. These results provide some support for the resource-dependence theory. Pearce and Zahra (1992) examined 119 Fortune 500 companies and found that the number of directors of the board (board size) and the number of outsiders on the board were positively associated with environmental uncertainty.

However, the majority of studies show that time given by non-executive directors to the corporation—typically a day a month—is minimal and this would seem to serve as evidence against the potential for co-optation (Donaldson 1995). If co-optation depends on gaining strong commitment from the non-executive director to the host organization, this will be extremely difficult to do, given that they spend the large proportion of their time away from the organization. The support for this theory from the interlocking directorates tradition must also be viewed with caution. Burt's (1983) study of the link between corporate interlocks and profit-raising found no relationship, and, as Donaldson (1995: 155) concludes: 'the co-optative functions imputed to directorate ties are not confirmed empirically.'

Class-hegemony theory

Support for the class-hegemony theory is considerable. Mills's study into the 'Power Elite' examined a number of elite cadres in the USA and concluded that a conjunction of historical circumstances has led to an elite of power concentrated in the hands of comparatively few citizens. Useem's (1984) study used interview data from 129 large UK and US companies between 1979 and 1980 and found, amongst other things, that, the more directorships a person held, the more likely he or she was to have a public-school background. These directors formed the 'inner circle' of the upper class and were responsible for promoting class cohesion and consensus building. The pioneering work of Domoff (1967, 1970) showed that the highest social stratum is based in ownership of large businesses, and that members of the corporate community are deeply involved in major political parties. The importance of similar backgrounds and socialization in transmitting a unified worldview was also a clear finding. Scott and Griff (1984) examined 200 non-financial and fifty financial firms in the UK over three time periods (1976, 1938, and 1904), and, in developing a network analysis of interlocking directorships' showed that a managerial theory has the least to offer as an explanation of corporate power. Finance capitalism and primary interlocks produce an inner circle within the corporate directorate of business leaders (Scott and Griff 1984: 180). The work of Scott (1985, 1987, 1991*a*, *b*), among others, forms a solid body of literature concerning elite theory and its implications for the conduct of business.

Managerial-hegemony theory

Mace's (1971) classic study showed that boards do not always fulfil their requirements to monitor the performance of the company in general and the top management in particular. They
do not establish strategic objectives, select the chief executive, or ask discerning questions.
Typically, they do provide advice and counsel to the president, act as a kind of discipline for
the executive ('the requirement of formally appearing before a board of directors consisting of
respected, able people of stature, no matter how friendly, causes the company organisation to
do a better job of thinking through their problems and of being prepared with solutions,
explanations, or rationales' (1971: 180)), and make decisions in crisis situations. The work of
Pahl and Winkler (1974) lends some support to the managerial view. Their emphasis on positional elites indicates that much of board work is conducted by cabals, usually comprising
executive directors who have allocative control (rather than merely operational control),
though they do state that members of some cabals emanate from outside the boardroom.
Fidler's (1981) study of sixty chief executives found that they had difficulty in articulating
what the duties of directors were and saw no real distinction between the work of the board
and the work of senior management, indirectly confirming the managerial-hegemony thesis.
The research by Lorsch and MacIver (1989) found that the number of constraining factors on
non-executive director participation meant that boards had little opportunity to exercise any
power and influence over the organization.

Herman's (1981) analysis of corporate power and control found no superiority of shareholder returns in firms with owner control over those with management control. The study by
Francis (1980) also found little direct support for managerial domination, but, as Parkinson
(1994: 71) states, 'this is perhaps unsurprising given there is likely to be an under-reporting of
what respondents consider will be perceived as deviant behaviour'.

Other empirical evidence for this theory tends to be dominated by single case studies and
anecdotes (Kosnik 1987). Again, this may be a function, as was seen to be partly the case with
transaction-cost economics, of the fact that managerial-hegemony and agency theories share
a similar focus (Kosnik 1987). Apart from their different disciplinary origins, both are concerned with the potential conflict of interests between shareholders and managers. But, while
agency theory puts its faith in the board of directors as an instrument of corporate control,
managerial-hegemony theory views the board as an ineffective mechanism (Kosnik 1987).
Indirect evidence for the claims of managerial-hegemony theory can therefore be gleaned
from some strands of organizational economics research.

Appendix B
Selected empirical studies on the strategic role of the board

Authors	Description of study	Major findings
Mace (1971)	Interviews with 50 directors of medium and large US corporations in terms of board roles and responsibilities.	Boards do not impact on strategic decision-making, except in times of crisis. Typically, boards are under managerial domination and are 'the creatures of the chief executive'.
Norburn and Grinyer (1974)	91 executives from 21 companies interviewed.	Managing director identified as responsible for setting of primary company objectives. Strong lack of agreement within boards as to corporate direction.
Pahl and Winkler (1974)	Research in 19 companies, involving open interview with directors (number not specified); diary analysis from 71 directors, discussion groups, and shadowing of main board directors for a day.	Standard expectation is that boards collectively do not decide or discuss anything, with most proposals 'going through on the nod'. Board a legitimating institution rather than a decision-making one.
Tricker (1984)	Corporate Policy Group studies on the work of directors and the activities of boards.	Boards are involved in the formulation of strategy, setting policies, and the acquisition and allocation of resources. But emphasis within companies is with internal issues, rather than with focusing externally on matters affecting shareholders.
Henke (1986)	Survey of 234 large US corporations on manner of board involvement in strategy.	Boards influence the decision of many strategic issues but majority of boards do not know they are involved in strategic decision-making. Boards, therefore, do not influence their firm's direction in a coherent manner.
Rosenstein (1987)	4 case studies of US firms.	Board is 'not a proper locus for making or originating strategy'. Major role is to monitor and dismiss the chief executive.
Lorsch and MacIver (1989)	Interviews with 80 directors, 4 case studies, and a mail questionnaire in USA.	Boards act mainly as advisers to the chief executive on strategy, counselling the chief executive and evaluating options. The use of strategic committees is considered important.

136

Appendices

Pearce and Zahra (1991)	Survey of 139 Fortune 500 companies.	Participative boards are associated with superior financial performance, based on earnings per share.
Demb and Neubauer (1992)	Interviews with 71 directors of companies of a variety of nationalities (predominately UK and USA), plus survey of 127 directors.	Survey found that 75% of respondents considered setting strategy as the main job of the board. Interviews established idea of continuum of board involvement in strategy.
Judge and Zeithaml (1992)	Interviews with 114 board members from four US industry sectors, collecting both qualitative and quantitative data. Archival records.	Board size and levels of diversification and insider representation were negatively related to board involvement, and organizational age was positively related to it. Board involvement positively related to financial performance, after controlling for industry and size effects.
Ferlie *et al.* (1994)	Longitudinal and comparative case studies of 11 NHS sites, using interviews, archival analysis, attendance at board meetings.	Three levels of board involvement—rubber stamp, probing and questioning of strategic options, and active involvement in deciding between options, including shaping the vision. Factors influencing progression through levels include experience, expertise, and confidence of the non-executive director, and whether the executives want them to make the transition.
Goodstein (*et al*). (1994)	334 hospital boards surveyed over 6-year period.	Large and diverse boards hinder strategic change.
Hill (1995)	Interviews with 42 directors from 11 large UK companies.	Strategic direction is what directors see as their main purpose. Evidence of inner cabinets. Non-executives saw a wide role for themselves—bringing breadth of vision, environmental scanning, and acting as a sounding board for the chief executive.
O'Neal and Thomas (1995)	18 interviews in 6 for-profit firms in the USA.	Directors want to be 'more involved than they currently are'. Keys to board involvement are the degree to which the chairman wants the board involved, and the information provided to board members.

Pettigrew and McNulty (1995)	Study of part-time board members in the top 200 UK industrial and commercial firms (by turnover) and the top 50 UK financial institutions. Pilot study presents data from 20 in-depth interviews.	Characterize some board cultures as minimalist, others as maximalist, depending on the part-time members' will and skill, and also the presence of contextual factors, such as crisis conditions or changing board dynamics.
Conference Board (1996)	Survey of 82 US and European companies.	49% of the respondents described their board's current role as 'actively engaged in the choice of strategic options'.
McNulty and Pettigrew (1999)	108 UK directors interviewed.	Boards actively involved in strategic choice, change, and control.

References

ABRAHAMSON, E., and PARK, C. (1994), 'Concealment of Negative Organizational Outcomes: An Agency Theory Perspective', *Academy of Management Journal*, 37: 1302–34.

ALBERT, M. (1993), *Capitalism against Capitalism* (London: Whurr Publishing).

ALFREDER, C. P. (1986), 'The Invisible Director on Corporate Boards', *Harvard Business Review*, 64: 38–52.

ALI (1992): American Law Institute, *Principles of Corporate Governance: Analysis and Recommendations* (Philadelphia: American Law Institute).

ANDREWS, K. R. (1980), 'Directors' Responsibility for Corporate Strategy', *Harvard Business Review*, 58: 30–42.

ANSOFF, H. I. (1965), *Corporate Strategy: An Analytical Approach to Business Policy for Growth and Expansion* (New York: McGraw-Hill).

ARAM, J. D., and COWEN, S.A. (1986), 'The Directors' Role in Planning: What Information do They Need?', *Long Range Planning*, 19: 117–24.

BARNEY, J. B. (1990), 'The Debate between Traditional Management Theory and Organizational Economics: Substantive Differences or Intergroup Conflict?', *Academy of Management Review*, 15: 382–93.

—— (1991), 'Firm Resources and Sustained Competitive Advantage', *Journal of Management*, 17: 99–120.

—— and OUCHI, W. (1986) (eds.), *Organizational Economics* (San Francisco, Jossey-Bass).

BARTLETT, C. A., and GHOSHAL, S. (1989), *Managing across Borders* (Boston: Harvard Business School Press).

—— —— (1993), 'Beyond the M-form: Towards a Managerial Theory of the Firm', *Strategic Management Journal*, 14 (special issue, Winter), 23–46.

BAYSINGER, B. D., and BUTLER, H. N. (1985), 'Corporate Governance and the Board of Directors: Performance Effects of Changes in Board Composition', *Journal of Law, Economics, and Organization*, 1: 101–24.

—— and HOSKISSON, R. E. (1989), 'Diversification Strategy and R&D Intensity in Multiproduct Firms', *Academy of Management Journal*, 32: 310–32.

—— —— (1990), 'The Composition of Boards of Directors and Strategic Control: Effects on Corporate Strategy', *Academy of Management Review*, 15: 72–87.

BAZERMAN, M. H., and SCHOORMAN, F. D. (1983), 'A Limited Rationality Model of Interlocking Directorates', *Academy of Management Review*, 9: 206–17.

BELLIVEAU, M A., O'REILLY, C. A., and WADE, J. B. (1995), 'Social Capital at the Top: Effects of Social Similarity and Status on CEO Compensation', *Academy of Management Journal*, 39: 1568–93.

BENITO, A., and CONYON, M. (1995), 'Top Directors' Pay, Product Market Influences and Internal Control Systems', mimeo (University of Warwick).

BERLE, A., and MEANS, G. C. (1932), *The Modern Corporation and Private Property* (New York: Macmillan).

BEYER, J. M., CHANOVE, R. G., and FOX, W. B. (1995), 'The Review Process and the Fates of Manuscripts Submitted to the AMJ', *Academy of Management Journal*, 38: 1219–60.

BHIDE, A. (1994), 'Efficient Markets, Deficient Governance', *Harvard Business Review*, 72: 128–39.

BLAIR, M. M. (1995), *Ownership and Control* (Washington: Brookings Institution).

BOEKER, W. (1992), 'Power and Managerial Dismissal: Scapegoating at the Top', *Administrative Science Quarterly*, 37: 400–21.

BOULTON, W. R. (1978), 'The Evolving Board: A New Look at the Board's Changing Roles and Information Needs', *Academy of Management Review*, 3: 827–36.

BOWER, J. L. (1970), *Managing the Resource Allocation Process* (Boston: Harvard Business School Press).

—— and DOZ, Y. (1979), 'Strategy Formulation: A Social and Political Process', in D. Schendel and C.W. Hofer (eds.), *Strategic Management* (Boston: Little, Brown), 253–72.

—— and WEINBERG, M. W. (1988), 'Statecraft, Strategy and Corporate Leadership', *California Management Review*, 30: 39–56.

BOYD, B. K. (1990), 'Corporate Linkages and Organizational Environment: A Test of the Resource Dependence Model', *Strategic Management Journal*, 11: 419–30.

—— (1994), 'Board Control and CEO Compensation', *Strategic Management Journal*, 15: 335–44.

BRASS, D. J., and BURKHARDT, M.G. (1993), 'Potential Power and Power Use: An Investigation of Structure and Behaviour', *Academy of Management Journal*, 36: 441–70.

BRUCE, A., and BUCK, T. (1997), 'Executive Reward and Corporate Governance', in K. Keasey, S. Thompson, and M.Wright (eds.), *Corporate Governance: Economic, Management and Financial Issues* (Oxford: Oxford University Press), 80–102.

BUCKINGHAM, L., and WHITEBLOOM, S. (1996), 'The Gold Diggers of Britain plc', *Guardian*, 1 June, 40.

BURGELMAN, R. A. (1983), 'Corporate Entrepreneurship and Strategic Management: Insights from a Process Study', *Management Science*, 29: 1349–64.

—— (1991), 'Intraorganizational Ecology of Strategy Making and Organizational Adaptation: Theory and Field Research', *Academy of Management Review*, 16: 262–90.

BURRELL, G., and MORGAN, G. (1979), *Sociological Paradigms and Organizational Analysis* (Aldershot: Gower).

BURT, R. S. (1980), 'Models of Network Structure', *Annual Review of Sociology*, 6: 79–141.

—— (1983), 'Cooptive Corporate Action Networks: A Reconsideration of Interlocking Directorates Involving American Manufacturing', *Administrative Science Quarterly*, 25: 557–81.

CADBURY, SIR ADRIAN (1990), *The Company Chairman* (London: Director Books).

—— (1992), *The Financial Aspects of Corporate Governance* (Committee on the Financial Aspects of Corporate Governance; London: Gee & Co.).

—— (1993), 'Highlights of the Proposals of the Committee on Financial Aspects of Corporate Governance', in D. D. Prentice and P. R. J. Holland (eds.), *Contemporary Issues in Corporate Governance* (Oxford: Clarendon Press), 45–55.

—— (1997), *Board Focus: The Governance Debate* (Zurich: Egon Zehneder International).

CAMPBELL, A., and YEUNG, S. (1990), 'Do You Need a Mission Statement?', *The Economist*, Special Report No. 1208.

CARROLL, A. B. (1989), *Business and Society: Ethics and Stakeholder Management* (Cincinnati, Oh.: South Western).

CASSELL, C., and SYMON, G. (1994), *Qualitative Methods in Organizational Research* (London: Sage Publications).

CHAGANTI, R. S, MAHAJAN, V., and SHARMA, S. (1985), 'Corporate Board Size, Composition and Corporate Failures in the Retailing Industry', *Journal of Management Studies*, 22: 400–17.

CHANDLER, A. D. (1962), *Strategy and Structure* (Cambridge, Mass.: MIT Press).

CHARKHAM J. (1986), *Effective Boards* (London: Chartac).

—— (1994a), *Keeping Good Company* (Oxford: Oxford University Press).

CHARKHAM J. (1994*b*), 'A Larger Role for Institutional Investors', in N. H. Dimsdale and M. Prevezer (eds.), *Capital Markets and Corporate Governance* (Oxford: Clarendon Press), 99–110.

—— and SIMPSON, A. (1998), *Fair Shares: The Future of Shareholder Power and Responsibility* (Oxford: Oxford University Press).

CHITAYAT, G. (1985), 'Working Relationships between the Chairman of the Board and the CEO', *Management International Review*, 25: 6570.

CIMA (1992): Chartered Institute of Management Accountants, *A Framework for Internal Control* (London: CIMA).

CLARK, A. (1997), 'Gartmore Chief Speaks out on Corporate Governance', *Daily Telegraph*, 21 Nov.

CLUTTERBUCK, D., and WAINE, P. (1995), *The Independent Board Director* (Maidenhead: McGraw-Hill).

COASE, R. (1937), 'The Nature of the Firm', *Economica*, 4: 386–405.

COCHRAN, P. L., and WARTICK, S. L. (1988), *Corporate Governance: A Review of the Literature* (Morristown, NJ: Financial Executives Research Foundation).

—— WOOD, R. A., and JONES, T. B. (1985), 'The Composition of Boards of Directors and the Incidence of Golden Parachutes', *Academy of Management Journal*, 28: 664–71.

COFFEE, J. C. (1991), 'Liquidity versus Control: The Institutional Investor as Corporate Monitor', *Columbia Law Review*, 91/6: 1277–368.

COMBINED CODE (1998), *Combined Code for Corporate Governance* (London: London Stock Exchange).

COMMONS, J. R. (1934), *Institutional Economics* (Madison: University of Wisconsin Press).

CONFERENCE BOARD (1996), *The Corporate Board: A Growing Role in Strategic Assessment* (New York: Conference Board).

CONYON, M. J. (1997), 'Institutional Arrangements for Setting Directors' Compensation in UK Companies', in K. Keasey, S. Thompson, and M. Wright (eds.), *Corporate Governance: Economic, Management and Financial Issues* (Oxford: Oxford University Press), 103–21.

—— GREGG, P. , and MACHIN, S. (1995), 'Taking Care of Business: Executive Compensation in the United Kingdom', *Economic Journal*, 105: 704–14.

COOPERS & LYBRAND (1986), *Becoming a Director* (London: Coopers & Lybrand).

COSH, A. (1975), 'The Remuneration of Chief Executives in the United Kingdom', *Economic Journal*, 85: 75–94.

—— and HUGHES, A. (1987), 'The Anatomy of Corporate Control: Directors, Shareholders and Executive Remuneration in Giant US and UK Corporations', *Cambridge Journal of Economics*, 11: 285–313.

COUGHLAN, A. T., and SCHMIDT, R. M-(1985), 'Executive Compensation, Managerial Turnover and Firm Performance: An Empirical Investigation', *Journal of Accounting and Economics*, 7: 43–66.

COULSON-THOMAS, C. (1995), *Creating Excellence in the Boardroom* (Maidenhead: McGraw-Hill).

COURTIS, J. K. (1993), 'Recent Developments and Frustrations in the Corporate Reporting Process', *Corporate Governance—An International Review*, 1: 18–25.

COWE, R. (1993) (ed.), *The Guardian Guide to the Top 100 UK Companies* (London: Guardian Books).

CYERT, R. M., and MARCH, J. G. (1963), *A Behavioural Theory of the Firm* (Englewood Cliffs, NJ: Prentice-Hall).

DAILY, C. M. (1994), 'Bankruptcy in Strategic Studies: Past and Promise', *Journal of Management*, 20: 263–95.

—— (1996), 'Governance Patterns in Bankruptcy Reorganizations', *Strategic Management Journal*, 17: 355–76.

—— and DALTON, D. R. (1994*a*), 'Corporate Governance and the Bankrupt Firm', *Strategic Management Journal*, 15: 643–54.

—— —— (1994*b*), 'Bankruptcy and Corporate Governance: The Impact of Board Composition and Structure', *Academy of Management Journal*, 37: 1603–17.

DALTON, D. R., and KESNER, I. F. (1985), 'Organizational Performance as an Antecedent of Inside/Outside Chief Executive Succession: An Empirical Assessment', *Academy of Management Journal*, 28: 749–62.

—— —— (1987), 'Composition and CEO Duality in Boards of Directors: An International Perspective', *Journal of International Business Studies*, 18: 33–42.

DAVIS, G. F. (1991), 'Agents without Principals? The Spread of the Poison Pill through the Intercorporate Network', *Administrative Science Quarterly*, 36: 583–613.

DAVIS, J. H., SCHOORMAN, F. D., and DONALDSON, L. (1997), 'Towards a Stewardship Theory of Management', *Academy of Management Review*, 22: 20–47.

DAVIS, P. (1993), 'Institutional Investors in the United Kingdom', in D. D. Prentice and P. R. J. Holland (eds.), *Contemporary Issues in Corporate Governance* (Oxford: Clarendon Press), 69–95.

DEAKIN, S., and HUGHES, A. (1997*a*), 'Comparative Corporate Governance: An Interdisciplinary Agenda', in S. Deakin and A. Hughes (eds.), *Enterprise and Community: New Directions in Corporate Governance* (Oxford: Blackwells), 1–9.

—— —— (1997*b*), *Enterprise and Community: New Directions in Corporate Governance* (Oxford: Blackwells).

DEMB, A., and NEUBAUER, F. F. (1992), *The Corporate Board* (New York: Oxford University Press).

DEPARTMENT OF EMPLOYMENT (1977), *Report of the Committee of Enquiry on Industrial Democracy (Bullock Committee)* (Cmnd. 6706. London: HMSO).

DEUTSCH, M. (1973), *The Resolution of Conflict* (New Haven: Yale University Press).

DICKSON, M. (1992), 'Revolution behind Closed Doors', *Financial Times*, 13 April, 10.

DIMSDALE, N. H., and PREVEZER, M. (1994) (eds.), *Capital Markets and Corporate Governance* (Oxford: Clarendon Press).

DOMOFF, G. W. (1967), *Who Rules America?* (Englewood Cliffs, NJ: Prentice-Hall).

—— (1970), *The Higher Circles* (New York: Random House).

DONALDSON, L. (1990), 'The Ethereal Hand: Organizational Economics and Management Theory', *Academy of Management Review*, 15: 369–81.

—— (1995), *Anti-Managerial Theories of the Firm* (Cambridge: Cambridge University Press).

—— and DAVIES, J. H. (1991), 'Stewardship Theory and Agency Theory: CEO Governance and Shareholder Returns', *Australian Journal of Management*, 16: 49–64.

—— —— (1994), 'Boards and Company Performance: Research Challenges the Conventional Wisdom', *Corporate Governance—An International Review*, 2: 151–60.

DONALDSON, T., and PRESTON, L. E. (1995), 'The Stakeholder Theory of the Corporation: Concepts, Evidence and Implications', *Academy of Management Review*, 20: 65–91.

DOZ, Y. L., and PRAHALAD, C. K. (1991), 'Managing DMNCs: A Search for a New Paradigm', *Strategic Management Journal*, 12 (special issue, Summer), 145–64.

DRUCKER, P. F. (1991), 'Reckoning with the Pension Fund Revolution', *Harvard Business Review*, 69: 106–14.

DTI (1998): Department of Trade and Industry, *Modern Company Law for a Competitive Economy* (London: HMSO).

EASTERBY-SMITH, M., THORPE, R., and LOWE, A. (1991), *Management Research: An Introduction* (London: Sage).

THE ECONOMIST (1994), 'Watching the Boss: A Survey of Corporate Governance', 29 Jan.

EISENHARDT, K. L. (1985), 'Control: Organization and Economic Approaches', *Management Science*, 31: 134–49.

—— (1989a), 'Agency Theory: A Review and Assessment', *Academy of Management Review*, 14: 57–74.

—— (1989b), 'Building Theories from Case Study Research', *Academy of Management Review*, 14: 532–50.

—— and BOURGEOIS, L. J. (1988), 'Politics of Decision-Making in High Velocity Environments', *Academy of Management Journal*, 31: 737–70.

EVAN, W. M., and FREEMAN, R. E. (1988), 'A Stakeholder Theory of the Modern Corporation: Kantian Capitalism', in T. Beauchamp and N. Bowie (eds.), *Ethical Theory and Business* (Englewood Cliffs: Prentice-Hall), 75–93.

EZZAMEL, M., and WATSON, R. (1993), 'Organizational Form, Ownership Structure and Corporate Performance: A Contextual Empirical Analysis of UK Companies', *British Journal of Management*, 4: 161–76.

—— —— (1997), 'Executive Remuneration and Corporate Performance', in K. Keasey and M. Wright (eds.), *Corporate Governance: Responsibilities, Risks and Remuneration* (Chichester: Wiley), 61–92.

FAMA, E. F. (1980), 'Agency Problems and the Theory of the Firm', *Journal of Political Economy*, 88: 288–307.

—— and JENSEN, M. C. (1983), 'Separation of Ownership and Control', *Journal of Law and Economics*, 26: 301–25.

FERLIE, E. F., ASHBURNER L., and FITZGERALD L. (1994), 'The Non-Executive Director and the Board—Some Evidence from the NHS', unpublished paper, Centre for Corporate Strategy and Change, University of Warwick.

—— —— —— and PETTIGREW, A. (1996), *The New Public Management in Action* (Oxford: Oxford University Press).

FIDLER, J. (1981), *The British Business Elite: Its Attitudes to Class, Status and Power* (London: Routledge & Kegan Paul).

FIELDING, N. G., and FIELDING, J. L. (1986), *Linking Data* (Beverly Hills: Sage).

FINKELSTEIN, S. (1992), 'Power in Top Management Teams: Dimensions, Measurement and Validation', *Academy of Management Journal*, 35: 505–38.

FINKELSTEIN, S., and D'AVENI, R. A. (1994), 'CEO Duality as a Double Edged Sword: How Boards Balance Entrenchment Avoidance and Unity of Command', *Academy of Management Journal*, 37: 1079–108.

—— and HAMBRICK, D. C. (1988), 'CEO Compensation: A Synthesis and Reconciliation', *Strategic Management Journal*, 9: 543–58.

—— —— (1989), 'Chief Executive Compensation: A Study of the Intersection of Markets and Political Processes', *Strategic Management Journal*, 10: 121–34.

FORBES, D. P. , and MILLIKEN, F. J. (1999), 'Cognition and Corporate Governance: Understanding Boards of Directors as Strategic Decision-Making Groups', *Academy of Management Review*, 24: 489–505.

FORBES, W., and WATSON, R. (1993), 'Managerial Remuneration and Corporate Governance: A Review of the Issues, Evidence and Cadbury Committee Proposals', *Accounting and Business Research*, 23: 331–8.

Fox, M. A., and Hamilton, R. T. (1994), 'Ownership and Diversification: Agency Theory or Stewardship Theory', *Journal of Management Studies*, 31: 69–81.

Francis, A. (1980), 'Company Objectives, Managerial Motivation and the Behaviour of Large Firms: An Empirical Test of the Theory of Managerial Capitalism', *Cambridge Journal of Economics*, 4: 349–62.

Franks, J., and Mayer, C. (1991), 'Hostile Takeovers and the Correction of Managerial Failure', *Journal of Financial Economics*, 40: 163–81.

Freeman, R. E. (1984), *Strategic Management: A Stakeholder Approach* (Boston: Pitman).

—— and Evan, W. M. (1990), 'Corporate Governance: A Stakeholder Interpretation', *Journal of Behavioural Economics*, 19: 337–59.

Friedlander, F. (1970), 'The Primacy of Trust as a Facilitator of Further Group Accomplishment', *Journal of Applied Behavioural Science*, 6: 387–400.

Friedrickson, J., Hambrick, D. C., and Baumrin, S. (1988), 'A Model of CEO Dismissal', *Academy of Management Review*, 13: 255–70.

Gambetta, D. (1988) (ed.), *Trust: Making and Breaking Co-operative Relations* (Oxford: Basil Blackwell).

Garratt, B. (1996), *The Fish Rots from the Head* (London: HarperCollins).

Gautschi, F. H., and Jones, T. M. (1987), 'Illegal Corporate Behaviour and Corporate Board Structure', *Research in Corporate Social Performance and Policy*, 9: 93–106.

Ghemawhat, P. (1991), *Commitment: The Dynamic Theory of Strategy* (New York: Free Press).

Ghoshal, S., and Moran, P. (1996), 'Bad for Practice: A Critique of Transaction Cost Theory', *Academy of Management Review*, 21: 13–47.

Giddens, A. (1977), *Studies in Social and Political Theory* (London: Hutchinson).

—— (1979), *Central Problems in Social Theory* (Hemel Hempstead: Harvester-Wheatsheaf).

Gilson, R. J., and Kraakman, R. (1991), 'Reinventing the Outside Director: An Agenda for Institutional Investors', *Stanford Law Review*, 43: 863–906.

Gioia, D. A., and Thomas, J. B. (1996), 'Identity, Image and Issue Interpretation: Sensemaking during Strategic Change in Academia', *Administrative Science Quarterly*, 41: 370–3.

Glaser, B. G., and Strauss, A. L. (1967), *The Discovery of Grounded Theory: Strategies for Qualitative Research* (Chicago: Aldine).

Goldenberg, P. (1998), 'Shareholders v Stakeholders: The Bogus Argument', IALS Company Law Lecture, *Company Lawyer*, 19: 34–9.

Gomez-Mejia, L. R., and Balkin, D. B. (1992), *Compensation, Organizational Strategy and Firm Performance* (Cincinnati, Oh.: Southwestern).

Goodpaster, K. E. (1991), 'Business Ethics and Stakeholder Analysis', *Business Ethics Quarterly*, 1: 53–73.

Goodstein, J., and Boeker, W. (1991), 'Turbulence at the Top: A New Perspective on Governance Structure Changes and Strategic Change', *Academy of Management Journal*, 34: 306–30.

—— Gautam, K., and Boeker, W. (1994), 'The Effects of Board Size and Diversity on Strategic Change', *Strategic Management Journal*, 15: 241–50.

Goold, M., and Campbell, A. (1987), *Strategies and Styles* (Oxford: Basil Blackwell).

—— —— (1990), 'The Non-Executive Director's Role in Strategy', *Long Range Planning*, 23: 118–19.

—— and Quinn, J. J. (1990a), 'The Paradox of Strategic Controls', *Strategic Management Journal*, 11: 43–58.

—— —— (1990b), *Strategic Control: Milestones for Long-Term Performance* (London: Hutchinson).

GRANOVETTER, M. S. (1973), 'The Strength of Weak Ties', *American Journal of Sociology*, 78: 1360–80.

GREENBURY, R. (1995*a*), *Directors' Remuneration: Report of a Study Group Chaired by Sir Richard Greenbury* (London: Gee & Co.).

—— (1995*b*), 'On Board Meetings', *Corporate Governance—An International Review*, 3: 7–8.

GREGG, P. , MACHIN, S., and SZYMANSKI, S. (1993), 'The Disappearing Relationship between Directors' Pay and Corporate Performance', *British Journal of Industrial Relations*, 31: 1–9.

GUPTA, A., and GOVINDARAJAN, V. (1984), 'Business Unit Strategy, Managerial Characteristics and Business Unit Effectiveness at Strategy Implementation', *Academy of Management Journal*, 27: 25–42.

HABERMAS, J. (1971), *Knowledge and Human Interests* (London: Hutchinson).

HAMBRICK, D., and MASON, P. (1984), 'Upper Echelons: The Organization as a Reflection of its Top Managers', *Academy of Management Review*, 9: 193–206.

HAMEL, G. (1990), 'Competitive Collaboration: Learning, Power and Dependence in International Strategic Alliances', unpublished doctoral dissertation, Graduate School of Business Administration, University of Michigan.

—— and PRAHALAD, C. K. (1994), *Competing for the Future* (Boston: Harvard Business School Press).

HAMPEL REPORT (1998), *Committee on Corporate Governance, Final Report* (London: Gee Publishing).

HARRE, R., and SECORD, P. F. (1973), *The Explanation of Social Behaviour* (Totowa, NJ: Littlefield, Adams).

HARRISON, J. R. (1987), 'The Strategic Use of Corporate Board Committees', *California Management Review*, 30: 109–25.

HARVEY-JONES, SIR JOHN (1988), *Making it Happen: Reflections on Leadership* (London: Collins).

HAWLEY, J. P. , and WILLIAMS, A. T. (1997), 'The Emergence of Fiduciary Capitalism', *Corporate Governance—An International Review*, 5: 206–13.

HENDRY, J. (1997), 'An Alternative Model of Agency Theory and its Application to Corporate Governance', Judge Institute of Management Studies Working Paper, University of Cambridge.

—— JOHNSON, G., and NEWTON, J. (1993) (eds.), *Strategy Thinking, Leadership, and the Management of Change* (Chichester: Wiley).

HENKE, J. W. (1986), 'Involving the Directors in Strategic Planning', *Journal of Business Strategy*, 7: 87–95.

HERMALIN, B. E., and WEISBACH, M. S. (1991), 'The Effects of Board Composition and Direct Incentives on Firm Performance', *Financial Management*, 20: 101–12.

HERMAN, E. (1981), *Corporate Control, Corporate Power* (New York: Cambridge University Press).

HERZBERG, F., MAUSNER, B., and SNYDERMAN, B. B. (1967), *The Motivation to Work* (2nd edn.; New York: Wiley).

HICKSON, D. J., HININGS, C. R., LEE, C. A., SCHNECK, R. E., and PENNINGS, J. M. (1971), 'A Strategic Contingency Theory of Interorganizational Power', *Administrative Science Quarterly*, 16: 216–29.

HILL, C. W. L., and JONES, T. M. (1992), 'Stakeholder-Agency Theory', *Journal of Management Studies*, 29: 131–54.

HILL, S. (1995), 'The Social Organization of Boards of Directors', *British Journal of Sociology*, 46: 245–78.

HILMER, F. G. (1993*a*), 'The Functions of the Board: A Performance-Based View', *Corporate Governance—An International Review*, 2: 170–9.

—— (1993*b*), *Strictly Boardroom* (Melbourne: Information Australia).

—— and TRICKER, R. I. (1994), *An Effective Board: Corporate Governance for Directors* (London: Director Books).

HOSKING, D. M. (1996), 'Negotiated Order', in N. Nicholson (ed.), *Encyclopaedic Dictionary of Organizational Behaviour* (Oxford: Blackwell Business), 342.

HOSMER, L.T. (1985), 'Trust: The Connecting Link between Organizational Theory and Philosophical Ethics', *Academy of Management Review*, 20: 379–403.

—— (1991), *The Ethics of Management* (Homewood, Ill.: Irwin).

HUGHES, J. A. (1990), *The Philosophy of Social Research* (2nd edn., Harlow: Longman).

HUSELID, M. (1995), 'The Impact of Human Resource Management Practices on Turnover, Productivity and Corporate Financial Performance', *Academy of Management Journal*, 38: 635–72.

HUSSERL, E. (1946), 'Phenomenology', in *Encyclopaedia Britannica*, 14th edn., xvii. 699–702.

ICA (1991): Institute of Chartered Secretaries and Administrators, *Good Boardroom Practice: A Code for Directors and Companies and Secretaries* (London: Institute of Chartered Secretaries and Administrators).

ICAEW (1991): Institute of Chartered Accountants of England and Wales, *Report of the Study Group on the Change in the Role of the Non-Executive Director* (London: ICAEW).

IOD (1995): Institute of Directors, *Standards of Good Practice for Boards of Directors* (London: Institute of Directors).

— (1996), *Guidelines for Directors* (London: Director Books).

ISABELLA, L. M. (1990), 'Evolving Interpretations as a Change Unfolds: How Managers Construe Key Organizational Events', *Academy of Management Journal*, 33: 7–41.

ISAKSSON, M., and SKOG, R. (1994) (eds.), *Aspects of Corporate Governance* (Stockholm: Corporate Governance Forum, Juristforlaget).

ISC (1991): Institutional Shareholders' Committee, *The Roles and Duties of Directors—A Statement of Best Practice* (London: ISC).

JACKSON, T. (1998), *Morality Meets Mammon: Responsible Business in the Global Economy* (London: FT Publications).

JANIS, I. (1983), *Groupthink: Psychological Studies of Policy Decisions and Fiascos* (2nd edn.; Boston: Houghton Mifflin).

JENSEN, M., and MECKLING, W. (1976), 'Theory of the Firm: Managerial Behaviour, Agency Costs and Ownership Structure', *Journal of Financial Economics*, 3: 305–60.

JICK, T. D. (1979), 'Mixing Qualitative and Quantitative Methods: Triangulation in Action', *Administrative Science Quarterly*, 24: 602–11.

JOHNSON, G., and SCHOLES, K. (1988), *Exploring Corporate Strategy* (2nd edn., London: Prentice-Hall).

JOHNSON, J. L., DAILY, C. M., and ELLSTRAND, A. E. (1996), 'Boards of Directors: A Review and Research Agenda', *Journal of Management*, 22: 409–38.

JONES, G. R., and GEORGE, J. M. (1998), 'The Experience and Evolution of Trust: Implications for Cooperation and Teamwork', *Academy of Management Review*, 23: 531–46.

JONES, T. M. (1986), 'Corporate Board Structure and Performance: Variations in the Incidence of Shareholder Suits', in L. Preston (ed.), *Research in Corporate Social Performance and Policy*, 8: 345–59.

—— and GOLDBERG, L. D. (1982), 'Governing the Large Corporation: More Arguments for Public Directors', *Academy of Management Review*, 7: 603–11.

JUDGE, W. Q., and ZEITHAML, C. P. (1992), 'Institutional and Strategic Choice Perspectives on Board Involvement in the Strategic Decision Process', *Academy of Management Journal*, 35: 766–94.

KAY, J. (1994), 'Corporate Strategy and Corporate Accountability', in N. H. Dimsdale and M. Prevezer (eds.), *Capital Markets and Corporate Governance* (Oxford: Clarendon Press), 50–64.

—— and SILBERSTON, A. (1995), 'Corporate Governance', *National Institute Economic Review*, 84: 84–97.

KEASEY, K., and WRIGHT, M. (1997) (eds.), *Corporate Governance: Responsibilities, Risks and Remuneration* (Chichester: Wiley).

—— THOMPSON, S., and WRIGHT, M. (1997) (eds.), *Corporate Governance: Economic, Management and Financial Issues* (Oxford: Oxford University Press).

KERR, J., and BETTIS, R. A. (1987), 'Boards of Directors, Top Management Compensation and Shareholders' Returns', *Academy of Management Journal*, 30: 645–64.

—— and KREN, L. (1992), 'Effect of Relative Decision Monitoring on CEO Compensation', *Academy of Management Journal*, 35: 370–97.

KESNER, I. F. (1987), 'Directors' Stock Ownership and Organizational Performance: An Investigation of Fortune 500 Companies', *Journal of Management*, 13: 499–508.

—— and JOHNSON, R. B. (1990), 'An Investigation of the Relationship between Board Composition and Stockholder Suits', *Strategic Management Journal*, 11: 327–36.

—— VICTOR, B., and LAMONT, B. T. (1986), 'Board Composition and the Commission of Illegal Acts: An Investigation of Fortune 500 Companies', *Academy of Management Journal*, 29: 789–99.

KESTER, W. C. (1992), 'Industrial Groups as Systems of Contractual Governance', *Oxford Review of Economic Policy*, 8: 24–44.

KNOEBER, C. R. (1986), 'Golden Parachutes, Shark Repellents and Hostile Tender Offers', *American Economic Review*, 76: 155–67.

KOENIG, T., GOGEL, R., and SONQUIST, J. (1979), 'Models of the Significance of Interlocking Directorates', *American Journal of Economics and Sociology*, 38: 173–86.

KOSNIK, R. (1987), 'Greenmail: A Study of Board Performance in Corporate Governance', *Administrative Science Quarterly*, 32: 163–85.

KRAMER, R., and TYLER, T. (1996) (eds.), *Trust in Organizations: Frontiers in Theory and Research* (London: Sage).

LAMBERT, R. A., and LARCKER, D. F. (1985), 'Golden Parachutes, Executive Decision-Making and Shareholder Wealth', *Journal of Accounting and Economics*, 5: 3–30.

LANG, J. R., and LOCKHART, D. E. (1990), 'Increased Environmental Uncertainty and Changes in Board Linkage Patterns', *Academy of Management Journal*, 33: 106–28.

LAUENSTEIN, M. (1977), 'Preserving the Importance of the Board', *Harvard Business Review*, 55: 36–46.

LAWLER, E. E. III. (1987), 'Pay for Performance: A Motivational Analysis', in H. R. Nalbantian (ed.), *Incentives, Cooperation and Risk Sharing* (Totowa, NJ: Rowman and Littlefield), 69–86.

LAWRENCE, P. R., and LORSCH, J. (1967), *Organization and Environment* (Boston: Harvard Business School Press).

LEAVITT, H. J., and LIPMAN-BLUMAN, J. (1985), 'Hot Groups', *Harvard Business Review*, 73/4: 109–17.

LEWICKI, R. J., MCALLISTER, D. J., and BIES, R. J. (1998), 'Trust and Distrust: New Relationships and Realities', *Academy of Management Review*, 24: 438–58.

LIPTON, M., and LORSCH, J. W. (1992), 'A Modest Proposal for Improved Corporate Govern- ance', *Business Lawyer*, 48: 59–77.

—— and PANNER, M. (1993), 'Takeover Bids and United States Corporate Governance', in D. D. Prentice and P. R. J. Holland (eds.), *Contemporary Issues in Corporate Governance* (Oxford: Clarendon Press), 115–34.

LOOSE, P. , and YELLAND, J. (1987), *The Company Director: His Functions, Powers and Duties* (6th edn., London: Jordans).

LORANGE, P, MORTON, M. F. S., and GHOSHAL, S. (1986), *Strategic Control* (St Paul, Minn: West Publishing).

LORSCH, J. W., and MACIVER, E. (1989), *Pawns or Potentates: The Reality of America's Corporate Boards* (Boston: Harvard Business School Press).

LUHMANN, N. (1979), *Trust and Power* (Chichester: Wiley).

McCLELLAND, D. C. (1961), *The Achieving Society* (Princeton: Van Nostrand).

McNULTY, T., and PETTIGREW, A. (1999), 'Strategists on the Board', *Organization Studies*, 20: 47–74.

MACE, M. L. (1971), *Directors: Myth and Reality* (Boston: Harvard University Graduate School of Business Administration).

MAIN, B. (1993), 'Pay in the Boardroom: Practices and Procedures', *Personnel Review*, 22: 3–14.

—— and JOHNSON, J. (1992), 'Deciding of Top Pay by Committee', *Personnel Management*, 22: 32–5.

MALLETTE, P. , and FOWLER, K. L. (1992), 'Effects of Board Composition and Stock Ownership on the Adoption of Poison Pills', *Academy of Management Journal*, 35: 1010–35.

MARSH, P. R. (1990), *Short-Termism on Trial* (London: Institutional Fund Managers Association).

MARSTON, C. (1993), 'Investor Relations Project', university paper (University of Northumbria at Newcastle, Newcastle Business School, and University of Glasgow).

MARTIN, C. (1985), 'Accessing and Interviewing Senior Managers', *Graduate Management Research*, 2: 13–23.

MEYER, C. (1997), 'Corporate Governance, Competition and Performance', in S.Deakin and A. Hughes (eds.), *Enterprise and Community: New Directions in Corporate Governance* (Oxford: Basil Blackwell), 152–76.

MILES, M. B., and HUBERMAN, A. M. (1994), *Qualitative Data Analysis: A Source Book of New Methods* (2nd edn., Beverly Hills, Calif.: Sage).

MILLER, D., and FRIESEN, P. H. (1984), *Organizations—A Quantum View* (Englewood Cliffs: Prentice-Hall).

MILLER, D. J. (1995), 'CEO Salary Increases may be Rational after all: Referents and Contracts in CEO Pay', *Academy of Management Journal*, 38: 1361–85.

MILLS, C. W. (1956), *The Power Elite* (London: Oxford University Press).

MILLS, G. (1981), *On the Board* (Chichester: Wiley).

MINTZBERG , H. (1973), *The Nature of Managerial Work* (New York: Harper & Row).

—— (1978), 'Patterns in Strategy Formation', *Management Science*, 24: 934–48.

—— (1983), *Power in and around Organizations* (Englewood Cliffs, NJ: Prentice-Hall).

—— and WATERS, J. A. (1985), 'Of Strategies, Deliberate and Emergent', *Strategic Management Journal*, 6: 257–72.

MIZRUCHI, M. S. (1983), 'Who Controls Whom? An Examination of the Relation between Management and Boards of Directors in Large American Corporations', *Academy of Man- agement Review*, 8: 426–35.

Mizruchi, M. S. (1992), *The Structure of Corporate Political Action: Interfirm Relations and their Consequences* (Cambridge, Mass: Harvard University Press).

—— and Schwarz, M. (1988), *Intercorporate Relations: The Structural Analysis of Business* (New York: Cambridge University Press).

Molz, R. (1985), 'The Role of the Board of Directors: Typologies of Interaction', *Journal of Business Strategy*, 5: 86–93.

—— (1988), 'Managerial Domination of Boards of Directors and Financial Performance', *Journal of Business Research*, 16: 235–50.

Monks, R.A.G., and Minow, N. (1990), *Power and Accountability* (New York: HarperCollins).

—— —— (1995), *Corporate Governance* (Oxford: Basil Blackwell).

Moyser, G. M., and Wagstaff, M. (1987a), 'Studying Elites: Theoretical and Methodological Issues', in G. M. Moyser and M. Wagstaff (eds.), *Research Methods for Elite Studies* (London: Allen & Unwin), 1–24.

—— —— (1987b) (eds.), *Research Methods for Elite Studies* (London: Allen & Unwin).

Murphy, K. (1985), 'Corporate Performance and Managerial Remuneration: An Empirical Examination', *Journal of Accounting and Economics*, 7: 11–42.

Myners, P. (1995), *Developing a Winning Partnership: How Companies and Institutional Investors are Working Together* (London: HMSO).

Nader, R. (1984), 'Reforming Corporate Governance', *California Management Review*, 26: 126–32.

Nicols, T. (1969), *Ownership, Control and Ideology* (London: George Allen & Unwin).

Noda, T., and Bower, J. L. (1996), 'Strategy Making as Iterated Processes of Resource Allocation', *Strategic Management Journal*, 17 (special issue: Summer), 159–92.

Norburn, D. (1989), 'The Chief Executive: A Breed Apart', *Strategic Management Journal*, 10: 1–15.

—— and Grinyer, P. (1974), 'Directors without Direction', *Journal of General Management*, 1: 30–9.

—— and Schurz, F. (1988), 'The British Boardroom: Time for a Revolution?', in B. Taylor (ed.), *Strategic Planning, the Chief Executive and the Board* (Oxford: Pergamon Press).

Nystrom, P. C., and Starbuck, W. H. (1984), 'To Avoid Crises, Unlearn', *Organizational Dynamics*, 13: 53–65.

OECD (1998), *Corporate Governance* (Paris: OECD).

Oliver, C. (1991), 'Strategic Responses to Institutional Processes', *Academy of Management Review*, 16: 145–79.

O'Neal, D., and Thomas, H. (1995), 'Director Networks/Director Selection: The Board's Strategic Role', *European Management Journal*, 13: 7990.

O'Reilly, J. (1994), *Banking on Flexibility* (Aldershot: Avebury Press).

Osborne, R. N., Jauch, L. R., Martin, T. N., and Glueck, W. F. (1981), 'The Event of CEO Succession, Performance and Environmental Conditions', *Academy of Management Journal*, 24: 183–91.

O'Toole, J. (1991), 'Do Good, Do Well: The Business Enterprise Trust Awards', *California Management Review*, 33: 9–24.

Oviatt, B. M. (1988), 'Agency and Transaction Cost Perspectives on the Manager–Shareholder Relationship: Incentives for Congruent Interests', *Academy of Management Review*, 13: 214–25.

Oxford Analytica (1992), *Board Directors and Corporate Governance: Trends in the G7 Countries over the Next Ten Years* (Oxford: Oxford Analytica Ltd.).

Pahl, R. E., and Winkler, J. T. (1974), 'The Economic Elite: Theory and Practice', in P. J.

Stanworth and A. Giddens (eds.), *Elites and Power in British Society* (Cambridge: Cambridge University Press), 103–28.

PARKER, H. (1990), *Letters to a New Chairman* (London: Director Books).

PARKHE, A. (1993), ' "Messy" Research, Methodological Predispositions, and Theory Development in International Joint Ventures', *Academy of Management Review*, 18: 227–68.

PARKINSON, J. E. (1993), *Corporate Power and Responsibility* (Oxford: Oxford University Press).

PATTON, A., and BAKER, J. C. (1987), 'Why won't Directors Rock the Boat?', *Harvard Business Review*, 65: 10–18.

PAUL, A. (1993), 'Corporate Governance in the Context of Takeovers of UK Public Companies', in D. D. Prentice and P. R. J. Holland (eds.), *Contemporary Issues in Corporate Governance* (Oxford: Clarendon Press), 135–50.

PEARCE, J. A. (1983), 'The Relationship of Internal versus External Orientations to Financial Measures of Strategic Performance', *Strategic Management Journal*, 4: 297–306.

—— and ZAHRA, S. A. (1991), 'The Relative Power of CEOs and Boards of Directors: Associations with Corporate Performance', *Strategic Management Journal*, 12: 135–53.

—— —— (1992), 'Board Composition and Strategic Contingency', *Journal of Management Studies*, 20: 410–38.

PECK, E. (1995), 'The Performance of an NHS Trust Board: Actors' Accounts, Minutes and Observations', *British Journal of Management*, 6: 135–56.

PENNINGS, J. M. (1980), *Interlocking Directorates* (San Francisco: Jossey-Bass).

PERROW, C. (1986), *Complex Organizations: A Critical Essay* (New York: McGraw-Hill),

PETTIGREW, A. M. (1973), *The Politics of Organisational Decision-Making* (London: Tavistock).

—— (1985), *The Awakening Giant: Continuity and Change in ICI* (Oxford: Basil Blackwell).

—— (1990), 'Longitudinal Field Research on Change: Theory and Practice', *Organization Science*, 1: 267–92.

—— (1992), 'On Studying Managerial Elites', *Strategic Management Journal*, 13: 163–82.

—— and McNULTY, T. (1995), 'Power and Influence in and around the Boardroom', *Human Relations*, 8: 845–73.

PFEFFER, J. (1972), 'Size and Composition of Corporate Boards of Directors: The Organization and its Environment', *Administrative Science Quarterly*, 17: 218–29.

—— (1973), 'Size, Composition and Function of Hospital Boards of Directors: A Study of Organization–Environment Linkage', *Administrative Science Quarterly*, 18: 349–64.

—— (1987), 'A Resource Dependence Perspective on Intercorporate Relations', in M. S. Mizruchi and M. Schwartz (eds.), *Intercorporate Relations: The Structural Analysis of Business* (Cambridge: Cambridge University Press), 25–55.

—— (1994), *Competitive Advantage through People* (Boston: Harvard Business School Press).

—— and SALANCIK, G. R. (1978), *The External Control of Organizations: A Resource Dependence View* (New York: Harper & Row).

PIRC (1998): Pensions Investment Research Consultants, *Non-Executive Directors in FTSE 350 Companies: Assessing Independence* (London: PIRC).

PLENDER, J. (1997), *A Stake in the Future: The Stakeholding Solution* (London: Heinemann).

PORTER, M. E. (1988), *Competitive Strategy* (New York: Free Press).

—— (1991), 'Towards a Dynamic Theory of Strategy', *Strategic Management Journal*, 12: 95–117.

—— (1992), *Capital Choices: Changing the Way America Invests in Industry* (Washington: Council on Competitiveness).

POUND, J. (1992), 'Beyond Takeovers: Politics Comes to Corporate Control', *Harvard Business Review*, 70: 83–93.

PREBLE, J. F. (1992), 'Towards a Comprehensive System of Strategic Control', *Journal of Management Studies*, 29: 391–410.

PRENTICE, D. D. (1993), 'Some Aspects of the Corporate Governance Debate', in D. D. Prentice and P. R. J. Holland (eds.), *Contemporary Issues in Corporate Governance* (Oxford: Clarendon Press), 25–42.

—— and HOLLAND, P. R. J. (1993), (eds.), *Contemporary Issues in Corporate Governance* (Oxford: Clarendon Press).

PREVEZER, M., and RICKETTS, M. (1994), 'Corporate Governance: The UK Compared with Germany and Japan', in N. H. Dimsdale and M. Prevezer (eds.), *Capital Markets and Corporate Governance* (Oxford: Clarendon Press), 237–56.

PRONED (1987), *A Practical Guide for Non-Executive Directors* (London: ProNed).

PROSHARE (1998), *Share Ownership in the UK: Investor Update Newsletter* (London: ProShare).

PROVAN, J. G. (1980), 'Board Power and Organizational Effectiveness among Human Service Agencies', *Academy of Management Journal*, 23: 221–36.

PUGH, D. S. (1983), 'Studying Organizational Structure and Process', in G. Morgan (ed.), *Beyond Method* (Beverly Hills, Calif.: Sage).

RECHNER, P. L., and DALTON, D. R. (1991), 'CEO Duality and Organizational Performance: A Longitudinal Analysis', *Strategic Management Journal*, 12: 155–60.

REDLING, E. T. (1981), 'Myth vs Reality. The Relationship between Top Executive Pay and Corporate Performance', *Compensation Review*, 4: 16–24.

ROBERTS, J. (1998), 'Trust and Control in the UK System of Corporate Governance: The Constitutive Effects of Different Forms of Accountability on Agency', paper presented to the 14th EGOS colloquium, Maastricht.

ROE, M. J. (1996), *Strong Managers, Weak Owners: The Political Roots of American Corporate Finance* (Princeton: Princeton University Press).

RORTY, R. (1980), *Philosophy and the Mirror of Nature* (Oxford: Basil Blackwell).

ROSENSTEIN, J. (1987), 'Why don't US Boards get More Involved in Strategy?', *Long Range Planning*, 20: 20–34.

ROSS, S. (1973), 'The Economic Theory of Agency: The Principal's Problem', *American Economic Review*, 63: 134–9.

RSA (1995): Royal Society of Arts, *Tomorrow's Company* (London: RSA Publications).

RUMELT, R. P. , SCHENDEL, D., and TEECE, D. J. (1991), 'Strategic Management and Economics', *Strategic Management Journal*, 12: 5–29.

SAHLMAN, W. A. (1990), 'Why Sane People shouldn't Serve on Public Boards', *Harvard Business Review*, 68: 28–36.

SCHLEIFER, A., and VISHNY, R. W. (1997), 'A Survey of Corporate Governance', *Journal of Finance*, 52: 737–83.

SCHREYOGG, G., and STEINMAN, H. (1987), 'Strategic Control: A New Perspective', *Academy of Management Review*, 12: 91–103.

SCOTT, J. P. (1985), *Corporations, Classes and Capitalism* (2nd edn., London: Hutchinson).

—— (1987), 'Intercorporate Structures in Western Europe: A Comparative Historical Perspective', in M. S. Mizruchi and M. Schwartz (eds.), *Intercorporate Relations: The Structural Analysis of Business* (Cambridge: Cambridge University Press), 208–32.

—— (1990) (ed.), *The Sociology of Elites* (Aldershot: Edward Elgar), ii.

—— (1991*a*), 'Networks of Corporate Power: A Comparative Assessment', *Annual Review of Sociology*, 17: 181–203.

—— (1991*b*), *Who Rules Britain?* (Cambridge: Polity).

—— (1997), *Corporate Business and Capitalist Classes* (Oxford: Oxford University Press).

—— and GRIFF, C. (1984), *Directors of Industry* (Cambridge: Polity).

SHEPPARD, B. H. (1995), 'Negotiating in Long-Term Mutually Interdependent Relationships among Relative Equals', in R. J. Bies, R. J. Lewicki , and B. H.Sheppard (eds.), *Research on Negotiations in Organizations* (Greenwich, Conn.: JAI Press), 5: 3–44.

SHORT, H., and KEASEY, K. (1997), 'Institutional Shareholders and Corporate Governance', in K. Keasey and M. Wright (eds.), *Corporate Governance: Responsibilities, Risks and Remuneration* (Chichester: Wiley), 23–60.

SIMON, H. A. (1976), *Administrative Behaviour* (3rd edn., New York: Free Press).

SIMONS, R. (1991), 'Strategic Orientation and Top Management Attention to Control Systems', *Strategic Management Journal*, 12: 49–62.

—— (1994), *Levers of Control: How Managers Use Innovative Control Systems to Drive Strategic Renewal* (Boston: Harvard Business School Press).

SINGH, H., and HARIANTO, F. (1989), 'Top Management Tenure, Corporate Ownership Structure and the Magnitude of Golden Parachutes', *Strategic Management Journal*, 10: 143–56.

SMITH, T. (1996), *Accounting for Growth: Stripping the Camouflage from Company Accounts* (2nd edn., London: Century Business).

SNELL, S. A., and DEAN, J. W. (1992), 'Integrated Manufacturing and Human Resource Management: A Human Capital Perspective', *Academy of Management Journal*, 35: 467–504.

SNOW, C. C., and THOMAS, J. B. (1994), 'Field Research Methods in Strategic Management: Contributions to Theory Building and Testing', *Journal of Management Studies*, 31: 457–80.

SOREF, M., and ZEITLIN, M. (1988), 'Finance Capital and the Internal Structure of the Capitalist Class in the United States', in M. S. Mizruchi and M. Schwartz (eds.), *Intercorporate Relations: The Structural Analysis of Business* (Cambridge: Cambridge University Press), 56–84.

SPENCER, A. (1983), *On the Edge of the Organization: The Role of the Outside Director* (New York: Wiley).

STANWORTH, P. J., and GIDDENS, A. (1974) (eds.), *Elites and Power in British Society* (Cambridge: Cambridge University Press).

STEWART, R. (1991), 'Chairman and Chief Executives: An Explanation of their Relationship', *Journal of Management Studies*, 28: 511–27.

STRAUSS, A. L. (1978), *Negotiations: Varieties, Contexts, Processes and Social Order* (San Francisco: Free Press).

SULLIVAN, M. K. (1988), 'Outsider versus Insider Boards Revisited: A New Look at Performance and Board Composition', paper presented to the Academy of Management, Anaheim, California.

SZYMANSKI, S. (1992), 'Directors' Pay Incentives in the 1980s: The UK Experience', London Business School Centre for Business Strategy, Working Paper.

TASHAKORI, A., and BOULTON, W. (1985), 'A Look at the Board's Role in Planning', *Journal of Business Strategy*, 3: 64–70.

TAYLOR, B. (1988) (ed.), *Strategic Planning, the Chief Executive and the Board* (Oxford: Pergamon Press).

—— and TRICKER, R. I. (1990) (eds.), *The Director's Manual* (London: Director Books).

TAYLOR, S. A. and BOGDAN, R. (1984), *Introduction to Qualitative Research Methods* (New York: Wiley-Interscience).

TOOTELIAN, D. H., and GADEAKE, R. N. (1987), 'Fortune 500 List Revisited 12 Years Later: Still an Endangered Species for Academic Research', *Journal of Business Research*, 5: 359–63.

TOSI, H. L., and GOMEZ-MEJIA, L. R. (1989), 'The Decoupling of CEO Pay and Performance: An Agency Theory Perspective', *Administrative Science Quarterly*, 34: 169–89.

TRICKER, R. I. (1984), *Corporate Governance* (Aldershot: Gower).

TRICKER, R. I. (1994), Editorial, *Corporate Governance: An International Review*, 2: 2–3.

—— (1995), *International Corporate Governance: Text, Readings and Cases* (London: Simon & Schuster).

TRUSS, C., GRATTON, L., HOPE, V., MCGOVERN., P. , and STILES, P. (1997), 'Strategic Integration and the Employment Contract: New Forms of Human Resource Management', *Journal of Management Studies*, 34: 70–86.

TSUI, A. S. (1990), 'A Multiple Constituency Model of Effectiveness: An Empirical Examination at the Human Resource Sub-Unit Level', *Administrative Science Quarterly*, 35: 458–83.

—— (1994), 'Reputational Effectiveness: Towards a Mutual Responsiveness Framework', in B. M. Staw and L. L. Cummings (eds.), *Research in Organizational Behaviour* (Greenwich, Conn.: JAI Press), 16: 257–307.

TURNBULL, S. (1997), 'Corporate Governance: Its Scope, Concerns and Theories', *Corporate Governance: An International Review*, 5: 180–205.

TURNBULL REPORT (1999), *Internal Control: Guidance for Directors on the Combined Code* (London: ICAEW).

USEEM, M. (1979), 'The Social Organization of the American Business Elite and Participation of Corporation Directors in the Government of American Institutions', *American Sociological Review*, 44: 553–71.

—— (1984), *The Inner Circle: Large Corporations and the Rise of Business Political Activity in the US and UK* (New York: Oxford University Press).

—— (1993), *Executive Defense: Shareholder Power and Corporate Reorganization* (Boston: Harvard Business School Press).

—— BOWMAN, E. H., MYATT, J., and IRVINE, C.W. (1993), 'US Institutional Investors Look at Corporate Governance in the 1990s', *European Management Journal*, 11: 175–89.

VANCE, S. C. (1983), *Corporate Leadership: Boards, Directors and Strategy* (New York: McGraw-Hill).

VAN MAANEN, J. (1979), 'The Fact of Fiction in Organizational Ethnography', *Administrative Science Quarterly*, 24: 539–55.

VOGEL, D. (1983), 'Trends in Shareholder Activism: 1970–1982', *California Management Review*, 25: 68–87.

WALSH, J. P. , and SEWARD, J. K. (1990), 'On the Efficiency of Internal and External Control Mechanisms', *Academy of Management Review*, 15: 421–58.

WANG, J., and DEWHIRST, D. H. (1992), 'Boards of Directors and Stakeholder Orientation', *Journal of Business Ethics*, 11: 115–23.

WARNER, J. B., WATTS, R. L., and WRUCK, K. H. (1988), 'Stock Prices and Top Management Changes', *Journal of Financial Economics*, 20: 461–92.

WEICK, K. E. (1979), *The Social Psychology of Organizing* (Reading, Mass.: Addison Wesley).

WEIDENBAUM, M. L. (1985), 'The Best Defence against the Raiders', *Business Week*, 23 (Sept.), 21.

—— (1986), 'Updating the Corporate Board', *Journal of Business Strategy*, 7: 77–230.

WEISBACH, M. S. (1988), 'Outside Directors and CEO Turnover', *Journal of Financial Economics*, 20: 431–60.

WESTPHAL, J. D. (1996), 'Illuminating the Black Box: Board Structure and Behavioural Processes in Management/Board Relationships', unpublished doctoral dissertation, Northwestern University.

—— and ZAJAC, E J. (1995a), 'Defections from the Inner Circle: Social Exchange, Reciprocity and the Diffusion of Board Independence in US Corporations', *Academy of Management Best Papers Proceedings*, 281–5.

—— —— (1995*b*), 'Who shall Govern? CEO/Board Power, Demographic Similarity and New Director Selection', *Administrative Science Quarterly*, 40: 60–83.

—— —— (1997), 'Defections from the Inner Circle: Social Exchange, Reciprocity and the Diffusion of Board Independence in US Corporations', *Administrative Science Quarterly*, 42: 161–83.

WHITTINGTON, G. (1993), 'Corporate Governance and the Regulation of Financial Reporting', *Accounting and Business Research*, 23: 311–20.

WILLIAMS, B. A. O. (1985), *Ethics and the Limits of Philosophy* (Cambridge, Mass.: Harvard University Press).

WILLIAMSON, O. E. (1975), *Markets and Hierarchies* (New York: Free Press).

—— (1984), 'Corporate Governance', *Yale Law Journal*, 93: 1197–230.

—— (1985), *The Economic Institutions of Capitalism* (New York: Free Press).

WINKLER, J. T. (1987), 'The Fly on the Wall of the Inner Sanctum: Observing Company Directors at Work', in G. M. Moyser and M. Wagstaff (eds.), *Research Methods for Elite Studies* (London: Allen & Unwin), 129–46.

WOOD, M. M. (1983), 'From the Boardroom: What Role for College Trustees?', *Harvard Business Review*, 61: 52–62.

WORKING GROUP ON CORPORATE GOVERNANCE (1991), 'New Compact for Owners and Directors', *Harvard Business Review*, 69: 142–3.

YIN, R. K. (1984), *Case Study Research: Design and Methods* (Beverly-Hills, Calif.: Sage).

ZAHRA, S. A. (1990), 'Increasing the Board's Involvement in Strategy', *Long Range Planning*, 23: 109–17.

—— and PEARCE, J. A. (1989), 'Boards of Directors and Corporate Financial Performance: A Review and Integrative Model', *Journal of Management*, 15: 291–334.

ZAJAC, E. J. (1990), 'CEO Selection, Succession, Compensation and Firm Performance: A Theoretical Integration and Empirical Analysis', *Strategic Management Journal*, 11: 217–30.

—— and WESTPHAL, J. D. (1996), 'Director Reputation, CEO-Board Power, and the Dynamics of Board Interlocks', *Administrative Science Quarterly*, 41: 507–29.

ZALD, M. N. (1967), 'Urban Differentiation, Characteristics of Boards of Directors, and Organizational Effectiveness', *American Journal of Sociology*, 73: 261–72.

—— (1969), 'The Power and Functions of Boards of Directors: A Theoretical Synthesis', *American Journal of Sociology*, 74: 97–111.

ZEITLIN, M. (1974), 'Corporate Ownership and Control: The Large Corporation and the Capitalist Class', *American Journal of Sociology*, 79: 1073–119.

Index

Burmah Castrol (*cont.*)
  strategic role 54–5, 57–8
Burman, C. 8
Burt, R. S. 16, 86 n., 133
Business in Community 7
business definition and strategic role 38–40, 53–6

cabal and strategic role 49–50
Cadbury, Sir Adrian: Cadbury Report (1992) on
      financial aspects of corporate governance
      v, vi, 4, 6
  and control role 62, 65, 69–70, 75, 121
  and dynamics of process 107, 112
  and institutional role 87, 92, 93, 95
  and strategic role 51
  and theoretical debates 10, 11–12
Campbell, A. 39, 45
capital:
  access to 87
  see also finance; shareholders
care and skill, duty of 12, 62
Carlton 5
case studies 28–9, 30
  of control role 80–5
    audit committees 84
    diagnosis, control as 82–4
    informal reviews 84–5
    rewards and sanctions 85
  institutional role 101–5
    boundary-spanning 104–5
    external relations 101–3
    stakeholders 103–4
  of strategic role 53–9
    business definition 53–6
    confidence-building 58–9
    discipline 57–8
    gatekeeping 56–7
CEO (chief executive) 4, 19, 115
  and AGMs 93
  assessment of 73–8
  and chairman 107–8
  chairman as former 107–8, 111, 132
  compensation and remuneration 75–7
  and control role of board 63, 66–7, 73–8, 79
  and director selection 125
  disciplining directors 77–8
  dismissal 21, 45, 50, 63, 78, 89, 120, 121
  and duality 16
  and finance meetings 90–1, 100
  hiring and firing, see CEO, dismissal; CEO,
    selection
  isolation of 107

monitored 23, 67
  on other boards 99
  personality of 77–8
  selection 6, 21, 45–6, 77, 120
  and strategic role 42, 45–6, 47, 49, 50, 120
  see also executives
Chaganti, R. S. 130, 132
chairman of board 4
  and AGM 93
  and appointments 46–7
  and CEO 107–8
  as former CEO 107–8, 111, 132
  in inner cabinet 49
  and institutional role 93, 122, 128
  and mission and values 39–40
  as non-executive 111, 132
  role in managing relationships 111–13
  and strategic role 39–40, 42, 46–7, 49, 120
Chandler, A. D. 34, 62
changing expectations 1–9
  corporate governance, rise of 5–8
  domain of Board 4–5
Charkham, J. 1, 10, 87, 88, 90, 92–3
chief executive, see CEO
Chisholm, S. 5
class-hegemony theory 10, 11, 17–18, 19–20
  and control role 62
  empirical support 133
  and strategic role 53
coalition 109
Coase, R. 14
Cochran, P. L. 131, 132
Coffee, J. C. 7
collaboration 106
Coloroll 5, 95
Combined Code (1998) v, 6, 10
committees 112
  auditing 69–70, 84
  board 4
  executive 41–2
  institutional shareholders 27, 31
communication:
  clarity and saliency 125
  electronic 95, 129
  see also information
Companies Acts v, 11–12, 32
compensation, see pay
complementarity 109
confidence-building and strategic role 44–5,
      51–2, 58–9, 120
conflict:
  and creativity 108, 113

160   *Index*

Loose, P. 10
Lorange, P. 64
Lorsch, J. W. and McIver, E. 5
  and control role 73, 78, 110
  and empirical support 134, 135
  and strategic role 31, 32, 34, 52
  and theoretical debates 10, 16, 22, 24, 27
Luhmann, N. 3

Maanen, J. van 30
McAllister 114
McClelland, D. C. 16
Mace, M. L. 27, 78, 110, 119
  and empirical support 134, 135
  and strategic role 31, 34, 43, 45
  and theoretical debates 12, 18, 19, 22
McIver, E., *see* Lorsch
McNulty, T. 106, 110, 123, 137
  and research 22, 25–6, 33, 36, 52
Main, B. 5, 75
make-or-buy question, *see* transaction-cost
Mallette, P. 131
management, *see* executives
managerial-hegemony theory 10, 11, 18–19, 20,
    21, 123
  and control role 60, 62, 79
  empirical support 130, 134
  and strategic role 51
March, J. G. 34
Marsh, P. R. 5
Marston, C. 90
Martin, C. 26
Marxism 17
Maxwell case vi, 5, 6
Mayer, C. 7, 8
Means, G. C. 6, 13, 18, 60, 61
Meckling, W. 13, 14
meetings:
  annual general 92–4, 129
  board 66, 73–4, 111–13, 120, 125
  and CEO 90–1, 100
  chairman and CEO 107
  executives 109
  finance 90–1, 100
  formality at 112
Miles, M. B. 29–30
Milliken, F. J. 3–4
Mills, C. W. 17, 18
Mills, G. 10
Minow, N. 4, 5, 10, 130, 131
Mintzberg, H. 4, 17, 86
  and strategic role 32, 34, 35, 51, 52

mission and vision 39–40, 124
Mizruchi, M. S. 14, 17, 18, 19, 21, 119
Molz, R. 36, 50
monitoring 23, 118
  environment 66, 67–8, 124–5
  performance 62, 63, 67
Monks, R. A. G. 4, 5, 10, 130, 131
Moran, P. 20
motivation and rewards 76
Moyser, G. M. 24
Murphy, K. 76
mutual societies demutualized 89
Myners Report 127

National Health Service, *see* NHS
NEDs, *see* non-executive
negotiation 2, 107
Neubauer, F. F., *see* Demb
NHS and hospital boards 25, 33, 133, 136
Nicols, T. 17
Noda, T. 34, 35, 45, 119, 120, 124
non-executive and part-time directors v, 4, 33
  as chairmen 111, 132
  and control role 61, 62, 66–70, 73–7 *passim*, 79,
    121, 128
  and dynamics of process 110, 111, 113–14
  and executives 108–11, 113–14
  and institutional role 86, 99–100, 101, 104–5,
    121
  qualities of 110
  and strategic role 39, 42–4, 46, 51, 120, 125
  and teams 113
  and trust 113–14
Norburn, D. 34, 135
normative theory 106
norms, *see* values
Nystrom, P. C. 79, 123

objectives, strategic 65–6
OECD countries: Corporate Governance
    Guidelines v
O'Neal, D. 22, 136
operational control 63–5, 71
  budgetary and planning cycles 63–4
  reserved powers 65
opportunism and self-interest, *see* agency theory
Ouchi, W. 13

Pahl, R. E. and Winkler, J. T. 22, 119, 121, 134,
    135
  and strategic role 34, 36, 41, 48, 49, 50, 337
Panner, M. 5

Index